OXFORD HISTORICAL MONOGRAPHS

Editors
BARBARA HARVEY A.D. MACINTYRE
R.W. SOUTHERN A.F. THOMPSON
H.R. TREVOR-ROPER

The Chronicle of Ernoul and the Continuations of William of Tyre

BY

M. R. MORGAN

OXFORD UNIVERSITY PRESS
1973

Oxford University Press, Ely House, London W. 1

GLASGOW NEW YORK TORONTO MELBOURNE WELLINGTON
CAPE TOWN IBADAN NAIROBI DAR ES SALAAM LUSAKA ADDIS ABABA
DELHI BOMBAY CALCUTTA MADRAS KARACHI LAHORE DACCA
KUALA LUMPUR SINGAPORE HONG KONG TOKYO

ISBN 0 19 821851 6

Printed in Great Britain
William Clowes & Sons, Limited
London, Beccles and Colchester

ACKNOWLEDGEMENTS

The thesis on which this monograph is based was submitted to the faculty of Medieval and Modern Languages under the title 'The Old French Continuations of the Chronicle of William, Archbishop of Tyre, to 1232.' My first thanks go to my research supervisor, Professor T.B.W. Reid, a debt all the more pleasant to acknowledge since he also taught my father before me. While he was absent for a short period in Canada, Mr. A.D. Crow kindly deputised for him, and gave me most generous help.

Adapting for a historical series a thesis written by a modern linguist presented all the problems associated with studies crossing two disciplines, and I am indebted to Miss Barbara Harvey for her patient help in the work of revision, and to Professor Southern for a great number of useful suggestions and comments. I have also been grateful for various kinds of help from Professor R.H.C. Davis, Dr. Jaroslav Folda, and Dr. R.C. Smail, and most of all from my husband, R.W. Morgan, without whom this book would not have been written at all, and to whom it is dedicated.

                                                            M.R. MORGAN.

CONTENTS

ABBREVIATIONS

Babcock and Krey   Emily Babcock and A.C. Krey, *A History of Deeds Done Beyond the Sea.* Records of Civilisation, 35. New York, 1943.

HLF   *Histoire Littéraire de France.*

M-L   *La Chronique d'Ernoul et de Bernard le Trésorier,* ed. Louis de Mas-Latrie. Paris, 1871.

PL   *Patrologia Latina,* ed. J.P. Migne (221 vols., Paris, 1844-64).

RHC   *Recueil des historiens des croisades.* Published by members of the Académie des Inscriptions et Belles Lettres. Paris, 1841-1906. Used alone, this abbreviation indicates the series of the *Recueil* most commonly referred to in this study, the *Historiens occidentaux.* Where another series is meant it is specified, e.g. *RHC Lois* i.

RIS   *Rerum Italicarum Scriptores,* ed. L.A. Muratori. Milan, 1723-51.

Runciman   J.C.S. Runciman, *A History of the Crusades.* Cambridge, 1951.

Smail   R.C. Smail, *Crusading Warfare, 1097-1193.* Cambridge, 1956.

TABLE OF MANUSCRIPTS

In this table the sigla given first are those used in this study. The following columns indicate the number of each manuscript, its sigla, if any, in the editions of Mas-Lastrie and the *Recueil*, its number in Riant's *Inventaire sommaire*, and a brief indication of what text it contains. Only the manuscripts mentioned frequently in the study are included.

		M-L	*RHC*	Riant	
a	B.N.f.fr. 2634	-	a	47	*Eracles* continued to 1261. Rothelin continuation from 1248 onwards.
A	Arsenal 4797	A	-	21	Bernard the Treasurer, with the name of the author, to 1231
b	B.N.f.fr. 2628	-	b	63	*Eracles* to 1265. With *a*, this text forms, up to 1248, what Mas-Latrie calls the Colbert-Fontainebleau continuation.
B	Berne 340	B	-	24	Bernard the Treasurer, with the name of the author, to 1231. Cf. *A*.
cJ	B.N.f.fr. 9086	J	c	34	*Eracles* to 1231.
d	Lyon 828	-	d	71	*Eracles* to 1248, the 1184-97 section being peculiar to this manuscript.
gG	B.N.f.fr. 9082	G	g	67	*Eracles* to 1275.
z	Saint-Omer 722	-	-	13	Ernoul, with the name of the author, to 1227.

Throughout the study, the term 'the abrégé' is used to mean the texts of *A* and *z* taken together.

More detailed descriptions of all the manuscripts in this table will be found on pp. 6-7.

INTRODUCTION

THE OLD FRENCH continuations of the chronicle of William
of Tyre, and the independent chronicles related to them, are
in content chronicles of the crusades and in form examples
of early French prose writing, and so have in the past attracted
the attention of both historians and linguists in good measure.
But they remain for all that problematic.

Historians, who like
Grousset, Richard, Runciman, and Prawer, to name but the
most obvious, use 'Ernoul' and the 'Eracles' as a major source
for much of the history of the Latin Kingdom of Jerusalem
in the late twelfth and early thirteenth centuries, are well
aware in doing so that it is not known with any degree of
certainty what Ernoul did write, or what kind of text the
'Eracles' really is. As far as Ernoul is concerned, their reliance
on the chronicle known by his name is grounded largely on
the assumption that Ernoul was a close companion of the
Ibelins,[1] and so must have had first-hand knowledge of what
happened, and that, allowing for bias, his witness is therefore
true. So it seems desirable to know exactly what Ernoul's
witness was. Similarly, it is a matter of common knowledge
that the continuations of William of Tyre, usually know collectively as the 'Eracles', and the so-called 'Chronique
d'Ernoul et de Bernard le Trésorier' are somehow related to
each other; but the precise nature and extent of that relationship,
and the significance it might have for the establishment of both
texts, and for the evaluation of their relative merits as historical
sources, have never been clearly defined.

The literary interest of the texts too, though vaguely recognized by most critics, composers of literary histories, and the
like, lies hidden beneath a number of textual problems so
weighty and forbidding as to hamper seriously, if they do not
entirely prevent, any clear appreciation of the literary skill
that went to the making of the texts. The main obstacle, for
historian and literary critic alike, is the fact that there are so

---

[1] See for example J. Prawer, *Histoire du royaume latin de Jérusalem* (Paris, 1969),
p.551 n. 11 where Ernoul is described as 'un familier de la maison Ibelin,
chevalier au service de Balian II.'

many texts, all unmistakably separate entities, but all equally unmistakably related to each other in a variety of subtle ways. These texts are: the *Historia Rerum in Partibus Transmarinis Gestarum*, by William, Archbishop of Tyre; the Old French translations of the *Historia*, and a number of Old French continuations, these two usually being collectively called the *Estoire* (or *Livre*, or *Roman*) *d'Eracles*; another continuation, in Latin;[2] and finally two works whose titles do not indicate any connection with the rest, but which are in fact related to the Old French continuations, the *Chronique d'Ernoul et de Bernard le Trésorier*[3] already mentioned, and the unpublished work generally known as the *Estoires d'Oultremer et de la Naissance Salahadin*.[4]

So the primary problem is to sort out these texts, and to try to define their relationship to each other. It was already known from previous studies that the first branch of the continuations, that ending in 1232, provided by far the most interesting and complicated problems; indeed it seemed that if these could be solved, the problems concerning the rest of the text would cease to be problems at all, a supposition which in the event has proved quite true. This study is therefore confined to this first branch of the continuations. The main aims are two: to clarify the structure of these, and to reconstruct from them and the related texts the original form of the lost chronicle of Ernoul.

Apart from these major questions there are also one or two loose ends left by previous studies which need to be dealt with if the major questions are to be satisfactorily settled. Most of these points are minor and occur quite naturally at certain stages of the argument in any case, but one is rather larger and will be considered separately in Chapter V. The identities of the two putative authors, Ernoul and Bernard, and their chronicles, will be considered separately before the texts are all taken together, and compared in an attempt to discover the structure of the continuations and their relationship to one another and to the short

---

[2] M. Salloch (ed.), *Die lateinische Fortsetzung Willelms von Tyrus* (Leipzig, 1934).
[3] Ed. L. de Mas-Latrie, Paris, 1871.
[4] MSS B.N.f.fr. 770 and 12203.

chronicles. From this analysis will emerge the reconstruction of Ernoul's original work and this in turn will allow the structure and sources of the short chronicle attributed to Bernard to be clearly defined. The ninth chapter is devoted to an assessment of the texts' place among the literature of their period, and the tenth examines the ways in which the conclusions of this study affect our view of their value as historical evidence.

The manuscript tradition of the continuations and the related chronicles is necessarily highly complex, partly because of the large number of manuscripts[5] but chiefly because of the infinite variety of the texts they contain. However, the ground has been cleared to a large extent by two pieces of work, Mas-Latrie's *Essai de classification*[6] and the *Inventaire sommaire* of Comte Riant,[7] which, though modestly claiming to be no more than a modification of Mas-Latrie's classification, has become the standard reference for subsequent researches in the field. His system was to divide the texts into classes according to the date at which their continuations ended. Thus class I is the manuscripts of William of Tyre without continuation, class II is William of Tyre abridged and continued to 1228 or 1231, with three subdivisions (the so-called 'Ernoul', 'Estoires d'Oultremer', and 'Bernard the Treasurer'), class III is William of Tyre translated and continued to 1261, and class V is the continuations to 1275. There are two obvious weaknesses in the method. The first and less serious one is that each class in fact includes highly disparate texts (class V even includes Lyon 828 which ends at 1248, and not 1275 at all); secondly and more gravely, the classes cut across manuscript families, so that manuscripts which are virtually identical over much of their length may be separated by Riant's classification simply because one has an extra section tacked on the end. Nevertheless the classification is still valuable as a means of reducing an almost

---

[5] There are at present extant fifty-one MSS containing the translation of William with continuations of greater or lesser extent, eleven of the translation alone, and thirteen of the three short chronicles (counted together), making seventy-five in all.

[6] *Bibliothèque de l'École des Chartes,* 5th Ser. i. Reprinted in *La Chronique d'Ernoul et de Bernard le Trésorier.*

[7] In *Archives de l'Orient Latin,* i (1880-1).

impossibly complex situation to more approachable proportions, and it does enable us to distinguish, though sometimes with qualification, between one text and another. Riant's inventory, then, provides us with a *point de repère* in the textual wilderness. The individual manuscripts too have been for the most part adequately described, in some cases more than once, and it seems superfluous to repeat all these descriptions at length. I have therefore confined myself to describing, in Appendix I, two manuscripts only—Saint-Omer 722, which has not been described before at all, but only mentioned by Riant (no. 13 in his list), and Lyon 828, formerly 732 and 815 (Riant no. 71), which is very inadequately described in the *Recueil*. The contents of both these manuscripts are essential to my argument.

It seemed undesirable too to invent a new set of sigla, since there are already in existence the sigla used by Mas-Latrie and those used by the *Recueil* editors, which partly overlap, and differ, and historians who use these texts are accustomed to refer to them as 'the *d* text' and so forth, so that to change the sigla would certainly invite confusion. The answer seemed to be to adapt the existing systems without adding to the multiplicity of names and numbers already surrounding the texts, and so for the manuscripts which are mentioned very frequently in my argument I have used the sigla of Mas-Latrie and the *Recueil* editors, distinguishing between them, since they sometimes use the same letter to refer to different manuscripts (e.g. *a* and *b* are used differently in the two editions), by putting Mas-Latrie's sigla in capitals and those of the *Recueil* in small letters. Thus A refers to the manuscript so designated by Mas-Latrie, Arsenal 4797 (formerly 677A), while *a* indicates B.N.f.fr. 2634, manuscript *a* of the Académie edition. In two cases a manuscript is described by both editors, and in these cases I have combined the sigla thus: cJ, gG. Since both editors describe, and give sigla to, manuscripts they use very little in their editions, as well as those which receive most of their attention, all the main manuscripts are covered in this way, except Saint-Omer 722, to which I have given the letter z, not hitherto used for any manuscript.

So much for the individual manuscripts. The more difficult question now arises of how to refer to the texts themselves in some way which should be clear and concise, since the terms used have to be repeated very frequently indeed in certain sections, and yet which would not prejudge the questions in hand. For example it is clearly undesirable to refer to anything as the chronicle of Ernoul when it has not yet been established just what the chronicle of Ernoul was. Each text is found in at least two manuscripts, and usually more, except the text of Lyon 828, which is unique. Among the manuscripts of any one text are found the kind of differences one normally expects among any group of manuscripts which may be called a family, and it is these differences which would interest, and do interest, someone attempting an edition of any one of the texts. But the problem under discussion in this study concerns another level of difference altogether—the difference not between the several manuscripts of one text, but between one text and another. To this end I have chosen for each text one manuscript which may fairly be taken as representative of that text, so that for example when the text of manuscript cJ is discussed, the same is taken to apply to all manuscripts containing the same text as cJ. Thus differences of reading between the various manuscripts of any one text are left aside as insignificant for the purpose of this study, which is to examine the relationship of the contents of each text to the contents of the others, and ultimately of each text to the original chronicle of Ernoul.

The choice of these representative texts has been in some cases suggested by the work of previous editors and in others departs from their classifications. Thus the choice of manuscripts a, b, cJ, gG, and A by the Académie editors and Mas-Latrie as the best manuscripts of their respective texts does seem on examination to be justified, and I have kept them as representatives of their texts. For the so-called 'chronicle of Ernoul' on the other hand I have chosen a manuscript, Saint-Omer 722, which Mas-Latrie did not know, and which seems superior to his base manuscript, Brussels 11142, for reasons expounded at length elsewhere.[8] Similarly, the Lyon manuscript, d, though known to the Académie editors and printed by them in variants, has never been accorded the prominence it deserves. Its text is unique, and it will be treated here as a separate family of one member,

[8] See below, pp. 57-58, and Appendix I.

whose immense importance will become progressively apparent. The *Estoires d'Oultremer* (Riant class II B) does not generally enter into the most complex sections of the textual argument because of all the texts it is the one least closely related to any other. It is moreover impossible to describe either B.N.f.fr. 770 or 12203 as 'representative' of this text,[9] and so wherever it is mentioned I have referred to it simply as *Estoires*.

The manuscripts in question are:

A   Paris, Bibliothèque de l'Arsenal 4797 (formerly 677A).[10] 13th century. Provenance unknown. Chronicle of Bernard the Treasurer, who is named in the colophon, f. 128a. Described by Mas-Latrie, p. xxxvj, and used by him as his base manuscript for the 1229-32 section of the text. See also below, pp. 12-13.

a   Paris, Bibliothèque Nationale fonds français 2634. Late 13th century or early 14th. Probably of eastern provenance (possibly Cyprus). *Estoires d'Eracles* continued to 1261, the 1248-61 section being the Rothelin continuation. Used together with *b* below as a base manuscript for the first branch of the continuations by the *Recueil* editors; for their description of it see *RHC* ii, pp. xiv-xv. See also below, pp. 18-19 and 20.

b   Paris, Bibliothèque Nationale fonds français 2628. 13th century; provenance probably eastern. *Estoires d'Eracles* with continuations to 1264. Cf. *a* above and description *RHC* ii, p. xiv. See also below, pp. 18-19.

cJ   Paris, Bibliothèque National fonds français 9086.[11] Late 13th or early 14th century. Probably of eastern provenance. *Estoires d'Eracles* continued to 1231. Described by Mas-Latrie, p.xlj, but used very little by him. Used for variants by the *Recueil* editors who describe it *RHC*, ii, p.xv. See also below, pp. 16-18 and 19-20.

d   Lyon, Bibliothèque Municipale 828 (formerly 815 and 732). Late 13th century. Probably written in Acre: the miniatures are certainly the work of the Acre atelier. *Estoires d'Eracles* continued to 1248, long sections of the text being unique to this manuscript. Inadequately described *RHC* ii, pp. xv-xvi; for a full description see below, pp. 192-3. Printed in variants in the *Recueil*, often very inaccurately. See Hugo Buchthal, *Miniature Painting in the Latin Kingdom of Jerusalem* (Oxford, 1957), pp. 87 ff. See also below, p. 19.

---

[9] For further discussion of this text see below, pp. 13-16 and 25-26; only MS B.N.f.fr. 770 contains the *Ordene de Chevalerie*.
[10] Misprinted as 677, M-L p. xxxvj.
[11] Misprinted as 9006, M-L p. xlj.

gG   Paris, Bibliothèque Nationale fonds français 9082. Written in
     Rome, 1295. *Estoires d'Eracles* continued to 1275. Printed in
     E. Martène and U. Durand, *Veterum Scriptorum et Monumentorum
     Historicorum, Dogmaticorum, Moralium, Amplissima Collectio*
     (Paris, 1724-33), vol. xxv, and in variants in the *Recueil*. Described
     RHC ii, pp. xix-xxi. See below, pp. 16-18 and 19-20.

z   Saint-Omer, Bibliothèque Municipale 722. 13th century. From
     the abbey of Saint-Bertin. Chronicle of Ernoul, who is mentioned
     by name, f. 32b. Described below in Appendix I, pp. 190-92. See
     also below, pp. 11-12.

As for the titles such as 'Chronique d'Ernoul' and such-like
often used by editors in referring to the texts, I have used only
those which have an unmistakable reference, e.g. 'Colbert-
Fontainebleau continuation', and not those which are variably
used, or whose usage is not justified by what is known about
the text to which they are usually applied. It has been necessary to make one exception, for the term used by Mas-Latrie
to describe the text published by him, the so-called 'Chronique
d'Ernoul et de Bernard le Trésorier'; following his practice I
have referred throughout to that text in all the forms in which
it is found by the blanket term of 'the abrégé' to distinguish
it from the continuation proper on the one hand, and from
the other short chronicle, the *Estoires d'Oultremer,* on the
other. This term is a reasonably colourless one, and it was
absolutely necessary to have some name by which to indicate
the texts of *A* and *z* taken together without perpetually
repeating both numbers. As the argument progresses, this
problem of how to refer to the texts diminishes as their true
natures become apparent, and they can be given names which
are genuinely appropriate and not merely arbitrary.

I

THE EXTANT TEXTS

THE *Historia Rerum in Partibus Transmarinis Gestarum* of William of Tyre[1] is justly one of the most famous works of medieval historiography. It has those qualities of careful documentation, objectivity of judgement, and stylistic elegance which are now considered essential to the writing of history, but which in its day were all too uncommon. It also has that vivacity which is common to all but the worst of medieval chronicles, and, most important of all for its immediate success, it was topical. It was this last quality which made it eminently suitable for translation into the vernacular, and made of that vernacular in turn the basis of a variety of compilations which were best-sellers in their day and remained popular long afterwards. The *Historia* ends, somewhat abruptly, in the year 1184, with the appointment of Raymond of Tripoli as regent by the dying Baldwin IV, but the vernacular version was continued, in several phases, until it finally reached 1277.

The *Historia* itself is a unified and straightforward work. We know a great deal about the circumstances of its composition from what the author himself tells us, and with the exception of one recently discovered chapter, hitherto missing,[2] there are no mysteries about it. Quite the contrary is true of the corpus of French writings attached to it.

The French continuations were added to the translation of the *Historia* cumulatively at intervals throughout the thirteenth century, and the works thus formed are usually known collectively as the *Estoires* (or *Livre* or *Roman*) *d'Eracles*, from the opening words of the translation: 'Les anciennes estoires dient que Eracles qui mout fu bons Crestiens governa l'empire de Rome.'[3] The constitution of the continuations, one of the subjects of this study, may best be described as kaleidoscopic: a certain number of elements form constantly shifting patterns. What is now a detail becomes in another formation a major feature; what

---

[1] *RHC* i, parts i and ii.
[2] R.B.C. Huygens, 'Guillaume de Tyr étudiant'. *Latomus*, xxi (1962) 811-29.
[3] *RHC* i. 9.

is central, and sometimes most admirable, in one, will not appear at all in any other; and sometimes a completely new element appears without warning or explanation.

When comparing the main texts of the continuations one with another, it immediately becomes obvious that the terms 'same' and 'different' are of limited use in describing their relationships one to another, since there are many degrees of similarity and of difference. It is necessary to deal separately with each level of similarity (e.g. of content, of wording, etc.) and separately also with each section of the texts, since a particular relationship between two of them in one section is not necessarily an indication, and never a guarantee, of a similar relationship in any other section. All these texts, with the sole exception of the *Historia* itself, are compilations, and must be treated as such.

The following table indicates the variety of groupings into which the texts fall, each text being represented by the manuscript chosen earlier.[4] Manuscripts *a* and *b* are what Mas-Latrie calls the Colbert-Fontainebleau continuation; *d* is the unique Lyon manuscript; *cJ* and *gG* are two versions of the *Eracles*, ending in 1231 and 1275 respectively; *A* is the text called the chronicle of Bernard the Treasurer; *z* is that called the chronicle of Ernoul, and mentioning his name; and the term *Estoires* refers to the *Estoires d'Oultremer*. The dates all refer to the contents of the texts and not their date of composition, e.g. *A* is represented as ending at 1231 because that is the date of the last event mentioned in the text, although we know from the colophon that it was composed in 1232; similarly *gG* is dated 1275 and not 1295. Each section is marked off by a date at which a text ends or, in the case of 1185 and 1218, a date at which hitherto similar texts begin to disagree or dissimilar texts to agree.

1095-1185:	*a, b, cJ, d*, and *gG* agree. *A, z* and *Estoires* agree.
1185-1197:	*a* and *b* agree. *cJ, gG, A*, and *z* agree. *d*. *Estoires*.
1197-1218:	*a, b, cJ, d, gG, A*, and *z* all agree.

⁴ Above, pp. 5-7.

1218-1227:	a and b agree.
	cJ, d, gG, A, and z agree.
1227-1229/31	a and b agree.
	cJ, d, gG, and A agree.
1229/31-1248:	a, b, d, and gG agree.
1248-1261:	a.
	b and gG agree.
1261-1264:	b and gG agree.
1264-1275:	gG.

It is clear from this that the first period of the continuations, i.e. up to 1231, is by far the most involved, or, in Mas-Latrie's word, chaotic. After that the development of the texts is a fairly obvious and predictable one; before that it is not at all clear on first sight how the shifting groupings could have been produced. The best place to begin comparing the texts with one another in order to classify them by their content would seem to be the section in which there is the greatest number of groups, i.e. 1185-97. Here, and, as it happens, elsewhere too, the two texts nearest each other are A and z.

'Ernoul'

The text represented in this table by manuscript z is known as the chronicle of Ernoul, from its mention of his name in the text. It begins: 'Or entendés conment le terre de Iherusalem et le sainte crois fu conquise des Sarrasins sor Crestiens.'[5] It is a chameleon work, clerkly then anti-clerical, factual then legendary, serious and frivolous by turns. The central portion is that which fulfils the author's intention as stated in the opening sentence quoted above, but around this core are clustered things relevant and irrelevant, in a series of digressions which begin immediately after this first sentence and extend for several chapters. These include long Biblical and quasi-Biblical passages, legends concerning serpents to be found in Palestine, and descriptions of parts of Galilee, all mixed into a résumé history of the Latin Kingdom from its beginning up to the period which is the author's proper subject, i.e. the mid-1180s onwards. From here on the diversions fade away and the book becomes a perfectly serious

[5] MS z, f. 4b.

and very full account of those crucial years. During the
narration of the battle of Nazareth occurs the mention of the
name of Ernoul unique to this text, from which it derives the
name given it by Mas-Latrie, whose practice is now universally
followed: 'Dont fist descendre .i. sien vallet qui avoit non
Ernous. Ce fu cil qui cest conte fist metre en escrit.'[6] Before
the siege of Jerusalem in 1187 there is a detailed description
of the town, which seems to have been borrowed from an
earlier text. It begins: 'Ainçois que je vous die coment
Salehadins assegei Iherusalem et coment il le prist vous dirai
je l'estat coment Jherusalem siet.'[7]

So although the opening sentence of z would seem to
indicate a beginning *in medias res,* this is in fact far from
being the case. Similarly, the author does not call a halt when
he has completed his self-appointed task, but continues his
history for some time, covering the Third and Fourth
Crusades, the Damietta campaign, the crusade of Frederick II,
and his private war against Jean de Brienne. The chronicle
finally comes to a stop in the middle of this war (A.D. 1229):
'Quant li empereres fu arivés si i enveia par toute se terre por
saisir les maisons dou temple et quanques il avoit d'avoir et
fist chacier tous les freres fors de se terre. Aprés s'amassa
grant gens et grant ost et ala encontre le roi Jehan. Et
manda son fil en Alemaigne.'[8] In other manuscripts of this
text (e.g. Brussels 11142) there follows a fragment beginning
'L'an de l'incarnation . . .' enumerating some of the events
in the history of the Latin Kingdom.

'Bernard the Treasurer'

From the text of z just described, the next one, *A,* differs
very little. The fragment 'L'an de l'incarnation . . .' is here
transposed to the beginning, the mention of Ernoul is simply
omitted, and there are a few minor additions and alterations,
e.g. an explanation *en passant* of what the term *Latins* means
when used to describe the inhabitants of Outremer.[9] Otherwise *A* is a reproduction of *z,* right up to the end of *z,* after
which *A* continues without a break (the new material being

---

[6] MS z, f. 32[b], col. 2   [7] MS z, f. 39[b].
[8] MS z, f. 91[b].   [9] See M-L p.365 nn. 3 and 4.

apparently original) up to September 1231. It ends 'Li
empereres et li chevaliers de la terre firent volentiers quanque
li rois Jehan lor devisa si com il avoient en couvent et li rois
atant s'en tint.'[10] In manuscript *A* and one other of the family
(Berne 340, Mas-Latrie's MS *B*), there follows a colophon:
'Ceste conte de la terre d'outre mer fist faire li tresoriers
Bernars de Saint Pierre de Corbie. En la carnation millesimo
cc.xxij.' From this colophon the text is generally known as
the *Chronique de Bernard le Trésorier*. But the fact that it is
so nearly identical to the so-called *Chronique d'Ernoul* has
been the source of not a little confusion, and means that
whenever a critic mentions either of these texts it is essential
to make very sure exactly what he intends to refer to.
Mas-Latrie, having carefully compared these two families,
finally published in 1871 an edition which is based on a manuscript of the same family as *z* (Brussels 11142), but adding
in italic print at the beginning and end the 'L'an de
l'Incarnation . . . ' fragment and the 1227-31 section respectively, from manuscript *A*. To this edition he gave the composite title, *La Chronique d'Ernoul et de Bernard le Trésorier*.[11]
The choice was justifiable, but unfortunate, for it has pre-
judiced in the minds of readers ever since the question of the
authorship of these two chronicles and led them to think of
the two people named in the title as being in some sense
authors of the work so entitled. Mas-Latrie himself, as is
clear from all his criticism of the texts, though he is prepared
to refer to them by these names for the sake of convenience,
considers the question of authorship a very open one indeed.

Estoires d'Oultremer

So much for the texts of *z* and *A*. It seems appropriate to
deal next with the third and last of the texts not containing
the translation of William of Tyre, that is, the *Estoires
d'Oultremer*. Significantly, in the period we are referring to,
1185-97, it stands alone, and it must be added that even when
it is shown as agreeing with other texts the agreement is always
of the most approximate kind, and allows for more divergence
than does any other agreement between two texts in the

---

[10] MS *A*, f. 128ª, col. 1.
[11] L. de Mas-Latrie (ed.), *La Chronique d'Ernoul et de Bernard le Trésorier*
(Paris, 1871).

whole table. In absolute strictness, it should always be put by itself, but that would not indicate the resemblance it does bear, often quite closely in isolated parts of its text, to some of the other texts, and it seemed important to point out this resemblance in the table on p. 10-11 even though it must be qualified in the description of the texts. The fact is that the *Estoires* is a very mixed text indeed, whose compiler has treated his material with a freer hand than any other compiler of these texts, thus producing the most fragmented and confusing hotchpotch imaginable. He juxtaposes sound historical narrative with flagrant legend, cutting from one to the other and back with even more alacrity and less warning than his contemporaries. Nevertheless his text is of interest because it is clear from those sections which have counterparts elsewhere that it has been independently drawn from old sources, and it preserves not only many details not found elsewhere, but also whole sections concerning Salahadin and the King of Nubia, Renaud de Châtillon, and Raoul de Bembrac. Most interestingly of all, the last part of the chronicle, covering the years 1197-1230, is heavily condensed by comparison with *A* and *z*.

The *Estoires* opens like the other short chronicles, *A* and *z*, 'Oiiés et entendés comment la tiere de Iherusalem fu conquise' etc.,[12] and resembles them without major difference until the arrival of Renaud de Châtillon in Palestine, where the narrator changes subject without ceremony: 'Mais or se taist ici endroit une piece li contes de lui et dira dont li bons rois Salehadins ki tant fu preudom et renoumés de bien vint et de quel gent il fu estrait. Au tans passé ot un conte en Pontiu ki mout ama chevalerie et le siecle.'[13]

There follows the story of the Comtesse de Ponthieu, and of how Salahadin was descended through her from a noble French house. The other major section which is found only in the *Estoires,* and which is not history, also concerns Salahadin, and is inserted after the battle of Montgisart.[14] It is a prose version of the *Ordre de chevalerie,* well known in verse[15] but apparently not found elsewhere in prose.

[12] MS B.N.f.fr. 770, f. 313a.   [13] f. 315b.   [14] Ff. 326a-327b. Cf. M-L pp. 43-5.
[15] Ed. and trans. William Morris, *L'Ordène de chevalerie* (Hammersmith, 1893).

The hero, Humfroi de Toron in other versions, is here Hugues
de Tabarie: it is to be supposed that the *prosateur* found the
initials H. de T. in the verse and expanded them to suit himself. Indeed he may well have had some interest in making
into the hero of the story a member of the Tiberiade family,
for this family sprang from the Castellans of Saint-Omer, the
Fauquemberghes, and the two manuscripts of the *Estoires*
(B.N.f.fr. 770 and 12203) are identified by art-historians as
having been illustrated, and probably also copied, in an atelier
in the north-east of France.[16] These two fictitious interpolations
serve a single purpose, and are typical of the many legendary
or semi-legendary anecdotes to which chroniclers writing for
European audiences were obliged to resort in order to get out
of the considerable ethical difficulties with which the person
of Salahadin presented them. He was a pagan, yet morally
good; not a knight, and yet chivalrous. There could only be
one solution of the paradox: despite all evidence to the
contrary, Salahadin must in fact be both a Christian and a
knight. So a number of stories were produced to demonstrate
that this was so, and these two illustrating respectively how
Salahadin was of European, better still of French descent,
and how he wrested from a captive Frank the secrets of
knighthood, are classic examples of the genre.[17]

In short, the text of the *Estoires* differs from *z* and *A* in
two chief ways. It includes the two stories outlined above,
which are easy to discern and need no explanation for their
presence, since they are simple interpolations, and it also
includes a quantity of apparently serious historical narrative
not found elsewhere which, like the two legends, centres on
Salahadin. The text ends in 1230: 'En celui point s'asemblerent
.x. mille Sarrasin et vinrent en Jherusalem et le quidierent
prendre. Et cil de la vile les requellirent bien et les ochisent
tous et prisent et misent fors y larra cinc [*sic*. B.N.f.fr. 12203:
ocisent tous fors .ij.] ke li emperes y avoit laissiés pour garder le
sepucre'.[18]

---

[16] I am grateful to Dr. Jaroslav Folda of the University of North Carolina,
Chapel Hill, for this information, orally communicated.

[17] Cf. also for example the story of Salahadin baptizing himself on his death-bed
in *Récits d'un menestrel de Reims*, ed. Natalis de Wailly (Paris, 1876), § 212,
pp. 111-12.

[18] f. 354a.

Before leaving the *Estoires* it is necessary to mention a printed book which has caused some controversy in the past and about which there is still some mystery.[19] It is obviously a version of the *Estoires*, and bears the same title, but as published by Citry de la Guette, in modern French, differs from the text of the two extant manuscripts in one aspect which could be very important when it comes to establishing the original form of the text. We have already noted that in the extant text the section covering the years 1197-1230 is very condensed by comparison with the corresponding section in *z* and *A*. In Citry de la Guette's version it is more condensed still; indeed it would not be an exaggeration to say that there is virtually nothing that one could call historical narrative after the death of Henri de Champagne in 1197. There are two possible explanations. The first is that Citry de la Guette has been less faithful to his manuscript than he claims, and has simply condensed this section himself. An argument in favour of this is that MS B.N.f.fr. 770, if that is the one he used, has now, and may well have had then, several folios missing immediately before the last one, and the quickest way of dealing with this deficiency would have been simply to run the text of the two last existing folios together, the condensation effectively concealing the gap in the narrative. Against this, however, one must balance the indisputable fact that elsewhere he is really very scrupulous about following his source, and also that throughout the text, small but significant details suggest a difference between his manuscript and the extant ones. Until such time as a new manuscript of the *Estoires* may come to light the only safe assumption is that there was another in existence, with the proviso that Citry de la Guette's version must be treated cautiously and not accepted as certain proof that another manuscript did exist.[20]

Estoire d'Eracles, MSS cJ and gG

Apart from these three texts, *z, A*, and the *Estoires,* all the others shown on the table on p. 10-11 begin with a French

---

[19] Samuel de Broë. Seigneur de Citry et de la Guette, *Histoire de la conqueste du royaume de Jérusalem sur les Chrestiens par Saladin* (Paris, 1679).
[20] Cf. also below, pp. 25-26.

translation of William's *Historia,* and attach to it continuations of greater or lesser extent. When we begin comparing them with each other we see immediately the drawbacks to Riant's system of classification.[21] He splits the texts into classes on the criterion of the date at which they end, and this has the effect of separating texts which in fact are almost identical for the major part of their content. For example, it can be seen in the table that *cJ* and *gG* always appear in the same group, in each section of their texts. But they are put into different categories by Riant simply because *cJ* ends some forty-six years earlier than *gG*. The content of these two texts can be quite simply described. Up to 1183 they consist of the French translation of William, and from 1183 to 1231 they correspond to the same section of *A* (from 'Li quens de Triple respondi'[22] to the end of *A*). The two parts are joined together by a connecting section of three chapters in *cJ*,[23] in *gG* by the first of the three only. After 1231, *gG* goes on with the same continuation as that found in *b* as far as 1264, and from 1264 to 1275 has another continuation of its own, while *cJ* ends in the same place as *A*, indeed with the same words (q.v. above p. 13), without the colophon of course. In the section 1183-1197, *cJ* and *gG* sometimes offer interesting variants of the *A* text, but these are always unmistakably variant renderings of the same basic text. Again, from 1218 to 1231, *cJ* is slightly more concise than *gG*, but this concision takes the form of economy of wording, and not any condensation of the material, which is the same in all details throughout this section. These two kinds of variation among the texts do not put in any doubt the fact that all three manuscripts contain, in their own versions, the same basic text for the period 1183-1231.

Before that of course they are totally different. Where *A* has its first nine and a half chapters, confused both as regards subject-matter and the manner of its exposition, *cJ* and *gG* have the translation of William, and so give a much more professional and unified aspect than *A*. It is clear, however, that the compilers of *cJ* and *gG* did know the early section of *A*. One of them, *gG*, gives in the middle of the battle of Hattin

---

[21] Cf. above, p. 3.   [22] M-L p. 116, *RHC* ii. 6.   [23] *Eracles* xxiii. 1-3. (*RHC* ii. 1-6).

the account of Heraclius's election to the patriarchate of
Jerusalem and of his notorious manner of life,[24] which *A* and
z have at an earlier point, in its proper chronological place.
The other, *cJ*, gives just before the siege of Jerusalem the
description of the town[25] found in the same place in *A*, while
gG omits it. These two texts are fairly typical of the *Eracles*
texts as a whole, in that their individuality comes not from
the inclusion of any new material, but from a new combination of elements found in various other texts, so that *cJ*, for
example, is unlike any other text, and yet each of its components individually has an exact counterpart elsewhere.

Estoire d'Eracles, MSS a and b

Rather different from *cJ* and *gG* are another two texts of
the *Eracles*, represented in the table by manuscripts *a* and *b*.
Up to 1248 these two can in fact be regarded as a single text,
but after that they differ completely. Like *cJ* and *gG*, they
begin with a translation of William, followed by the three
connecting chapters found in *cJ*, then they embark on what
looks at first like the same continuation as *cJ* and *gG*. But at
the narrative of the battle of Hattin they begin to present
frequent and lengthy passages quite unlike anything in *cJ* and
gG, and it is clear that here are not mere variants of the same
text, like the ones observed in the comparison of *cJ*, *gG,* and
A, but something which must be regarded as a different continuation altogether. The text of *a* and *b* continues to differ
intermittently from that of *cJ* and *gG*, up to the death of
Henri de Champagne in 1197. From there all the texts agree
with each other up to 1218 (death of Otto IV), when there
is a sudden jump in the chronology and in the subject-matter.
Since the Fourth Crusade the narrative had dealt only with
Europe and the Byzantine Empire. Now the scene shifts to
the Latin Kingdom, and all the texts take up the story at the
death of Amalric. But although the subject-matter is the same,
the texts are not, and from here to 1229, *a* and *b* again differ
radically from *cJ* and *gG*. Only on one topic—Jean de Brienne's
visit to Europe in 1223, his marriage to Berengaria of Castile,
and his war against Frederick II—is there any similarity. This
exception will be discussed in detail later.[26] The general

---

[24] *RHC* ii. 58 n. 44 and variant.
[25] *RHC* ii. 82 n. 4. Cf. M-L pp. 190-210.   [26] p. 141 ff.

picture of the relationship between *cJ* and *gG* on the one hand
and *a* and *b* on the other is that for the period 1183-97 the
two groups are partly similar, but in general differ quite a lot,
from 1197 to 1218 they are the same, and after 1218 are
totally different.

Estoire d'Eracles, MS d

The last text it remains to describe is *d*, the Lyon manuscript,
towards which it seems that Mas-Latrie would have turned his
attention if time had allowed,[27] and which will be given a
major place in the argument of the present study. It gives a
text unlike any other. As can be seen from the table on p. 10-11,
it tends generally to resemble *gG*, except in the section of
most importance, 1183-97. For this section, *d* does not have
a totally different text, but interspersed among passages
resembling the other texts are many extensive and invaluable
passages peculiar to *d* alone. Sometimes these are different
accounts of events which we already know about from the
narratives of the other texts, and on which *d* sheds a new and
different light, and sometimes they concern incidents which
are never heard of elsewhere at all.

Continuations from 1232

Having thus described in broad outline the contents of all
the texts in the first period of the continuations, 1183-1232,
which are our subject, it seems useful to add a brief note on
the remaining sections of the continuations after 1232, both
in order to gain a complete view of those texts which continue into the second and third periods, and also because it
will be necessary later, in comparing the continuations in the
period ending 1231/2, to make some references to the sections
immediately following.

At 1231, *gG* and *d* take up the same text as *a* and *b,* beginning at 1229, although this involves them in repeating some
events they have already mentioned. The four texts continue
in agreement up to 1248, where *d* ends, and *a* diverges from
the remaining two to join that of the Rothelin family. Manuscripts *b* and *gG* continue giving the same text as each

---

[27] M-L p. xxiij: 'Les MSS de Lyon mériteraient une étude spéciale dans cette
direction'.

other until *b* stops, in 1264, after which *gG* continues alone
up to 1275 (Council of Lyon).[28]

Rothelin continuation

At the same point, 1231, other manuscripts which have
hitherto been identical with *cJ* and *gG* now begin what is
known as the Rothelin continuation, after the owner of the
first known manuscript of the text, the abbé Rothelin.[29]
This continuation runs from 1229 to 1261, and includes the
description of Jerusalem, as in *z, A,* and *cJ,*[30] and several
chapters of descriptions of the Holy Land and legends associated with it, some of which are drawn from the Bible and the
apocryphal gospels, while others are merely legends current
in the Middle Ages, of no known literary origin. The Rothelin
continuation also includes a piece quite often tacked on to
histories of the crusades, and called the *Prophecie le Fil Agap,*
which is interpreted as foretelling certain events in the crusades;
a letter to Innocent III about Salahadin, also found in the
work of Jacques de Vitry; and short chapters on the Caliph of
Baghdad and the Assassins. All these come at the beginning of
the continuation, interrupting the narration of the events of
1229. Elsewhere there are passages freely adapted from
pseudo-Callisthenes and Lucan, and two songs, one popular
and the other attributed to Philippe de Nanteuil. Apart from
all these, the continuation is otherwise a straightforward, if
rather haphazard and sketchy history continuing to the year
1261.

How did this great variety of texts arise, with its complex
web of relationships? What basic elements lay at the root of
the process, and how did these different species of one genus
evolve? From the very beginning, when the ink was hardly
dry on the last manuscript, studies of all these works have
been vitiated by one or two erroneous but unchallenged
assumptions, so that in a short time the state of studies became as Daedalian as its subject. Before approaching the
texts themselves it is first essential to clear away the parasitic

[28] There exists in MS Pluteus LXI, 10 of the Laurentian Library in Florence a
   further continuation bringing the narrative down to the election of Nicholas III
   in 1277.
[29] *RHC* ii. 489 ff.
[30] See above, pp. 12 and 18.

confusion of misapprehension with which the works of
scholars, who all too often relied on one another's unreliable
observations, have surrounded it.

II

THE STATE OF STUDIES

BY THE end of the thirteenth century all the texts which can properly be said to belong to the William of Tyre corpus already existed in their final forms. After this there are no more prolongations, no more regroupings, no more elaborations of a significant sort. In the following century the popularity of the chronicles remained undiminished, to judge from the number of copies made then which have survived to the present, and in this century too there appeared almost simultaneously the first work to use the continuations as a source, and the first translation of them.

The *Liber Secretorum Fidelium Crucis* of Marinus Sanutus Torselli, a Venetian nobleman, is dated by its editor between 1305 and 1307.[1] It is a lengthy work dealing with several aspects of the crusades; its sub-title sufficiently indicates its scope: '. . . qui est tam pro conservatione fidelium quam pro conversione et consumptione Infidelium: quanquam etiam propter acquirandam et tenendam Terram Sanctam, et alias multas terras in bono statu pacifico et quieto'.

So it is partly historical and partly geographical, but consists for the most part of a treatise on how the Holy Land may best be retaken. Book 3 is a history of the Holy Land from Old Testament times to the present, in which the history of the Latin Kingdom of Jerusalem occupies parts 4 to 12. This is drawn from the *Eracles,* beginning at i. 11, fairly freely adapted and abbreviated. That it is a free rendering of the *Eracles* and not of the original Latin *Historia* is plain from the fact that in all the tiny differences between William and his translator, Sanutus always has the translator's version. Also he often leaves proper names in French, while for others he invents new and strange Latin forms quite unlike those which William had given them.[2] There can be no doubt that here for the first time is a historian using the French version and not the Latin as his source. Sanutus's use of the *Eracles* is not exclusive, nor continuous, but there are some passages

---

[1] Marinus Sanutus, dictus Torselli, *Liber Secretorum Fidelium Crucis,* in Bongars, *Gesta Dei per Francos,* Vol. ii (Hanover, 1611).

[2] See for instance the list of crusaders' names on pp. 131-2.

which are nothing less than accurate translations of parts of
the *Eracles,* evidently in the Colbert-Fontainebleau version
(i.e. the text of *a* and *b*).[3] It is unfortunately impossible to
tell precisely what was the extent and content of the text
Sanutus used. His abbreviations telescope chronology and
often digest several chapters into one, allowing us to do no
more than pick out sections either translated from the *Eracles,*
or clearly adapted from it. What we can say with certainty is
that in the first decade of the fourteenth century the *Eracles*
was evidently considered an authoritative source by an author
whose work manifests no small degree of earnestness.

Not long after the publication of Sanutus's work, in the
year 1320 to be precise, and again in Italy, Fra Francesco
Pipino, a Dominican of Bologna, completed his *magnum opus.*
This work, untitled, and generally referred to simply as the
Chronicon, is a universal chronicle, fairly typical of its genre
in that it covers a wide area and a very long period, and has
no pretensions to originality. It is the 25th book which concerns us here. This is basically a translation into Latin of part
of the French translation of William and part of the abrégé.
The most brief and superficial comparison of Pipino's work
and William's suffices to demonstrate the irony of Pipino's
task. As for the influence of his chronicle on later studies, it
was disastrous, less through his own fault than through that
of his editor Muratori, who published parts, though not the
whole, of Pipino's chronicle in his collection *Rerum Italicarum
Scriptores.*[4] In Volume vii, published in 1725, Muratori
printed the whole of Pipino's 25th book, and entitled it
Bernardi Thesaurarii: De Acquisitione Terrae Sanctae.
Muratori had got this idea from two mentions that Pipino
makes of Bernard in his work:

Haec ex Historia Damiatae sumta sunt. Sed de discessu Regis Johannis,
et qualiter Christiani Damiatam Soldano reddiderunt, et nonnulla quae
sequuta sunt, sic scribit Bernardus Thesaurarius.[5]

---

[3] For example Sanutus xi. i (p. 208, v. 28 ff.): 'Accidit autem hyeme per ora
cruraque populi pestilens morbus . . .' is a translation of the *Eracles* xxxii.
13-14 (*RHC* ii. 344 ff.). Again, Sanutus xi. 12, (p. 213, v. 10 ff.): Soldanus
igitur attendens pauperrimum Imperatoris adventum . . .' translates the *Eracles*
xxxiii. 6 (*RHC* ii. 371): Quant li sotans . . . sot que l'empereres estoit venus en
la terre povrement . . .'
[4] *Rerum Italicarum Scriptores,* ed. L.A. Muratori (Milan 1723-51), Vol. vii.
[5] Ibid. vii, col. 842

Haec de gestis Regis Johannis sumta sunt ex Historia Bernardi Thesaurarii. Qualis autem fuerit exitus non inveni, vel quod Historiam non compleverit, vel quod codex, unde sumsi, fuit imperfectus.[6]

Somehow or other Muratori took these references, and especially the second, which occurs in the penultimate chapter, to mean that the whole of book 25 was drawn from Bernard, and therefore he gave book 25 the title it bears in his edition. This led scholars and bibliographers alike to attribute to Bernard the original of the whole of book 25, notwithstanding the fact that Bernard's name is found only in two manuscripts of a short chronicle which could not possibly have provided all the material, and is never attached to any manuscript of the *Eracles,* which alone could have supplied the early parts of the book. This error persisted right up to 1871, when Mas-Latrie finally corrected it in his edition of Bernard, and even then Mas-Latrie limited himself to showing how and why Muratori, and all those who were misled by his edition, had erred.[7] So preoccupied was he, it seems, with eliminating this error, that he stopped completely short of examining the evidence that Pipino's work really does give us about the chronicle of Bernard, evidence which will be considered in detail later in relation to the question of authorship. For the moment, the features of Pipino's work which emerge as significant are that, like Sanutus, he knew not the *Historia* but a vernacular translation of it; that, again like Sanutus, he accepts it as authoritative; and that he is the first to cite Bernard the Treasurer as author of a chronicle. This is a landmark in the development of the continuations, in that for the first time the vernacular texts are used extensively as a source (Sanutus's use of the *Eracles* is a minor thing by comparison, and he did not know Bernard at all), and in that the foundation is laid for the most confusing and far-reaching error to vitiate further studies of the texts.

The advent of printing in the fifteenth century provides a useful indication of the literary tastes of the age: what books did they consider worth printing? Significantly the *Eracles,* or at any rate part of it, was one. Manuscripts of it were of course still being copied, for example the splendidly ornate

---

[6] Ibid., col. 846   [7] M-L pp. i-xiv.

copy done for the English court and now in the British Museum[8] dates from this period. In 1481, William Caxton published *The History of Godefrey of Boloyne and of the Conquest of Iherusalem*. This is Caxton's own translation of the first nine books of the *Eracles,* i.e. those covering the life of Godefroi de Bouillon, together with a short prologue and epilogue composed by Caxton himself. Caxton slants the work, as his title indicates; his prologue cites as the three great heroes Arthur, Charlemagne, and Godefroi, and the book is a biography of Godefroi rather than a history of the crusades as such. Here we see the vernacular text used once again, this time not as a historical source, as Pipino had used it, but as part of an established literary tradition, comparable to the traditions surrounding Arthur and Charlemagne, in fact nothing less than a new *matière.* Caxton's book was resuscitated in 1893 by William Morris, who reprinted at the Kelmscott Press Caxton's first edition,[9] and in the same year the Early English Text Society published an edition of Caxton's work by Mary Colvin.[10] It is unfortunate that as far as Caxton's sources are concerned, Miss Colvin's introduction is wholly derivative and largely misleading. She does not limit herself to William's *Historia* and its French translation, but makes fairly extensive comments on Ernoul and Bernard, all based on the various researches of Mas-Latrie published in the period immediately preceding her edition, but these do not always represent Mas-Latrie's findings accurately. Fortunately the influence of this edition on later studies seems to have been nil.

After Caxton's publication of 1481, the continuations and all the texts related to them seem to have been forgotten for some two hundred years. Not until 1679 does any new work on the texts appear, and then it is so amateurishly presented as to inspire among critics nothing but suspicion of its authenticity. The author of the work was Samuel de Broë, seigneur de Citry et de la Guette, who claimed to have

---

[8] Royal MSS 15. E. 1.

[9] William Caxton, *The History of Godefrey of Boloyne and of the Conquest of Iherusalem,* corrected by H. Halliday Sparling, reprinted by William Morris (Kelmscott Press, Hammersmith, Apr. 1893).

[10] William Caxton, *Godeffroy of Boloyne,* ed. Mary Colvin (Early English Text Society, London, 1893).

translated into modern French 'un MS fort ancien', and in his preface protested at some length his utter fidelity to the text.[11] Indeed he was generally considered to have protested too much. The drawback was that no one but himself had seen the manuscript, allegedly given him by Cabart de Villermont, nor has it in fact been identified to this day, and this circumstance, combined with the differences between his history and the then known facts about the crusades, naturally called down upon him the unanimous disbelief of literary pundits. The *Journal des Sçavans* gives him a sort of consolation prize for being 'pleasant to read therein', and otherwise does not even bother to inquire into the authenticity of his source.[12] But the narrative contained in Citry de la Guette's book is quite clearly a version of the text we now know as the *Estoires d'Oultremer*, which exists in two manuscripts, f.fr. 770 and 12203, of the Bibliothèque Nationale. As has already been stated in the review of the extant texts,[13] there are differences between the printed book and the two extant manuscripts sufficient to suggest that Citry de La Guette's manuscript was not either of them. But there is no possible shadow of doubt that he used another manuscript of the same text. Citry de la Guette is vindicated; it remains to discover, if it still exists, the manuscript he undoubtedly did use.

At last, in 1729, the first real edition of the continuations appeared. In Volume v of their *Amplissima Collectio* Martène and Durand published the continuation of William of Tyre found in the manuscript owned by Gaston de Noailles[14] with the title *Guillelmi Archiepiscopi Tyriensis Continuata Belli Sacri Historia* and no attribution.[15] They felt it necessary to add to this a glossary of Old French words which would not be easily recognized by readers having only a knowledge of modern French. But they did not provide any critical apparatus, the introduction consisting simply of a short eulogy of William, and some remarks on the linguistic difficulty of the continuation and its date of composition. But their edition

---

[11] Cf. above p. 16 and n. 19.

[12] *Journal des Sçavans*, vii. (for 1679, Amsterdam, 1680), 80. Cf. also Lelong, *Bibliothèque historique de la France,* ed. Fevret de Fontette (Paris, 1769), p. 141, no. 16700, which quotes this article.

[13] Cf. above p. 16.   [14] MS *gG*

[15] Martène and Durand, *Amplissima Collectio* (Paris, 1729), Vol. v, cols. 581-758.

served nevertheless the very necessary purpose of making one version of the continuations available in a printed form, and offering some point of comparison with Muratori's edition of Book 25 of Pipino's *Chronicon*. The similarity between the two texts was first noticed by Mansi in his edition of Raynaldi's *Annals*, and his judgement merits quotation *in extenso*, for it shows how Muratori's error, from being an unchallenged but also an unsubstantiated hypothesis, acquired 'evidence' of a sort to support it, and became that much more difficult to dismiss. After quoting passages from the texts published by Muratori and by Martène and Durand, Mansi concludes:

> Ex his patere arbitror Gallicum Latinumque scriptum unum idemque esse opus Bernardo Thesaurario tribuendum, quod a doctissimis Gallici editoribus ignoratum fuit. Discimus pariter F. Pippinum mutilum codicem Gallicum nactum fuisse, cum Latinam Historiam nonnisi ad annum 1230 circiter perduxerit. . . . Continuavit utique Thesaurarius historiam suam usque ad annum 1274 quo Lugdunense I Concilium celebratum fuit; ejusdem enim in fine historiae suae meminit. Hinc etiam de aetate Bernardi Thesaurarii, quam Muratorius ex conjectura tantummodo subodoratur argumentum capere licet.[16]

Now Mansi's first argument—that Martène and Durand's text and the source of Muratori's text were one and the same—was so plainly right that no one could possibly reject it, and it carried with it the rest of his assertions. His identification of the *Eracles,* in the version of manuscript *gG*, with the continuation up to 1275, as the source of Pipino's chronicle up to 1230, seemed perfectly plausible, for had not Pipino himself suspected that the manuscript he was using was incomplete?

Thus Muratori was vindicated, or so it seemed. There was, however, a rival opinion current, attributing the continuation to one Hugues Plagon, and while it is easy to see how and why the Muratori error arose, Hugues Plagon seems to have been created *ex nihilo*. His name appears in no manuscript of the continuations, or of the related texts, but is mentioned for the first time by Du Cange in the *Glossarium* of 1678 among the list of vernacular authors consulted. 'Hugues Plagon en la version de Guillaume de Tyr', runs the entry.[17] Du Cange, then, attributes to Plagon the translation of the *Historia*; but

---

[16] Baronius and Raynaldi, *Annales,* ed. Mansi (Lucques, 1747), vol. i p. 567.

[17] Du Cange, *Glossarium ad Scriptores Mediae et Infimae Latinitatis* (Paris 1678), Vol. i, col. cxcij.

Du Cange's editor, Dom Carpentier, added to this in the 1766 edition a reference to the text of Martène and Durand, thus attributing to Plagon the continuation as published in their *Amplissima Collectio.*[18] From now on these two equally false attributions of the continuations, to Bernard on the one hand and to Hugues Plagon on the other, vie with each other. Fevret de Fontette, editing Lelong's *Bibliothèque historique de la France* in 1769, followed Carpentier, as did Meusel in his revision of Struvius's *Bibliotheca Historica* in 1786.[19] Michaud, however, in the 1822 edition of his *Bibliothèque des croisades,* follows Mansi, whose note he translates, providing it with additional comparisons between the editions of Muratori and Martène to support Mansi's conclusions.[20]

Last and most important, Guizot, having observed that two schools of thought exist on the topic, opts for Mansi's view. He published his *Collection des mémoires relatifs à l'histoire de France* in thirty volumes, during the years 1823-1835, and Volume xix contains what he calls the *Chronique de Bernard le Trésorier.* It is in fact the French translation of William with the Martène and Durand continuation after it. Indeed his knowledge of the texts is hardly different from theirs, and his introduction reproduces all the stock observations of what might by now be called the Mansi tradition. But Guizot makes one important step forward. He points out that while Martène and Durand's text continues up to 1274, Pipino's manuscript of Bernard evidently stopped at 1230, and having apparently forgotten Pipino's claim that his manuscript was in any case incomplete, Guizot now propounds the useful (and incidentally true) theory that the 'continuation' of William of Tyre is in fact not one but a series of continuations. Apart from this his edition is unremarkable: a text already known, with a modern French translation on the facing page, and footnotes chiefly of historical and not textual interest.

Contributions to the field of study now began to succeed each other thick and fast. The first to appear, and in more than one sense the most weighty, was the edition, produced by members of the Académie des Inscriptions, of William's

---

[18] Ibid., ed. Carpentier (Paris 1766) Vol. iv, col. lxxxiij.
[19] Lelong, op. cit., ed. Fontette, Vol. ii, p. 139, no. 16681. Struvius, *Bibliotheca Historica,* ed. J.G. Meusel (Leipzig, 1786), Vol. ii, part 2, p. 294.
[20] Michaud, *Bibliographie des croisades* (Paris, 1822), i. 405 ff.

Historia, in the Latin text, together with the French translation, and the continuations in four versions,[21] plus the
'continuation de Rothelin'. These were published in the
Recueil des Historiens des Croisades, as Volumes i and ii of
the series Historiens Occidentaux. Volume i, in two parts,
appeared in 1844 and consists of the *Historia* proper, with the
French translation below, while the second volume, published
in 1859, gives all the continuations, a real *tour de force.* The
method the editors adopt is to take one continuation, that of
a and *b,* the Colbert-Fontainebleau text, as the main text up
to the end of Book 33 (A.D. 1247), and to print the variants
of *cJ, gG,* and *d,* in footnotes or, in the case of extended
passages, as a separate text at the foot of the page. The Rothelin
text[22] is printed separately at the end. Their edition is thus
invaluable for any study of the continuations, providing as it
does all the main versions in a form which permits easy comparison. There is one major drawback, however, namely the
temptation to allow the form of edition chosen by the editors
to prejudge for the reader the issue of the primacy of one
continuation over the others, and to lead him unconsciously
to accept their preference for *a* and *b*, and even to regard all
the other texts as variants of these two, simply because they
are printed as such. To be sure, there is a case to be made for
doing precisely this, indeed Mas-Latrie will later go so far as
to assert that the text of *a* and *b* is the nearest to the original
chronicle of Ernoul. But this is by no means an open and
closed question, and one of the main arguments of this study
will be that the claim thus made for the text of *a* and *b* is not
justified.

The editors' preface to the continuations in Volume ii is a
strange mixture of carefully drawn conclusions and wild
surmise. An example of the first is the passage[23] on the
genesis of manuscript *d*, while all the material on Ernoul and
Bernard must be consigned to the second category. The editors
may be right in concluding that the short chronicles which
bear these names cannot properly be classed with the continuations of William of Tyre for the purpose of their edition,
but the suggestions which in their preface lead up to this

---

[21] Those represented in the table on p. 10-11 by MSS *a* and *b* and by *d, cJ,* and *gG.*
[22] For which see above, p. 20.   [23] p. vii.

conclusion must be totally rejected. They have for example
no sufficient grounds for even suggesting[24] that Ernoul and
Bernard are both abbreviators of previous works rather than
authors in their own right. Another weak point in the preface,
though this is not a false assertion so much as a misleading
emphasis, is their analysis[25] of the existing continuations.
These they classify into two redactions, Eastern and Western,
but they tend to gloss over the precise relationship between·
the two for the period 1183-1229, saying simply that in this
section the Western redaction consists of the Eastern continuation in an abbreviated form. It seems at first a small point,
but taken at its face value it vitiates at the start any study of
the relationships between the continuations. Close comparison
of the texts shows that in the first place the connection between
the two is far more subtle than they suggest, indeed of a different kind altogether, and in the second place it rapidly becomes
evident that such a rigid division of the texts into two redactions is quite unrealistic. In short, the Académie edition of the
continuations is admirable as far as the texts are concerned
but the preface should be treated with caution in the sections
concerning the continuations, while the passages on Ernoul
and Bernard are best disregarded altogether.

The publication of this edition ushered in what may be
described as the *grande époque* of William of Tyre studies. In
1860, the year after the publication of the second volume,
Louis de Mas-Latrie published his *Essai de classification des
continuateurs de l'Histoire des croisades de Guillaume de Tyr.*[26]
In 102 pages he makes a direct attack on the central problem,
until then untouched: the origin of the variety of continuations
extant. His first move in the attempt to reduce the phenomenon
to comprehensible terms is the establishment of five classes of
manuscripts, the sole criterion being the date to which the
history is continued. This system is to some extent misleading,
in that it obscures the fact (of which Mas-Latrie was of course
perfectly well aware) that manuscripts belonging to different
classes may be identical with each other in certain sections of
their text: for example, cJ, gG, and d of the table on p. 10-11
all stop at different dates, and are therefore put into different

---

[24] p. vi.   [25] pp. iii-iv.
[26] *Bibliothèque de l'École des Chartes,* 5th Ser. i. 38 ff. and 140 ff. Reprinted in
La Chronique d'Ernoul et de Bernard le Trésorier (Paris, 1871).

classes by Mas-Latrie, but they all give the same text (see
table) for the period 1197-1231. In other words, Mas-Latrie's
classes cut across manuscript families. Also the *Essai* is so
densely written as to be at times confusing. Nevertheless it is
the first delineation of the problem in general terms, the first
successful attempt to evaluate existing beliefs about the William
of Tyre corpus and to distinguish between fact, fiction, and
speculation. Moreover Mas-Latrie's classification of the manuscripts provided a framework not only for his own subsequent
researches, but for those of all his successors in the field right
up to the present day.

Apart from classifying the manuscripts known to him,
Mas-Latrie also tackled several related problems, notably the
identity of Bernard, and also that of Ernoul, who now attracts
attention for the first time. Up to this point no attention had
been paid to the manuscripts of the short chronicles which
bear their names, except by the Académie editors, who mention them only to dismiss them.[27] Citry de la Guette had
translated the *Estoires*, and all other studies had dealt with
either the *Historia* or the continuations proper, though many,
as we have seen, attributed these in part or in whole to Bernard.
Now at last Mas-Latrie classified all the manuscripts known
to him, both of the continuations and of the short chronicles,
treating them as variant species of one genus, and this in itself
made clear that they were, in some way as yet unspecified,
related to one another. Just how they were related was a
question which exercised him, and which he went some way
towards defining, but in the end his work points to a solution
rather than reaching one. The hypothesis he evolved was this:
the continuations attached to the French text of William consist in part of texts written for the purpose, and therefore composed after the translation, and in part of independent
chronicles written in Europe and in Outremer before the translation was done, and later adapted for use as continuations.
The chronicles of Ernoul and Bernard, he concluded, were
two of the latter sort.

Concerning Ernoul, Mas-Latrie also suggested that the text
in which his name is mentioned, that is the abrégé, 1229
version, is not in fact the best-preserved version of his work,

[27] *RHC* ii, p. iv.

but that the Colbert-Fontainebleau continuation (*a* and *b*), which frequently gives a much fuller version of the same basic narrative, is the most faithful reproduction of it. This suggestion seems to have been completely lost on modern historians, who when they refer to 'Ernoul', invariably mean by it the chronicle naming him, as published by Mas-Latrie. Another suggestion that Mas-Latrie made, was that he thought it possible, though unproven, that the original chronicle of Ernoul stopped earlier than 1227 (the *terminus a quo* of the text containing his name), partly because there seemed to be a change in redaction at or around the death of Henri de Champagne in 1197, and partly because of an allusion by Ralph of Coggeshalle to a French chronicle translated by Richard, the Prior of Holy Trinity, London, which Mas-Latrie thought might well be the chronicle of Ernoul.[28] If it was, then there must have existed a version of that text stopping at or before 1220, when Ralph made his allusion to it. But Mas-Latrie remained vague about the exact nature and extent of Ernoul's work, referring to the pre-1197 section of the chronicle with his name as 'si ce n'est la chronique primitive d'Ernoul, du moins une chronique antérieure employée par Ernoul', and to Ernoul himself as 'premier rédacteur ou compilateur'.[29] In short, something may have stopped at 1197, but what? and had Ernoul composed or merely compiled? All these questions, left unsolved by Mas-Latrie, will be dealt with in later chapters.

As for the chronicle of Bernard the Treasurer, Mas-Latrie finally exposed completely Muratori's error, and established that Bernard did not translate William, but that his work was quite independent of the *Historia*, which Bernard may or may not have been acquainted with. At this juncture some confusion creeps into Mas-Latrie's argument. He states clearly on the one hand that Bernard composed his chronicle (*A* in the table on p. 10-11) by copying the short chronicle with Ernoul's name in it (*z*), and adding a short original continuation to bring it up to 1231, and also the prologue beginning 'L'an de l'incarnation'. But on the other hand he makes statements about Bernard which cannot possibly be inferred from the small sections of text he has just attributed to Bernard, but which regard him

---

[28] M-L p. 498. Cf. below, ch. V.   [29] M-L p. 499.

as the author, and not merely the compiler, of the whole of
the text of *A*.[30] This failure to distinguish sufficiently precisely and consistently between Bernard's own work and his
source, though one appreciates all too well the difficulty of
doing so in the maze of variant texts, is one of the most confusing features of the *Essai*. It is necessary to refer back constantly to Mas-Latrie's definitive statement of his view on
Bernard, and to read all his other material on Bernard in the
light of that.[31] Lastly, Mas-Latrie concludes from Pipino's
use of Bernard that by the time Pipino was writing, in 1320,
Bernard's chronicle had been completely absorbed into the
continuations. A new examination of Pipino will show, in a
later chapter, that while there certainly did exist by 1320
versions of the *Eracles* including parts of the chronicle
attributed to Bernard, it was not thus that Pipino knew
Bernard, but as a complete and independent work, similar
though not identical to the one we now possess in the text
of *A*. Mas-Latrie, while pointing out and correcting Muratori's
error, is yet haunted by its ghost.

Mas-Latrie then goes on, in the second part of the *Essai,* to
consider the continuations proper, in their first period, i.e. up
to 1232, which is also the scope of this study. He begins with
a useful résumé of the conclusions to which the first part had
led him, beginning with one in which he contradicts himself.
Earlier, attacking the notion that Bernard did not know
William's work, he had asserted that there exist translations
of William as old as the work of Bernard, and that therefore
it would have been perfectly possible for Bernard to have
known the *Historia* in a French translation.[32] He now
declares,[33] as his main conclusion, that Ernoul and Bernard
both wrote their chronicles before any translation of William
was made. Later still[34] he returns to his first idea again, and
rather grudgingly qualifies it: '. . . il se peut encore rigoureuse-
ment que le chroniqueur picard [i.e. Bernard] ait ignoré

---

[30] See for instance p. 509: 'Bernard le Trésorier reste donc pour nous l'auteur
personnel et certain des chroniques renfermées sous son nom dans les deux
manuscrits de Berne et de l'Arsenal.' Compare with this p. 520: 'Bernard le
Trésorier, qui a peut-être vécu en Orient, ne nous paraît être que le continuateur
de cet abrégé depuis l'année 1227 jusqu'à l'année 1231 seulement.'
[31] M-L p. 515: 'A son prologue historique' etc.
[32] p. 515.   [33] pp. 520-1.   [34] pp. 526-7.

l'existence de la grande histoire des croisades ou de la traduction
française.'

From the remainder of this section emerge several new ideas
which, though conjectures on Mas-Latrie's part rather than
conclusions from evidence, are among his most valuable contributions. Not infrequently careful examination of the texts
now extant, including one important manuscript which
Mas-Latrie did not know,[35] and several to which he paid no
real attention, leads to a logical conclusion which he had
already put forward as an imaginative hypothesis. Often he is
right, but unable to demonstrate it conclusively. These sign-
posts he provides to point along a path which he himself was
not able to follow to its end are at least as valuable as the conclusions he actually reached, and sometimes more so.

The *Essai* revolutionized the study of the continuations.
Unfortunately the effect was not felt immediately, for in
February 1861 there appeared a monograph by Ludwig
Streit which takes no account of the *Essai* at all. Since Streit
does refer to Mas-Latrie's work on Ernoul embodied in his
Histoire de l'île de Chypre it is reasonable to suppose that he
would also have referred to the *Essai* had he known it. Since
he must have been writing his own essay, to judge from the
date of publication, at virtually the same time as Mas-Latrie
was writing the *Essai*, it presumably reached him too late. At
all events in his *De Rerum Transmarinarum qui Guilelmum
Tyrium excepisse fertur Gallico auctore specimen*[36] (the
stylistic promise of the title is alas fulfilled in every page),
Streit duplicates to some extent the work Mas-Latrie had
done in the *Essai*. But he also covers some new ground not
touched by Mas-Latrie, and it is worth outlining briefly the
contents of his *libellus* as he calls it. He himself sets out the
plan of his work:

> Itaque ab initio, quo melius disputatio procedat, breviter superiorum
> sententias recensebo . . . , tum ad ipsam caussam [*sic*] ita aggrediar, ut
> primum de totius corporis transmarini compositione disseram . . . , deinde
> narrationis, quae primae continuationis loco habetur, originem et
> propagationem investigare studeam . . . , denique scrutari incipiam, num
> certa quaedam illi cum Guilelmi Tyrii historia intercedat condicio quidve
> auctor secutus sit.[37]

---

[35] Saint-Omer 722, MS *z*.   [36] Greifswald, 1861.   [37] Op. cit., p. 7.

These are large objectives for a *libellus* of some 70 pages, and this is the main trouble with Streit's paper: economy tends to degenerate into superficiality. Nevertheless he does have something to say about each of these topics, and leaving aside the unoriginal and the obvious, we may summarize his contributions thus. He rejects[38] the distinction made by the Académie editors between Western and Eastern redactions, pointing out that there are cross-connections between the two. He does not, however, arrive at the notion of a common pool of source material. But later he does give a helpful, if sketchy and incomplete, concordance of the various fragments occurring in more than one text. He also criticizes the Académie editors for putting their faith in the text of manuscripts *a* and *b*, but his arguments on this point are not really convincing. He gives[39] examples of bad readings in these two manuscripts, which is indeed an argument for saying that they are not good manuscripts of the text they give. But this is not what the Académie editors had claimed in the first place. Rather they had asserted that where the text of these two differs radically from that given by the other versions of the continuations, in content and not merely in wording, it is the version of *a* and *b* which is to be regarded as the older text. Streit seems rather to have confused manuscript and text. In any case the arguments he does produce[40] for the primacy of *cJ* over all the other versions are only moderately convincing. The most interesting part of his work is the short final chapter on Ernoul. Streit sets out a rehabilitate Ernoul, deprived hitherto of recognition because everyone has attributed to Bernard what Streit believes to be the work of Ernoul, namely the short chronicle represented above on p.10-11 by *z*. It must be remembered that Streit thinks he is being very original in making this point, because he has not read Mas-Latrie's *Essai*. He points out Ernoul's opportunities, as the squire of Balian d'Ibelin, for obtaining exact military information, and agrees with received opinion in recognizing as Ernoul's undisputed work that part of the chronicle which is most complimentary to the Ibelins. He believes, however, that Ernoul carried on far beyond the goal he had set himself in his opening

---

[38] pp. 19-20.   [39] pp. 45 ff.   [40] pp. 66-70.

sentence, continuing the history of Palestine for some forty
years after the loss of Jerusalem. In other words, Streit does
not accept the theory that Ernoul stopped at or before 1227,
but believes that Ernoul's work as we have it today, is split up.[41]
The vagaries of the chronology he dismisses as a feature of
Ernoul's method: 'Secutus igitur Arnoldus est non annorum
seriem, sed rerum quendam connexum'.[42] Again he reiterates
his preference for the version of *cJ*. As for the question of
whether Ernoul drew on the *Historia* for the early part of his
chronicle, Streit arrives at the curious conclusion that he did,
but that he frequently disagrees with William. They are, as he
had already observed, very different authors.

Streit, then, makes some minor points, but no major step
forward. It was another ten years before another sizeable work
did appear, this time in the form of a critical edition by Mas-
Latrie of what he entitled *La Chronique d'Ernoul et de Bernard
le Trésorier*.[43] This was an edition of the texts which name the
two authors and which are represented in the table on p. 10-11
by *z* and *A* respectively. A manuscript of the same family as
z, Brussels 11142, was adopted as the base, and the variants
of the named Bernard manuscripts[44] were given in footnotes.
In addition, the sections peculiar to the *A* family, and attributed by Mas-Latrie to Bernard himself, namely the prologue
beginning 'L'an de l'Incarnation . . .' and the last part covering the years 1227-31, are printed in italics at the beginning
and the end. The *Essai* of 1860 was reprinted as an appendix
to the edition, and Mas-Latrie also added a new *Avertissement*,
a concordance of his edition with those of Muratori, Martène,
Guizot, and the Académie, and with the continuations, and
finally, descriptions of the manuscripts and of previous printed
editions he had used.

In the *Avertissement* Mas-Latrie's views have, as one
might expect, developed somewhat from those he had expressed
in the *Essai* eleven years before. The most noticeable change
is that he now draws attention to the possible value of the
Lyon manuscript (*d*),[45] without however relinquishing his
previous opinion that the Colbert-Fontainebleau text (*a* and *b*)

---

[41] p. 73.   [42] p. 75.   [43] Paris, 1871.
[44] Arsenal 4797 (MS *A*) and Berne 340.
[45] M-L p. xxiij.

is the oldest and most valuable of all. Another manuscript too, Brussels 11142, had only recently come to his notice, indeed he had prepared his edition without it, and had almost finished when Kervyn de Lettenhove brought to his attention manuscript 11142 of the Bibliothèque Royale, Brussels, which Mas-Latrie now acclaimed as 'un texte qui a plus de chances que tous les autres d'être le texte d'Ernoul'.[46] He began all over again, using it as the base of his edition. He still did not know, indeed he never knew, a manuscript which he might well have preferred even beyond the Brussels one, Saint-Omer 722 (MS *z*). Still it is surprising that Mas-Latrie, taken up as he was by the discovery of the Brussels manuscript, did not realize that it ought to alter his views on the authorship of the fragment 'L'an de l'Incarnation' etc. which he still calls 'le prologue de Bernard' and which he prints accordingly in italics at the beginning of the work. We shall see later that this fragment was originally totally unconnected with the chronicle to which it is now attached, that it was not a prologue, and that it was not written by Bernard.[47]

Otherwise the *Avertissement* deals extensively with Pipino, tracing the history of Muratori's error. Again it is curious that Mas-Latrie by no means exploits to the full the evidence which Pipino offers us about the work of Bernard, but dismisses as unimportant the question of exactly what text it was that Pipino believed to be the work of Bernard.[48] Certainly to reject Muratori's misinterpretation of Pipino's evidence is vital, but it is no less essential to look at what Pipino really does say about his source.

There now existed usable, though not definitive editions of the Latin text of the *Historia,* of the French continuations, and of the short chronicles attributed to Ernoul and Bernard. The translation of William remained rather inadequately edited, for in the *Recueil* it had been given the status of a footnote extraordinary, and proportionately less effort seems to have been expended on it than on the text itself. Paulin Paris therefore proposed to bring out an edition of the *Eracles,* translation and continuations together, based on the manuscripts belonging to Ambroise Firmin-Didot. Volumes i and ii of this

---

[46] Ibid., p. xxv.   [47] Cf. below, pp. 56-58.   [48] M-L pp. x-xj.

projected work, containing the translation, with the descriptions
of Jerusalem and Galilee from the text published by Mas-Latrie
added as an appendix to Volume ii, appeared in 1879 and
1880.[49] Equipped with footnotes, glossary, and Longnon's
maps, these volumes make one regret very much indeed that
the rest never appeared.[50]

Since then, only one major piece of work has been published
which conerns the continuations, as opposed to William himself, or the translation of William, and that is Riant's *Inventaire
sommaire,* published in the *Archives de l'Orient Latin* for
1880-1.[51] This is a catalogue of all the known manuscripts of
all the texts, both the *Eracles* and the short chronicles, an
improvement on Mas-Latrie's classification, though based on
the same principles, and it remains the standard list to this
day.[52]

All researches since Riant have been devoted to other texts
of the corpus, either the *Historia* itself, or the Latin continuation, or the French translation, and none to the French
continuations or the short chronicles. These will all be found
listed in the bibliography; here it seems relevant to mention
only those which, although they do not concern the texts
which are the subject of this study, namely the continuations
and the short chronicles, do have some bearing on the question
in hand. Marianne Salloch edited in 1934 the Latin continuation found appended to the *Historia* in the British Museum
MS Reg. 14.c.x.,[53] and in 1943 Emily Babcock and A.C. Krey
published an English translation of the *Historia* under the
title *A History of Deeds Done Beyond the Sea.*[54] In recent
years R.C.B. Huygens has published several invaluable articles

[49] P. Paris (ed.) *Guillaume de Tyr et ses continuateurs* (Paris, 1879-80).
[50] The Preface, however, perpetrates some old errors about Bernard the Treasurer,
a surprising vagary since Paris had explicitly denounced these in his catalogue
of the Royal Library forty years earlier. See P. Paris, *Les Manuscrits français
de la bibliothèque du roi* (Paris, 1836), i. 81: 'L'un de ces écrivains, faussement
désigné par Muratori sous le nom de Bernard le Trésorier' etc.
[51] Comte Riant, *Inventaire.* cf. above p. 3.
[52] Several amendments can now be made. No. 38 is now in the British Museum,
as no. 12 of the Yates Thompson Collection. Nos. 42 and 55 are in the Walters
Art Gallery, Baltimore, Maryland, designated W. 137 and W. 142 respectively,
and this gallery also possesses two MSS not listed by Riant, which are numbered
524 and 528 in its collection.
[53] M. Salloch, *Die lateinische Fortsetzung Willelms von Tyrus* (Leipzig, 1934).
[54] Columbia Records of Civilisation, no. 35 (New York, 1943).

on William,[55] including an edition of the 'lost' autobiographical chapter of the *Historia*, and he is now preparing, with H.E. Mayer, a new edition of the *Historia*.[56]

What then remains to be done? Any study of the French continuations and the short chronicles is bound to some extent to take as a point of departure the work of Mas-Latrie, which in the last analysis is the only critical work on the continuations that is worth taking very seriously, and the only one on which it is reasonable to place any degree of reliance. Mas-Latrie describes explicitly some of the work he has left yet to be done: 'démêler le chaos de la première époque de formation des continuations de Guillaume de Tyr'.[57] This will be the broad aim of the present study; within that, the more precise aim is to reconstruct the chronicle of Ernoul, at least in outline, where the evidence does not allow more, and where possible in detail.

On the other hand, Mas-Latrie's conclusions, when closely examined, sometimes turn out to be less than watertight, and his whole method of analysing the texts begs a number of questions. For example, in saying at one point of the Colbert-Fontainebleau continuation (*a* and *b*) and at another of Brussels 11142[58] that they are the nearest text to the original chronicle of Ernoul, he does assume that there will be one text which will be nearer than all the others to the original, in every section of its text.[59] In view of the composite nature of all the texts this is obviously not a certainty to be counted on. He also tends, in common with everyone who has ever worked on the texts, to treat each as a whole, and though he recognizes that each is an assembly of parts which were once independent of each other, he does not treat the parts separately. The questions he asks about the text are always applied to the whole, though they may by their very nature relate to such an early stage in the evolution of the compilations that the texts

---

[55] See full list in Bibliography.
[56] In addition, Mr. O.G. Goulden of the University of North Staffordshire is working on the Old French translations of the *Historia,* and Dr. J. Folda of the University of North Carolina, Chapel Hill, recently presented at Johns Hopkins University a thesis on the miniatures in the MSS of both the *Historia* and the related French texts. Both of them have kindly allowed me to use information collected by them in the course of their own researches, and I am most grateful for their help.
[57] M-L p. xxiv.   [58] Riant, no. 16.   [59] M-L p. xxv.

we have now cannot possibly give any meaningful answer. For example, in asking how near any given compilation is to the original Ernoul, it is essential to allow for at least the possibility that several stages of development separate the two, and that some parts of the text may well have suffered more change than others in the process. It seems more logical, as well as potentially more profitable, to isolate the units which in ever-varying combinations go to make up the texts, and this is not difficult to do, in view of the relatively large number of texts we have available for comparison.

We shall begin, then, by considering how much is known about the identities of the two shadowy figures to whom constant reference must be made in studying the texts, Ernoul and Bernard, and what they wrote, before examining the structure of the various versions of the *Eracles*.

III

THE PUTATIVE AUTHORS:
ERNOUL AND BERNARD

1. *Ernoul*

IN APRIL 1187 Guy of Lusignan sent to his troublesome
vassal Raymond of Tripoli a delegation consisting of the
Archbishop of Tyre, the Grand Masters of the Hospital and
the Temple, Reynaud of Sidon, and Balian d'Ibelin. At Nablus
the party split up, Balian remaining behind in the town while
the others continued their journey, on the understanding that
he should rejoin them the next day at the castle of La Fève.
Thus he was not present at the engagement, ill-advised and
disastrous, between the knights of the Temple and the re-
connaissance party led by Salahadin's son al-Afdal, which is
sometimes called the battle of Nazareth. When Balian arrived
at La Fève the next day he found the place apparently desert-
ed. 'Dont fist descendre .i. sien vallet qui avoit non Ernous.
Ce fu cil qui cest conte fist metre en escrit.' (MS *z*, f. 32^b,
col. 1.) This is the wording of four manuscripts: the one
quoted, Berne 41, Berne 115, and Brussels 11142.[1] All the
other manuscripts of the abrégé, and most of those of the
Eracles, relate the incident in exactly the same way, merely
omitting the name of Balian's servant.[2] On this short mention
is ultimately based any connection of Ernoul's name with any
of the texts.

This is slight evidence by itself perhaps, but it is not without
strong support from other sources. To begin in general terms,
the part of the abrégé in which the mention of Ernoul's name
occurs is strongly and uniformly pro-Ibelin, and conflicts in
its assessment of Balian's character and motives with other
contemporary chronicles. There is the question, for example,
of Balian's relationship with Salahadin. The writer of the
abrégé makes it clear that they were quite close friends, but
he turns this to Balian's honour, as is shown especially well in
his account of Balian's negotiations with Salahadin for the
ransom of the poor of Jerusalem after the city had fallen to
the Saracens in 1187. According to the abrégé, Balian used

---

[1] Cf. M-L p. 149.   [2] *RHC* ii. 42.

the influence he had with Salahadin to bring the sum asked
for down to reasonable proportions, and then asked further
for five hundred people to be freed without ransom, as a
personal favour to himself. That Salahadin agreed to these
terms in consideration of his friendship with Balian, and not
simply as the outcome of the customary diplomatic haggling,
is put beyond doubt: 'Lors s'amolia Salehadins, et dist que,
pour Diu, avant, et pour l'amor de lui qui l'em prioit, metroit
le raençon a raison, si qu'il i poroient avenir.'[3]

Elsewhere Balian and his brother Baldwin of Rames are
referred to as the only Frankish barons in Outremer whom
the Saracens really feared. At the accession of Guy of Lusignan
in 1186, Baldwin refused to do him homage, for he believed
Guy, and Guy's wife Sybilla, through whom he claimed the
kingdom, to have been illegally crowned. He entrusted his
lands and his young son Thomas to his brother Balian, and
left the Kingdom of Jerusalem for Antioch, where he entered
the service of Bohemond. The abrégé says: 'Quant Bauduins
de Rames ot ensi fait, si vint a Balyan de Belin sen frere, se li
carja son fil et sa tiere a garder, et prist congiet, si s'en ala.
Dont che fu mout grans duels et grans domages a le tiere, et
dont Sarrasin furent mout lié, car il ne douterent puis homme
qui fust en le tiere, fors Balyan son frere seulement, qui
demoura.'[4]

This incident certainly did cause rejoicing in the Saracen
camp, for the opposition to Guy was widespread, and Baldwin
was not the only lord who left the Kingdom at his accession.
A general dissension was arising among the Frankish barons,
and the country soon split into two camps, those loyal to
Guy, and his opponents, who regarded Raymond of Tripoli
as their unofficial head. It was a division that the tiny state
could ill afford, and to which its downfall was unanimously
attributed. But the abrégé puts quite a different slant on the
incident quoted above, by making it illustrate, not the
generalized state of political trouble prevalent in the Kingdom,
but the importance of one man, Baldwin of Rames, and this
is typical of the abrégé's whole approach. Time and again, as
will be seen in the course of our examination of the texts, the
abrégé, and the other texts where they agree with the abrégé,

[3] M-L p.222.   [4] Ibid., pp. 138-9.

give a far greater importance to the Ibelin family than they
really had, and that was already a great deal.

Moreover, other chroniclers, though well aware of the
Ibelins' close relations with Salahadin, put a more doubtful or
even downright pejorative interpretation on them. Nor are they
so laudatory in describing Balian's moral character. The author
of the *Itinerarium Peregrinorum,* who admittedly represents
the extremist section of the Ibelins' critics, but who is not
alone in his views, makes these two references to Balian:

> Porro Balisantus, mortuo rege Amalrico, matrem puellae duxerat
> uxorem, quae Graia faece a cunis imbuta, virum moribus suis habebat
> conformem, saevum impia, levem mobilis, perfidum fraudulenta.[5]

> ... contigit Stephanum de Torneham, ipsis obviare exeuntibus a
> Salahadino de Jerusalem, quorum nomina tunc temporis ob notam
> infamiae satis erant notoria. Unus eorum vocabatur Balianus de Ybelino,
> alter Reginaldus de Sydone.[6]

In other words, the reputation and motives of the Ibelins
were not at all a clear-cut matter. Were they patriots who
used their personal influence for the good of their country, or
simply collaborators? subtle or treacherous? famous or notorious? The abrégé is unwaveringly on the side of the Ibelins.

More precisely, the assertion that the author of this part of
the text was Balian d'Ibelin's squire is also borne out by the
narrative. From his description of the battle of Hattin, it is
certain that he himself took part, and he describes the battle
from the point of view of the rearguard. In this text, and those
related to it at this point, and in no other chronicle, we read
the story of the Saracen witch found casting spells by a
rearguard sergeant,[7] and beyond that the whole account is
primarily of the action of the rearguard. It is well known
from other sources that the rearguard was led by Balian
d'Ibelin that day. Furthermore, after the battle, the abrégé
goes on to describe the escape of Balian, together with one or
two others, his journey to Jerusalem, and his conduct of the
negotiations for its surrender already described above. This
account, though not without the bias we have already observed

[5] *Itinerarium Peregrinorum et Gesta Regis Ricardi, auctore, ut videtur, Ricardo,
Canonico Sanctae Trinitatis Londoniensis,* ed. W. Stubbs (Rolls Series, London
1864), p. 121.
[6] Ibid., p. 337.
[7] M-L pp. 163-4. *Eracles* xxiii. 36, *RHC* ii. 53-4 main text, 54-5 variants.

as characteristic, is basically historically accurate, that is, it does not seem, when compared with other sources, to have distorted the facts, only to have put a peculiar interpretation on them. The whole section we have just examined, from the battle of Nazareth to the surrender of Jerusalem, is one of the parts of these chronicles most valued and used by modern historians.

There seems no reason, then, to disbelieve the statement made in the abrégé that it was Ernoul, a servant of Balian d'Ibelin, 'qui cest conte fist metre en escript', though the exact meaning to be attributed to those words is a large and vital question. For the present the identity of the man named is the question in hand. There are three pieces of evidence outside the text he is supposed to have written, which shed further light on him.

The first was discovered, and examined, by Mas-Latrie in his *Histoire de l'île de Chypre*. It is a Cypriot document, a treaty of alliance offensive and defensive for five years between Cyprus and Genoa, drawn up at Nicosia and dated 2 December 1233.[8] Among the names of the witnesses is that of *Arnaix de Gibelleto*. The editor states that other spellings are found elsewhere, but gives no references. As Mas-Latrie points out, it is of course not certain that this man and the man referred to in the abrégé are one and the same, and it probably cannot be proved one way or the other. But it is a possibility, and quite a strong one when one remembers that there was a close connection between the Ibelin and Gibelet families. Later, in examining the continuations, we shall find a clear instance of a Gibelet child being brought up in an Ibelin household.[9] It is at the least very likely that the Ernoul who in 1187 was learning the profession of arms as the squire of Balian d'Ibelin was the same Ernoul de Gibelet who in 1232 was a man of sufficient importance in Cyprus to witness a treaty of national importance. Cyprus at that time was effectively ruled by the Ibelins, who were thus in a position to reward with high office such loyalty as marks every page of the abrégé, the story that Ernoul the squire, it is claimed, caused to be put in writing.

[8] L. de Mas-Latrie, *Histoire de l'île de Chypre* (Paris, 1852-61), ii. 56. See also i. 136 for notes on the Giblet family.
[9] Cf. below, p. 112.

The second reference to Ernoul is made by Philip of Novara, in his list of the famous jurists and advocates from whom he got his thorough, if informal, legal education:

> Apres fui moult acointé de monseignor de Saeste a Baruth et a Acre et en Chypre; et moult de chozes m'aprist la soie merci volentiers. Et apres tout ces grans seignors et sages usai moult en cort entor messire Guillaume vesconte et messire Harneis et messire Guillaume de Rivet le joune, qui moult estoient grans plaideors. Et au reaume de Jerusalem fui je moult acointé de messire Nicole Anteaume et de sire Phelippe de Baisdoin, qui estoient grans plaideors en cort et hors court.[10]

Unfortunately Philip does not tell us where he knew Harneis, and as can be seen from this quotation, he travelled a great deal. But he brackets the name of Harneis with that of Guillaume de Rivet, whom we know to have been in Cyprus at the period in question, i.e. the 1220s, until immediately before his death in 1230.

The last reference to Ernoul occurs in the *Eracles,* though not in the section with which this study is concerned. In the summer of 1232 we find 'Arneis de Gybelet' besieged in the castle of Dieu d'Amour by the troops of Richard Filangieri:

> Or retornerons a Richart le mareschal. Apres ce que il ot fait l'eschec a Casal Ymbert, il envoia en Chypre les Chypreis qui o lui estoient, et de la soe gent ausi. Quant cil furent venus en Chypre, si firent ensi que il orent le chastel et la vile de Cherines et la Candare, et la tor de Famagoste, et assegerent Deu d'Amors. Dedens le chastel de Deu d'Amors estoient . ii. serors dou roi, damoiseles Marie et Ysabel; et si y avoient chastelein Felipe de Cafran, et y estoit Arneis de Gybelet, que li sires de Barut avoit laissé cheveteine de la terre, qui moult poi y mist de conroi, si que neis le chastel ou les serors dou roi estoient, et il meismes ne garni il mie; ains dut estre perdu par soffraite de viande; et a grant mesaise et a grant meschief se tindrent tant que il furent rescos.[11]

From these three references we can build up a sketchy but quite helpful picture of Arneis de Gibelet, a man of considerable importance in two fields, the legal and the political, which in the crusader states were even more intricately bound up than is usual at most times and in most places, whose life seems to have been spent in the entourage of the Ibelin dynasty, and who in the late 1220s and early 1230s was solidly established in Cyprus. All these factors will be taken into

---

[10] *Le Livre de Philippe de Navarre, in RHC Lois* i. 525.   [11] *RHC* ii. 399.

consideration in establishing exactly what he could or could
not have written of the corpus of chronicles which are our
subject. It is now time to turn to the figure behind the only
other name the chronicles preserve for us, that of Bernard
the Treasurer.

2. *Bernard the Treasurer*

As soon as we begin to consider Bernard the Treasurer, we
are presented with a paradox. As we have seen in reviewing
the state of studies, he was widely credited with the authorship of various large sections of the chronicles, either the
abrégé, or the continuations, or the translation of the *Historia,*
right up to Mas-Latrie's edition of 1871. Yet the manuscript
evidence for connecting his name with the chronicles at all is
minimal. To the end of two manuscripts, Berne 340 and
Arsenal 4797, is attached this colophon: 'Ceste conte de la
terre d'outre mer fist faire le tresoriers Bernars, de sant piere
de Corbie. En lacanacion .millo. ccxxxij.'[12]

That is all. Bernard is named in only two manuscripts of a
family of five containing the same text, and then only in a
colophon, not, like Ernoul, in the body of the text. Yet for
all that it would be foolish to dismiss lightly this connection
of the chronicle with Corbie, for the abbey had an extremely
high reputation as a centre of scholarship and of manuscript
copying, and was a highly likely place for the composition of
a contemporary vernacular account of the crusades.

From its foundation, the abbey of St. Peter enjoyed singular
good fortune. Between 657 and 661, Bathilde, widow of
Clovis II, transplanted a colony of the Order of Luxeuil to
Corbie, endowing the new community richly with money and
land, and her patronage was continued by six Merovingian
kings—Clothaire III, Childeric II, Thierry III, Clovis III,
Childeric III, and Dagobert III—and by Pepin the Short and
Charlemagne, so that when the abbey's privileges were
presented for confirmation by Abbot Leutchar, between 751
and 768, it was stated to possess extensive property *in
quibuslibet pagis.*

Another advantage of Corbie was the natural one of its
situation, only twelve and a half miles from the major centre

[12] Berne 340, f. 127ᵃ; Arsenal 4797, f. 128ᵃ, similarly.

of Amiens, the intersection of the main routes from north to south and from east to west, a factor of particular importance in the period of the crusades, which occasioned more movement than usual among most sections of the community. At all times Corbie would be closely in touch with the comings and goings of merchants, pilgrims, both clergy and laymen, missionaries, and soldiers. Many such people must even have accepted hospitality in the monastery itself.

These two factors contributed largely to the rapid growth of the scriptorium and school of Corbie. Symptomatic of its early preoccupation with scholarship is the provision made in the statutes of Adalhard the Elder in 822[13] for a parchmenter employed solely by the monastery. The 'Corbie script' became very famous indeed—one has only to look at Mabillon's *De Re Diplomatica*[14] to see what a disproportionate number of his illustrations are taken from Corbie manuscripts—and Corbie had extensive influence on other monastic schools, and on non-monastic affairs too, its monks going all over Europe for one purpose or another. Harbert, abbot of Lobbes, Eudes, bishop of Beauvais, Paschasius Radbertus and his rival Ratramnus, Druthmar the grammarian, who taught in the schools of Stavelot and Malmédy, and finally the monk John, who helped to found Alfred's palace school at Winchester, all came originally from Corbie. The reputation of the abbey continued well into the period which concerns us, to judge from accounts of its library, and catalogues made about the year 1220.[15]

All in all, Corbie in the early thirteenth century was an ideal place for the composition of a crusading chronicle. It had all the facilities necessary for such an undertaking, scriptorium, library, eye-witness evidence from returning crusaders, financial resources, and the means of disseminating the work once produced. It is therefore no surprise to read

---

[13] See L. Levillain, 'Les Statuts d'Adalhard', *Le Moyen Âge*, 2 e Sér., iv (1900), 333 ff. For the reference to the parchmenter see p. 352. The Bodleian Library has a typewritten copy of the Statutes, with many useful maps and plans of the abbey, entitled 'The Ancient Statutes of the Abbey of S. Peter of Corbie', and numbered 1107.b.4 in the catalogue.

[14] J. Mabillon, *De Re Diplomatica Libri Sex* (Paris, 1709), *passim*.

[15] L. Delisle, 'Recherches sur l'ancienne bibliothèque de Corbie', *Bibliothèque de l'École des Chartes*, 5th Ser. i. (1860) 420. See also an article which is effectively an amplified translation of this: L.W. Jones, 'The Scriptorium at Corbie', *Speculum*, xxii (1947) 191-204 and 375-94.

in the colophon quoted that the chronicle was made (in what sense 'made' is a later question) by Bernard, the treasurer of the abbey. There has been a certain amount of discussion as to whether this Bernard was a monk or not, centred on two pieces of evidence, the first suggesting that he had property of his own, the second that at the relevant time there was no monk of that name at Corbie.[16] The first is dealt with by Paulin Paris, who quotes thus from the Corbie cartulary: ' . . . sous la date de 1203, une charte de l'abbé, confirmant à notre trésorier la propriété de ce qu'il avait acheté d'un chevalier nommé Bernard de Moreuil, antérieurement à la donation que ce chevalier avait fait de ses biens à la même abbaye'.[17]

Now the Rule of S. Benedict is extremely emphatic on the question of personal property of all kinds,[18] and though there are circumstances under which one might find a Benedictine monk involved in property transactions, none of them fits the case described here. For example it might have been possible to suppose that the abbot was giving the treasurer the property in question for his use within the general financial structure of the monastery: Adalhard's statutes specifically mention such methods as being desirable and efficient. Again, to find the treasurer buying property would not be surprising: we should assume him to be acting on behalf of the community. But here it is the abbot who confirms the property to the treasurer, that is, it was intended to be his individually. Indeed the purpose of this charter would seem to be precisely to distinguish between the two parts of Bernard de Moreuil's property—the part he had sold to the treasurer, which the abbot here confirms is the treasurer's, and the part which he had subsequently donated to the abbey as a community. In short, the inevitable interpretation of the charter seems to be that the treasurer of Corbie in 1203 had personal property, and on this ground alone we must assert that he was not a professed monk.

It is not of course certain that the treasurer in 1203 and the treasurer in 1232 were one and the same person, though Paulin Paris evidently thinks they were. There is, however,

[16] M-L p. 510.
[17] P.Paris, *Guillaume de Tyr et ses continuateurs,* p. viii. The cartulary is not edited.
[18] *Sancti Benedicti Regula Monachorum,* ed. Butler (Friburg-im-Breisgau, 1912). See especially xxxiii, lviii, lix (pp. 64-5, 103 and 104-5).

another difficulty about Bernard the Treasurer, namely that
the records of the abbey about the year 1232 do not mention
anyone of that name, a circumstance which Mas-Latrie
suggested might be explained by Bernard's prolonged absence,
for example on pilgrimage.[19] This would mean that his work
was not in fact done at Corbie, and that he was only 'de
Saint Pierre de Corbie' in the sense that he came originally
from there. The strongest objection to this theory (which is
of course in any case pure hypothesis) is the indisputable
connection of the work with the north-east of France, a
connection which will become ever more apparent as the
examination of its sources and composition progresses. The
alternative possibility, that Bernard belonged to the abbey
without being a monk, is by contrast perfectly feasible. In any
medieval monastery there were nearly always a number of
laymen in one capacity or another; in an abbey of the size
and importance of Corbie the number was probably quite
considerable.[20] In fact the presence of such lay people in
monastic communities became something of a problem, and
the Hirschau reforms were designed to reduce their numbers
and their influence on the life of the community. Some were
attached in an official capacity, for example as domestic
servants, or as *ministeriales,* who might hold offices of some
importance, without being religious. Both these could be
regarded as members of the monastic family, but lay members.
Apart from these, however, there was a large category of
people for whom the monastery offered the only kind of
insurance policy available. It was common for individuals, or
sometimes whole families, to enter a monastery, making over
all their property to the community, though usually with
reservation of usufruct to themselves for their lifetime. The
monastery for its part undertook to provide them with all
the necessities of life, and thus gave them a security which,
in politically troubled times, the world could not give.[21]

---

[19] M-L p.510.

[20] U. Berlière, 'La *Familia* dans les monastères bénédictins du Moyen Âge', *Académie
Royale de Belgique. Classe des Lettres. Mémoires,* N.S. xxix (1930-2); see especially
pp. 12 ff; and for the situation at Corbie in the time of Adalhard, ibid., p.25.

[21] A. Luchaire, *La Société française au temps de Philippe-Auguste* (Paris, 1909),
gives one example of an entire family, father, daughter, and grandmother, entering
a convent under such terms.

Such oblates or corrodians, as they were called, promised obedience to the abbot in matters directly relating to their life in the abbey, but kept their judicial rights, which vowed monks did not. This arrangement was obviously beneficial to both parties: security was a valuable commodity to the one, and property to the other. There were also many people who simply retired to a monastery in old age; according to Professor Legge, this is what Denis Pyramus did, and as she points out, a monastery as busy as St. Edmund's would be unlikely to let his talents go unused.[22] Doubtless Corbie also exploited the talents of its lay people to the full, and if Bernard showed himself gifted as a compiler of chronicles, he would be given free rein in a house which was justly proud of its library.

In short, there were several ways in which a layman might find himself, in the year 1232, treasurer of a large Benedictine abbey, and in a position to have a book made for its library. Nor is it of great importance for our examination of his chronicle to know whether Bernard was monk or layman: what is certain is that he was attached to Corbie, and that his work will bear traces of the influence of the monastic milieu, regardless of his own precise status in the community. Thus in Ernoul and Bernard we have two men who in different ways were excellently equipped to compose such chronicles as make up the abrégé and the continuations. Both their names are associated with the abrégé. What precisely were their respective contributions to these texts?

[22] M.D. Legge, *Anglo-Norman in the Cloisters* (Edinburgh, 1950), pp. 6-7.

IV

THE WORK OF BERNARD THE TREASURER

THE CIRCUMSTANCES under which Ernoul and Bernard are named in the two versions of the abrégé[1] differ in a way which by itself gives us some indication of the difference in their contribution to this compilation. Ernoul is mentioned in passing, in such a way as to give us no real indication at all of how much he is being credited with, let alone how much he is in reality responsible for. But Bernard's name is added formally to a complete work. What his exact function was we do not yet know; but it is clear that he is in some way or other responsible for the work in its entirety, in the form in which we now have it in the named manuscripts, Berne 340 and Arsenal 4797.[2]

The first person to mention Bernard's connection with the chronicles at all was of course Francesco Pipino, whose references to Bernard have already been described in the review of the state of studies.[3] As we have seen, Pipino evidently did not intend to attribute to Bernard the material for the whole of the book in which he mentions him as a source, but only specific parts of it. Indeed he names elsewhere other sources— for example Oliver of Paderborn's *Historia Damiatae,* Vincent of Beauvais, Brochardus[4] —which by itself should have sufficed to prevent the error Muratori made in entitling the whole book *Bernardi Thesaurarii: De Acquisitione Terrae Sanctae.* The falsity of this title was amply demonstrated by Mas-Latrie, who showed that Bernard did not write anything beyond what is contained in the manuscripts bearing his name. But Mas-Latrie dismissed as unimportant the question of what exactly Pipino's source did contain, and whether he used a manuscript of the translation of William of Tyre with continuations up to 1230, or two separate manuscripts, one of the translation, and one of the chronicle of Bernard as we

---

[1] For the usage of the term *abrégé* throughout this study cf. above, p. 7 and Table of Manuscripts, and for the description of the two versions, above, pp. 11-13.
[2] Cf. above, p. 46.
[3] pp. 23-4.
[4] e.g. *RIS* Vol. vii, cols. 792, 801, and 842.

now have it in the manuscripts with the colophon.[5] This
dismissal seems somewhat peremptory, since in either case
the information would affect quite seriously our view of
Bernard in relation to the continuations as a whole. If the
first alternative is correct, then Pipino had a manuscript of a
recension of the *Eracles* ending in 1230 which is not now
extant in any manuscript; moreover it was marked at some
point with Bernard's name. This would suggest that it is at
least possible that Bernard's original intention was to write a
continuation to the French version of the *Historia,* which in
turn would mean that the present so-called chronicle of
Bernard must be some sort of abbreviation and re-working of
that original. Alternatively it might be interpreted as meaning
that the compilers of this lost 1230 version of the *Eracles*
drew on the work of Bernard for the years preceding 1230,
and that therefore his contribution cannot be limited to that
1229-31 section which is contained only in his version of the
abrégé and not in the version mentioning Ernoul. If on the
other hand it can be shown that Pipino used two manuscripts,
then his copy of Bernard's chronicle was shorter than any we
know now. In that case the question would again arise: of
how much is Bernard the original author? Is it not possible
that just as MS Berne 113 is a copy of the known Bernard
chronicle, without the name of the author (which as we have
seen we only know from two other manuscripts of the identical text),[6] so Brussels 11142 is a copy of the first recension
of Bernard's work, not named as his here, but which was so
named in the manuscript Pipino knew? Having defined what
Pipino's references to Bernard do not claim, we must now ask
what they do say about him.

Pipino in fact begins his 25th book with a fairly straightforward translation of the French version of the *Historia* back
into Latin, abbreviating here, expanding there, adding material
from other sources. He pursues this translation up to the first
chapter of Book xiv of the *Eracles* (accession of Fulk of Anjou
as King of Jerusalem), where he quite suddenly abandons it
in favour of the abrégé, which he uses as his basic source from
this point on, quite regardless of whether it is more informative
than the *Eracles,* which it almost always is not. In this, as in

[5] M-L pp. xj and 526.   [6] Cf. above, p. 46.

many other aspects, Pipino's work methods are mysterious
and not altogether laudable. He is no historian. For example
in his chapter 126 he transcribes the quite erroneous information given by the abrégé on the supposed siege of Ascalon
by Fulk of Anjou, Louis VII, and Conrad, of which the *Eracles*
gives an accurate, and incidentally far more interesting, account
in Book xvii, under the reign of Baldwin III.[7] But there can be
no doubt about what text Pipino is using as his source: it is
that early part of the abrégé found in the version attributed
to Bernard, and in the shorter version mentioning Ernoul,
but not found in any version of the *Eracles*,[8] in which it is unnecessary because the translation of William covers the same
ground. Pipino certainly possessed and used two texts, one a
copy of the *Eracles*, the other a chronicle attributed to
Bernard.

What did this second text contain? It certainly did not
correspond to the manuscripts we have now, for these go on
after the point at which Pipino's source ended. He says:
'Haec de gestis Regis Johannis sumta sunt ex Historia
Bernardi Thesaurarii. Qualis autem fuerit exitus non inveni,
vel quod historiam non compleverit, vel quod codex, unde
sumsi, fuit imperfectus.'[9]

Thus the text Pipino had cannot be identified with the
short version of the abrégé,[10] since it goes on after that text
stops, nor with the longer one. We are forced to conclude
that there existed yet another version of the same text, which
Pipino attributes to Bernard. From the fact that Pipino's
adaptation corresponds closely to the extant Bernard chronicle,
however, we may conclude that this shorter version of it differed only in length. The fact that Pipino knew Bernard was
the author although his manuscript was, he thought, incomplete,
implies something further about his text, namely that Bernard was
mentioned otherwise than in a colophon at the end, or Pipino
could not have been in much doubt as to the completeness of
his manuscript. So Mas-Latrie is vindicated: he postulated two
recensions of Bernard's chronicle, and it is now clear that he
was right in doing so.[11] But it must be added that the first

[7] *RIS* Vol. vii, col. 766: 'Deinde castrametati sunt apud Ascalonam' etc. M-L
pp. 12-23. *RHC* i, pt. 2, pp. 794-802 and 804-13.
[8] i.e. up to the year 1183, M-L p. 116.   [9] *RIS* vii. 846.
[10] For which see above, pp. 11-12.   [11] M-L p. 525.

was not simply, as he suggests, a re-working of the material existing in the shorter abrégé, to 1227, for Pipino's source stops only at 1230. Rather it would appear, therefore, that Bernard first produced a chronicle identical with the extant one in all respects except that it ended in 1230 (a work we may call Bi) and then added a further section bringing it up to 1231, thus producing the extant version (Bii).

This still leaves open the question of whether Bernard was an original author at all, a question on which authorities are completely divided, and which turns on the interpretation of the words of the colophon *fist faire*. Paulin Paris favoured the view that Bernard had the book made, perhaps drawing all the material from various written sources, while Mas-Latrie was equally sure that Bernard himself was the author at least of parts of the text, and that what he did not do was actually write the book out himself. All available evidence is on the side of Paris.

The two articles on the library and scriptorium of Corbie by Delisle and by Jones[12] give a selection of colophons. Though these are all taken from Corbie manuscripts, they are fairly typical of medieval manuscripts in general, and shed a good deal of light on that in Berne 340. They can be summarised as several distinct types thus:

(a)   Ego Audoinus scripsi. (B.N. lat. 13351)

(b)   Hic codex Hero insula scriptus fuit, jubente sancto patre Adalhardo dum exularet ibi. (Leningrad F.v.I.11)

(c)   Isaac, indignus monachus, propter Dei amorem et propter compendium legentium hoc volumen fieri jussit. Quicumque hunc librum legerit, Domini misericordiam pro eo exoret. (B.N. lat. 17234. A tenth-century copy of the Epistles of St. Paul.)

(d)   Ad honorem tocius Trinitatis et perpetue ac gloriose virginis Marie et beatorum apostolorum Petri et Pauli et omnium sanctorum quoru corpora et reliquie in hac Corbeiensi ecclesia continentur, compositus est liber iste a fratre Iohanne de Flissicuria, anno ab incarnatione Domini MCCLXXV. (B.N. lat. 13222. A liturgical collection made in 1275.)

(e)   Amalarius: *De Divinis Officiis.* (B.N. lat. 11580).
       This manuscript has at the beginning a large twelfth-century

---

[12] Cf. above, p. 47 n. 15.

> painting showing Saints Peter, Andrew, and Leonard, bishop
> Amalarius, the monk Herbert offering a book, and the monk
> Robert copying a book.

These inscriptions distinguish between the various elements
in the making of a book: the composition, the compilation,
the decision that it should be copied, the actual physical work
of writing. Colophon (a) indicates quite simply the scribe:
Audoinus wrote the manuscript, without having any part in
the composition of its contents. In (b) and (c) the patron is
named, that is, the person on whose initiative the manuscript
was made. In (b) he is a man of some standing, the same
Adalhard who on his return from exile drew up the statutes
of the abbey of Corbie, but in (c) he is a simple monk. In (c)
Isaac cannot possibly be claiming to have had any part in the
composition of the Pauline epistles, but he is said to have had
the book made—*fieri jussit, fist faire*. In (d) we are concerned
with a liturgical collection compiled—*compositus*— by Jean
de Flixécourt, who did not merely supervise the work but
actually chose the elements and assembled them himself. He
is still not the original author, however. The most interesting
of all is (e), which depicts the entire process. Jones's interpretation of the picture[13] is the obvious one: Amalarius composed
the book himself, i.e. he is the original author; Herbert had it
copied (*jussit fieri, fist faire*), and Robert copied it.

Which of these roles is indicated in the colophon of Berne
340? There is no question of Bernard's having been the scribe.
And because of the existence of the shorter version of the
abrégé, of which his is indisputably an adaptation and expansion, we know that he was not the original author of the whole
in the sense in which Amalarius was the author of the *De
Divinis Officiis*. Either, like Jean de Flixécourt, he assembled
the chronicle from several sources, the short version of the
abrégé being the main one, or like Isaac and Herbert, he
simply ordered a copy to be made for the monastery library
of a work which already existed in its full form. The strongest
objection to this last solution is the time element: given that
Bernard's manuscript was copied as the colophon tells us, in
1232, and that the last event narrated occurred in September
1231 in Constantinople, there is hardly time for the news to

---

[13] L. W. Jones, 'The Scriptorium at Corbie', *Speculum*, xxii (1947), 197.

be brought to France, incorporated into the newly composed
chronicle, and then recopied at Corbie, all between the spring
of 1232 (the first possible sailing to Europe) and the end of
the year. There is also the fact of the evident existence of two
Bernard chronicles, continued to different points; it is unlikely
that he would have found a written source exactly right for
filling the gap between Bi and Bii. Far more likely is the
alternative hypothesis that the short version of the abrégé
was available in the library at Corbie, and that the two suc-
cessive pieces that Bernard added to it were of his own
composition, possibly based on oral accounts of the events
by returning crusaders.

As well as the small interpolations made throughout the
abrégé by Bernard, and the last section of his chronicle,
Mas-Latrie also attributed to him as his own original work
the prologue which stands at the beginning of his chronicle,
'L'an de l'Incarnation' etc.[14] But Mas-Latrie is then in some
difficulty to explain the fact that this prologue is also found
in two manuscripts of the short version of the abrégé (Brussels
11142 and B.N. f.fr. 781) since he assumes on the one hand
that the text of these manuscripts, especially that of Brussels
11142, which he uses as his base, predates the composition of
Bernard's chronicle, and on the other, that the prologue is
Bernard's own original work. He is forced to the conclusion[15]
that the copyists of these manuscripts had to hand both the
short abrégé without prologue and also Bernard's longer
version, and that while transcribing Bernard's prologue at the
end of their work they preferred for the history itself to keep
to the shorter version, rather than include Bernard's interpolations and his 1229-31 section. Mas-Latrie himself recognized
how unsatisfactory this explanation is, contradicting as it does
everything that is known about the way compilers went about
their work. Apart from oddities like Pipino, they were not
usually inclined to waste good material, and though some of
Bernard's interpolations are merely an accumulation of
superfluous detail, many of them do add a good deal of
clarity to the narrative, and the final section covering the
years 1229-31 is of course new information. Are we to believe
that the compiler of Brussels 11142 deliberately chose to

[14] M-L p. 511.   [15] Ibid., p. xxv.

omit all this useful and interesting material, while at the same time including the superficial, fragmentary, and obviously incomplete prologue, and adding it moreover at the end of the work? It seems hard to believe, and we must clearly at least consider the contrary possibility.

There are two pieces of evidence which help here. The first is the form of the prologue (or epilogue as the case may be) itself. It is in substance a very brief sketch of events in, or relating to, the Latin Kingdom of Jerusalem between the death of Godfrey of Bouillon in 1100 and the accession of Amalric in 1162-3. This is quite an arbitrary point at which to end, unless the piece were to serve as an introduction to a chronicle beginning then, for which we have of course no evidence at all. Again, the events detailed are apparently chosen quite arbitrarily. Apart from the disastrous Second Crusade, the writer lights on the revolt of Edessa, much oversimplified and romanticized, the Flemish expedition under the Castellan of Dixmude which took Lisbon in 1147, and the death of Roger of Antioch, related with much censorious comment on his life. In other words, the only specifically local reference is to the Castellan of Dixmude, which does nothing more than reiterate what was already very obvious from the provenance of the manuscripts, that both versions of the abrégé are closely associated with north-east France and Flanders.

In short, the prologue is evidently an unfinished piece, and appears to be the beginning of something new, rather than the end of the text which precedes it. This prompts us to ask whether it is in fact related at all to the abrégé, and the answer is provided by a manuscript not known to Mas-Latrie. Saint-Omer 722 contains the same version of the abrégé as Brussels 11142, but it does not have this fragment at all, either at beginning or end. It is the only copy of the 1229 abrégé that does not, and in it we see for the first time the abrégé in this version completely dissociated from the fragment. We can now see the fragment for what it is—a piece of a text quite unrelated to the abrégé in any way, which some scribe of a manuscript like Brussels 11142 thought suitable to copy out. As it chanced, he began it after he had finished the 1229 abrégé, which he presumably took from a manuscript where it stood alone, as in Saint-Omer 722; and later scribes, such as the copyist of B.N.f.fr. 781, mistakenly assumed the fragment to belong to the text it followed. Bernard too, drawing the abrégé from a manuscript like these two, also assumed a connection, but, with more initiative, transposed the fragment to the beginning of the work. Here it finds, not as Mas-Latrie says, 'sa vraie place',[16] but certainly its most logical one, for if it has any value at all, it is as an introduction and Bernard's transposition constitutes an undoubted improvement.

Then, having copied the body of the work, suppressing the name of Ernoul, and adding details here and there, Bernard finishes it off with his own account of the events of 1229-30 to bring it up to date and thus produces his chronicle in its first version (Bi), now no longer extant. Later he comes back to the work, and produces the second version, the one we now have (Bii), a copy of Bi with a further section 1230-1. This theory is in several ways a very satisfactory explanation of the genesis of Bernard's chronicle as it now stands in MSS Berne 340 and Arsenal 4797. It explains why the prologue is there at all: Bernard did not add this almost completely superfluous piece merely, as has been suggested, for the sake of adding something of his own, even at the cost of producing a work inferior to the original, but actually improved on his source. What he did add that is not in that source, i.e. the 1229-31 section, was very much to the point and again constitutes an improvement. Finally, this revision and extension on his part amply justify, and exactly fulfil, the claim of the colophon: 'Bernard . . . fist faire ce livre.'

Bernard the Treasurer, then, compiled the chronicle contained in the manuscripts represented by A in the table on p. 10-11, by copying the version of z, transposing the fragment added at the end to the beginning, and adding various short interpolations of his own, and further narrative (which in default of evidence to the contrary we must assume to be original, but cannot prove to be so) to bring the history to 1230, and in a second version, to 1231. His contribution as an original author is thus very small, but he is the compiler of the 1232 abrégé. It is his name, and not that of Ernoul, which should stand at the head of the work, for the name of Ernoul is only associated with one incident, found in several works of which Bernard's is one. To Bernard belongs the *travail d'ensemble*.

[16] Ibid., p. xxxviij, in description of his MS *C*.

V

THE WORK OF ERNOUL i:
THE EVIDENCE OF RALPH OF COGGESHALLE

WITH BERNARD the Treasurer, the problem is to define his exact role in the creation of one particular text, the 1232 version of the abrégé which bears his name. This has been done by comparing the text attributed to him with related ones, and he has emerged as the compiler of the 1232 abrégé, and of another earlier lost version ending in 1230. To the *matière* of his chronicles he made at most a minimal contribution, but the *conjointure* is his alone.

In the case of Ernoul, however, the problem is of à quite different order. The only mention of his name which remains to us in manuscript is made in passing, its reference is even more obscure than that made to Bernard, and, worst of all, the obvious meaning of the statement made about him is soon seen not to be the true one. That is to say, that reading in the 1227 abrégé, 'Ce fu cil qui cest conte fist metre en escrit',[1] we should most naturally conclude that Ernoul is the author of that text, and the information one can gather or deduce about his identity would tend to confirm this view. He had the means of first-hand information about the subject-matter, the views expressed agree with what we should expect from the squire of an Ibelin, in short everything invites us to give the words the same value as they have in the chronicle of Robert de Clari, and to see in the 1227 abrégé the original chronicle of Ernoul.

This hypothesis turns out to be too good to be true. When we examine some of the continuations of William of Tyre it rapidly becomes apparent that they include much of the same material as the 1227 abrégé—but in much fuller form. The similarities of parts of the two texts are too great for them conceivably to be independent of each other. Though the abrégé is not simply an abbreviated form of the continuations, it is certainly condensed from their common sources. What is more, the sections which are peculiar to the abrégé alone, that is, which might be the work of Ernoul, are precisely not the

[1] Cf. above. pp. 12 and 41.

parts we should expect him to have written, but the miscellaneous material in the first ten chapters. Of the central parts, the narrative of the period from about 1186 onwards, which the texts have in common, and in which Ernoul is named, the version claimed to be his is clearly not the fullest or earliest, but a derivative of written sources which were also used by the compilers of the various versions of the *Eracles*.

This situation forced the editors of the *Recueil* into a very strange conclusion indeed: that Ernoul, having been an eye-witness of the battle of Hattin, the surrender of Jerusalem, and the other key events narrated in the texts, nevertheless did not write an original first-hand account of the period, but took a chronicle by someone else, and condensed it, since it was too long for his soldierly tastes.[2] This is to be sure a reasonable interpretation of the words 'cest conte fist metre en escrit', but that is about all one can say for the theory. Leaving aside the fact that the procedure they suggest is barely credible, it does not square with the contents of the continuations either. If Ernoul was merely an abbreviator as they suggest, the question arises, who did write the original chronicle from which he and the other compilers worked? As we shall see in examining the contents of the several texts, parts of them at least could hardly have been written except by someone answering exactly to Ernoul's description.

So we cannot accept either that the 1227 abrégé as it stands is Ernoul's original work, or that Ernoul compiled it by abbreviating sources also drawn on by the *Eracles* compilers. We must now examine a hypothesis proposed by Mas-Latrie, but never tested, which is raised by his reference in the *Essai de classification* to the work of Ralph of Coggeshalle, and his surmise that Ralph may have known a Latin translation of Ernoul.[3]

The facts of the case are these. Ralph of Coggeshalle wrote, about the year 1220, a *Chronicon Terrae Sanctae,* and in this chronicle, when relating the journey of Richard and Philippe-Auguste to the Holy Land, he refers his reader for a fuller account of these events to another chronicle:

[2] *RHC* ii, v.   [3] M-L pp. 496-8.

Post Pascha anno ab Incarnatione Domini MCXCI, rex Franciae
PHILIPPUS applicuit apud Achon et non multo post, scilicet circa
Pentecosten, venit rex Anglorum RICHARDUS: quorum seriem itineris
et quae in itinere gesserunt, seu ex qua occasione rex Philippus repatriavit,
si quis plenius scire desiderat, legat librum quem dominus prior Sanctae
Trinitatis de Londoniis ex gallica lingua in latinum tam eleganti quam
veraci stilo transferri fecit.[4]

This allusion opens up a number of problems almost as
complex as those posed by the continuations of William's
chronicle themselves. The work to which Ralph refers is
certainly that now known as the *Itinerarium Peregrinorum et
Gesta Regis Ricardi*. Its first editor, Stubbs,[5] rejected completely the notion that it was a translation of a French work,
and explained Ralph's reference by saying that he must have
heard of both the *Itinerarium* and the *'Chronique d'Oultremer'*
(that is, the abrégé), and had without justification assumed the
first to be a translation of the second, the more understandably since both were, in substance though not in intention,
continuations to the work of William of Tyre. Mas-Latrie does
not seem to have been familiar with this preface of Stubbs, but
strangely enough he also suggests a connection between the
Itinerarium and the abrégé, though unlike Stubbs he thinks
the connection may have been a real one, and not a figment
of Ralph's imagination. He quotes from the same passage of
Ralph's *Chronicon,* and points out that the question of what
chronicle Ralph is referring to, and what its French original
was, is no idle speculation, for if it could be shown that the
French chronicle was the work of Ernoul, then we should
know for certain that Ernoul's work was finished and in circulation before 1220, the date at or about which Ralph wrote
his *Chronicon.*[6] This in turn would tell us quite a number of
things about Ernoul's work as seen in the eyes of his contemporaries: that it was highly enough regarded to be circulated
as far away as England, and to be translated into Latin, with
a fairly high degree of care, for example. We should also be
able to conclude that it stopped short at 1220 at the very
latest, and probably a little before, and therefore that the
abrégé after 1220 is not dependent on Ernoul; in other words

---

[4] Martène et Durand, Vol. v, cols. 543 ff.
[5] Rolls Series, 1864. Cf. above, p. 43, and n. 5.   [6] M-L loc. cit.

we should be certain that the abrégé was of at least dual authorship. Mas-Latrie does not point out another fact which may be
deduced from Ralph's words: that the original French chronicle
as well as the Latin translation, must have been known to him,
since he is able to judge not only of the elegance of style of the
translation, but also of its faithfulness to the original. It was
not therefore a question of one isolated instance of the French
chronicle's being known in England. It had been read in at least
two separate monasteries, Holy Trinity London, and Ralph's
house in Essex.

In short, if Mas-Latrie's hypothesis did prove true, a large
part of the mystery surrounding Ernoul and the abrégé would
be cleared up. It would be possible to fix a division in the abrégé
between the pre-1220 and post-1220 sections, and this would in
turn influence our approach to the question of the relationship
of the abrégé to the *Eracles*. Probably it would also become
possible to say something more authoritative about the original
form of Ernoul's own work, now so scattered throughout the
various versions of this period of the continuations. Two
questions need answering: is the *Itinerarium* indeed a translation of a French chronicle? and if so, is the French chronicle
in question some form of Ernoul's work?

The first of these questions has been much debated. Gaston
Paris, in his edition of *L'Estoire de la guerre sainte,* published
as long ago as 1897, thought he had decided the matter, but
in reality he opened a debate which was to continue for a long
time.[7] The *Estoire* he edited is an account of the Third Crusade
in octosyllabic rhyming couplets by one Ambroise, a Norman
jongleur who claims to have taken part in the expedition led
by Richard Coeur-de-Lion, and Paris's detailed comparison of
this text with that of the *Itinerarium* proves beyond doubt a
very close connection. Not only the material but also many
of the locutions in the first part of the *Estoire* correspond
exactly to those of the *Itinerarium,* and Paris asserted that
the relationship was that of French original and Latin translation. Such a conclusion would of course eliminate Ernoul

---

[7] Ambroise, *Estoire de la guerre sainte,* ed. Gaston Paris, in Documents Inédits sur
l'Histoire de France (Paris, 1897). For discussion of the *Itinerarium* problem see
Introduction, pp. lix-lxxvi.

from the question altogether. But more recently two studies of Ambroise, one by J.G. Edwards,[8] the other by J.L. La Monte and J. Hubert,[9] have contradicted Paris, and replaced his theory, convincingly, with that of a lost common original. This original, they say, was most probably in French and in prose, a description which puts Ernoul once again strongly in the running.

In 1962, however, there appeared a new edition of the *Itinerarium,* by H.E. Mayer[10] who brings forward so much new evidence, and in consequence so many new theories, that not merely the answers to our questions, but the questions themselves must be completely reformulated. Basically, Mayer establishes that there are not one but two extant versions of the *Itinerarium,*which he names IP1 and IP2. IP1 ends in November 1190, and corresponds to Book i of Stubbs's text, up to the end of the *g* variant of chapter 65. IP2 is the complete chronicle as edited by Stubbs. Mayer asserts, without absolute proof, but with reasonably convincing argument, that IP1 was written about 1192 in Tyre, by an English Templar, a chaplain rather than a knight, and that it is basically an original work, but draws for the crusade of Barbarossa on an independent German account. Richard of Holy Trinity, who before the publication of Mayer's edition was generally taken to be the author of the *Itinerarium,* then took IP1, according to Mayer, and using Ambroise's *Estoire* to amplify and extend it, produced IP2.

The hypothesis thus propounded by Mayer has much to recommend it, reconciling as it does the assertions that the *Itinerarium* was, and was not, translated from French, but it is not entirely satisfactory. For example, there are substantial passages common to IP2 and Ambroise which are also found in IP1. The compiler of IP2 has not borrowed them from Ambroise to insert into IP1: they are already in IP1 before, on Mayer's theory, his work of compilation begins. In other words, there is clearly some connection between Ambroise and IP1,

[8] J.G. Edwards, 'The *Itinerarium Regis Ricardi* and the *Estoire de la Guerre Sainte',* in *Historical Essays in Honour of James Tait* (Manchester, 1933), pp. 59-77.
[9] J.L. La Monte with M.J. Hubert, *The Crusade of Richard the Lion-Heart,* (Records of Civilisation, New York, 1941).
[10] H.E. Mayer, *Das Itinerarium Peregrinorum* (Schriften der Monumenta Germaniae Historica, no. 18, Stuttgart, 1962). As Mayer's edition contains only IP1, all my references to the *Itinerarium* are to the Rolls Series edition.

quite independent of IP2 and its compiler. The finer points of this relationship are, however, extraneous to the present discussion. All we need accept for the moment is that while we may have some reservations about Mayer's theory of the authorship of the *Itinerarium,* it is on the whole acceptable, and for the practical purpose of determining the relationship of this text to the abrégé and the continuations, it does allow us to take the *Estoire* of Ambroise as containing nothing material that is not also found in the *Itinerarium* as edited by Stubbs. That is not to say that the *Estoire* and the *Itinerarium* are always in total and detailed agreement; but they do agree, by and large, on the broad outlines.

From the very beginning of even a cursory comparison of the *Itinerarium* with the continuations of William, one factor becomes clear: the sympathies of their authors are diametrically opposed on virtually everything and everybody. The villain of one is the hero of the other, and vice versa. No doubt the historical facts, if it is possible to unearth them from the tangle of equally, though differently, biased accounts, lie somewhere between, but cold objectivity is not the stock-in-trade of these chroniclers. Reading the abrégé, one is convinced that had Raymond of Tripoli been left to arrange matters diplomatically with Salahadin, there need have been no tragic battles, no loss of life. But the unintelligent blunderings of Guy of Lusignan, encouraged by the perfidious Master of the Temple, Gerard of Ridefort, brought total ruin to the Latin Kingdom.[11] For Richard of Holy Trinity, on the other hand, Raymond is the snake in the grass, the collaborator whose unpatriotic self-interest made things very difficult for the noble and upright king, and precipitated the train of events in the course of which Gerard himself died a martyr's death.[12]

It is therefore imperative to be even more wary than usual in separating fact, or rather what the authors present as fact, from what cannot be anything but opinion. It is after all not impossible for two compilers to adapt the same material radically in order to make history square with their own loyalties, and differences in interpretation do not eliminate the possibility of a single common source of factual information. As far

[11] See for example the description of the council before Hattin, M-L pp. 158-62.
[12] *Itinerarium,* pp. 13 (*De fraude comitis Tripolis*) and 121; and Gerard's death, p. 70.

as the facts themselves, the basic information, are concerned, agreement does not necessarily indicate dependence of two accounts on each other or on a common source; with historical narratives, unlike fiction, there is always the possibility of independent accuracy. But clear disagreement on straightforward matters of fact, which neither side can have any interest in falsifying, can indicate independence. As we shall see, a comparison of the *Itinerarium,* the *Estoire* of Ambroise, and the abrégé and continuations provides instances of similarity and dissimilarity which are not without interest, though the conclusions to be drawn are not what we might have expected at the outset.

The subject-matter of the *Itinerarium* is, as its title indicates, the journey of Richard and the pilgrims who followed him to the Holy Land, and the deeds he did there. But Book i is taken up with a background sketch of the events immediately preceding, and occasioning, his crusade, especially the siege of Acre.[13] Ambroise puts this same background information into a digression[14] and indicates that he had a written source for it.

> Si velt Ambroises faire entendre
> E saveir a cels qui aprendre
> Le voldront, par com faite enprise
> La citié d'Acre fud assise;
> Kar il n'en aveit rien veu,
> Fors tant come il en a leu.[15]

This period, that is the five or six years ending in 1192, is by far the most extensively treated in the abrégé, and also receives detailed treatment in all the versions of the continuations. But in Ambroise, and in the *Itinerarium,* it is so rapidly passed over that almost any source might have served. The battle of Hattin, for example, which may justly be regarded as the set-piece of the abrégé, and to which the continuations, even those not entirely agreeing with the abrégé, devote more space than to any other single incident, is hardly more than mentioned by Ambroise.[16] Richard, in the *Itinerarium* account, adds several appropriate Biblical quotations, and some

---

[13] *Itinerarium,* pp. 5-137.   [14] *Estoire,* vv. 2387-4568.

[15] *Estoire,* vv. 2401-6. Cf. also vv. 2743-4, 3526, 3563, etc.

[16] Ibid., vv. 2531 ff.

moralizing observations of his own, but has no more factual
material than Ambroise.[17] Again, on the siege and surrender of
Jerusalem, another episode very fully recounted in the abrégé
and the continuations, Ambroise says simply that Salahadin
took the city.[18] Here Richard does give a certain amount of
detail, though not as much as the texts related to Ernoul, and
he puts a different slant on the whole account.[19] As an avowed
anti-Ibelin he could not of course be expected to mention the
part played by Balian d'Ibelin in ransoming the poor of
Jerusalem. The ransom prices he gives are the same as those in
the abrégé: ten besants for a man, five for a woman, and one
for a child. But he asserts that those who could not pay the
price for their liberty were taken into captivity. In the abrégé
and the continuation on the other hand, we read that Balian
d'Ibelin and the Patriarch of Jerusalem carefully organized
the citizens of the town, obliging everyone to declare what
wealth he possed above the amount necessary for his own
ransom, and making a register of all those unable to ransom
themselves.[20] After this the story deserts cold fact for over-
imaginative eulogy. The details of the safe conduct of the
ransomed Christians also differ in the two texts: the texts
related to Ernoul spare no details of the shameful treatment
the refugees suffered at the hands of their fellow Christians,
both at Tripoli and at Alexandria, details which the Canon of
Holy Trinity would hardly have included in his chronicle even
if he knew them. But Richard also says, and here one can see
no motive for falsification, that they were allowed to choose
Antioch or Alexandria as their destination, while the abrégé
and continuations say that some also went to Tripoli and
some to Armenia.

The release of Guy was presumably of not much interest to
Ernoul, and the abrégé disposes of it in two paragraphs.[21] But
Ambroise considers Guy his real subject, and neglects the
politically more significant siege of Tyre to give us a touching
picture, or what he evidently means to be a touching picture,
of the king weeping over his lost land.[22] On the siege of Tyre,
the *Itinerarium* narrative is again closer to the abrégé: both

---

[17] *Itinerarium*, pp. 14-16.   [18] *Estoire*, v. 2590.
[19] *Itinerarium*, pp. 20-3.   [20] M-L pp. 221 ff. *RHC* ii. 84 ff.
[21] M-L pp. 252-3. Cf. *Itinerarium*, pp. 25-6.   [22] *Estoire*, vv. 2657-90.

have the story of Conrad of Montferrat being offered his father's life in exchange for Tyre, and refusing, and both give a certain amount of detail on Conrad's defence of the city.[23] Both also mention the funds sent to Outremer by Henry II of England, but in different contexts, and ascribing different motives—in the abrégé expiation for the death of Thomas à Becket, and preparation for an expedition to Palestine as a penance, in the *Itinerarium* sheer generosity. Richard, as a clerk, had no reason to whitewash Henry's motives, indeed he would rather be inclined to take the opportunity of reminding his readers of the martyrdom of Becket. According to the abrégé the money was used for the defence of the Kingdom of Jerusalem before Hattin, and for the ransom of the poor of Jerusalem after the fall of the city; according to Richard it was all spent on the defence of Tyre in 1188.[24] Ambroise does not mention the money at all. He also omits completely the reinforcements sent by William of Sicily, except for a passing reference elsewhere, in connection with William's death, while the abrégé and *Itinerarium* both give details on the subject.[25] They agree on the numbers of troops sent—500 knights—though the abrégé splits them into a party of 200 in March and a further force of 300 the following August. Richard adds the name of the commander of the fleet, Margarit, while the abrégé enlarges on the help given by William of Sicily to the Archbishop of Tyre when he passed through Sicily on his way to Europe, carrying the news of the fall of Jerusalem.

In the matter of Isabel of Jerusalem's divorce from Henfroi de Toron, and her subsequent marriage to Conrad of Montferrat, the lay and clerical standpoints of the abrégé and *Itinerarium* respectively become so obtrusive as to preclude any valid comparison at all. Richard feels it necessary to moralize extensively, emphasizing the case for the anti-Conrad party, and denigrating the characters of Conrad's supporters. This is the occasion for Richard's slanderous description of Balian d'Ibelin already quoted elsewhere.[26] The abrégé

[23] *Itinerarium*, pp. 23-5. M-L pp. 179 ff.
[24] *Itinerarium*, p. 26. M-L pp. 156-7 and 219.
[25] *Itinerarium*, pp. 27-8. M-L p. 247.
[26] *Itinerarium*, p. 121. Cf. above, 43.

by contrast is content to say, 'Teus i ot qui s'acorderent al departir, et tels i ot qui dist qu'il ne pooit estre.'[27] The versions of the *Eracles* which are not identical with the abrégé text at this point have much the most interesting and subtle account of the episode, pointing out the numerous ulterior motives on the part of the various protagonists, and how personal animosities played as great a part as political considerations. This account ends ominously, 'Encores deit l'on douter que li roiaumes de Jerusalem ne soit alé perillant et amenuisant par icestui fait.'[28] It includes too, as does the *Itinerarium* account, the assertion that Conrad bribed men to take his part, and a reference to Guy de Senlis, which, however, differs curiously from that made in the *Itinerarium*. In the *Itinerarium* he is captured by Turks on the day of Isabel's wedding to Conrad, and never seen again, while in the *Eracles* he presents himself as Isabel's champion and challenges Henfroi. In all these various accounts of the divorce, there are more contradictions than similarities, but in this episode one fact begins to emerge dimly, which will become clearer and more significant as our comparison of the texts proceeds. It is that when there is any fairly clear similarity between the texts of Ambroise or of the *Itinerarium* and those of the abrégé or the *Eracles,* the link is almost always between the *Itinerarium* and those versions of the *Eracles* which are least similar to the abrégé, that is the version of *a-b* habitually, and occasionally also *d,* when *d* is in agreement with *a-b*.

The siege of Acre, before the arrival of Richard Coeur-de-Lion, is given relatively little attention in either the abrégé or the *Eracles,* while Ambroise and the *Itinerarium* fill in all possible details, since this is the operation which will form the first concern of the English and French armies when they disembark.[29] Any suggestion that the 'siege journal' from which they are supposed to have drawn their material might be the original Ernoul or a text derived from it cannot be seriously supported for long. Nor can we even assume that it was a fuller and independent account on which the abrégé and the continuations also drew, for when they do touch on

[27] M-L p. 267.
[28] *RHC* ii. 151-4, main text. The *cJ* and *gG* variants agree with the abrégé.
[29] *Itinerarium,* pp. 61-138, i.e. more than half of Bk. i. *Estoire,* vv. 2729-4526.

the same subject as Ambroise and Richard there are differences
between them which really cannot be explained away as even
very radical differences in adaptation. One instance where they
do all treat a subject which is relatively free from political
import, where none of them has any perceptible interest in
distorting the facts, but where they manage nevertheless to
disagree on matters not of interpretation but of mere information, is the description of the famine suffered by the army
besieging Acre, and the prices at which various commodities
were sold at the height of the famine. It is not one of the most
aesthetic or the most gripping passages in the chronicles, indeed
it might reasonably be described as prosaic and even dull, but
for those very reasons it offers a good comparison: there is very
little in it except dry information, and that after all is what we
want to compare in the different accounts.

> Mult ert li muis de blé pesanz
> Qui costeit en l'ost cent besanz
> Que uns hom portast soz s'aissele
> Mult aveit ci freide novele.
> Chiers i esteit blez e farine,
> Doze solz valeit la geline
> E l'oef vendeit l'om sis deners,
> Tant esteit li tens pautoners.
>
> (*Estoire*, vv. 4217-4324.)

Quid plura? modii tritici, mensura modica quam videlicet quis facile
portaret sub ascella, centum aureis vendebatur: gallina quoque solidis
duodecim, ovum sex denariis. (*Itinerarium*, i. 66)

Grant cherté avoit en l'ost, si que li muis dou blé valoit .xx. besanz
Sarrasinas; une geline valeit .lx. solz; de buef ne de moton ne troveit l'en
point; un huef valoit .xij. deniers. La meaudre char que les gens de l'ost
manjassent, si estoit char de cheval ou de mule ou de asne. La mesaise
estoit si grant que, quant les povres gens poent trover aucune beste morte
il la mangeent a grant deintié. (*Eracles, a-b* and *d. RHC* ii. 150.)

Or vous di jou qu'il ot si grant cierté en l'ost des Crestiiens qu'il fu
tele eure c'on vendi le mui de forment .lx. besans et le mui de ferine
.lxx. Or vous dirai conbien li muys est: çou c'uns porteres porte a son
col est li muis de le tiere. Et .i. oef vendoit on .xii. deniers; et une geline
.xx. sols; et une pume .vi. deniers. Vins et cars parestoit si ciers c'on n'en
pooit avoir, se de ceval non, quant il moroit. (Abrégé, M-L p. 266.)

Lors ot tel foiz, fu si grant chierté en l'ost des Crestiens que l'en vendi
le mui de froment .lx. besanz et le mui de farine .lxx. Et le mui est ce que
un home puet porter a son col. Et vendoit l'en un oef. xii. deniers et une
geline .xx. solz; et une pome .vi. deniers. Vin et char par estoit si chier que
l'en n'en pooit point avoir, fors char de cheval, quant il moroit.
(*Eracles cJ. RHC* ii. 151-2.)

Une si grant chierté fu en l'ost aucune foiz c'om vendoit .i. mui de forment .l. besanz, et le mui de farine .lx. Le mui de la terre est tant com .i. porteor porte a son col a une foiz. L'en vendoit .i. oef .xx. deniers, une geline .x. solz, une pome .vi. deniers. Vin et char par estoit si chier c'om n'en pooit avoir se de cheval non, quant il moroit.

(*Eracles gG. RHC* ii. 152-3.)

Here the pattern which we saw vaguely in evidence in the accounts of Isabel's divorce emerges more clearly. The abrégé and the *cJ* and *gG* versions of the *Eracles* agree virtually word for word. The figures given by *gG* are not always the same, but the copying of Roman numerals is particularly liable to error. Here we have one figure the same—vi— an xx for xii, a very understandable mistake, and the final x omitted from the other three. Apart from this, the abrégé, *cJ,* and *gG* are in exact agreement. This is very often the case throughout the continuations, and not only in this section, as we shall see clearly later. The *Estoire* and the *Itinerarium* similarly agree exactly with each other on the prices, as we should expect, and also on the definition of a measure as the amount a man can carry under his arm, whereas all the other texts say on his shoulders. Between these two groups, the *Estoire* and *Itinerarium* on the one hand, and the abrégé and *cJ* and *gG* on the other, stands the remaining version of the *Eracles,* that of *a-b,* the main text of the *Recueil* edition, with which the version of *d* happens here to be in agreement, though this is by no means the usual state of affairs, as we shall see.[30] This version does not very closely resemble either of the others. The commodities it chooses as illustrations are those chosen also by Ambroise and Richard—like them, and unlike the abrégé, *cJ,* and *gG,* it does not mention either the apple or the unobtainable wine and meat—but it is in total disagreement with Ambroise and Richard on the prices. It remains true nevertheless that it does agree with them in some measure, small though it is, and that it is the only one of the *Eracles* texts to do so.

For the whole of the Third Crusade narrative the texts of the continuations are found in these two groups, the abrégé agreeing with *cJ* and *gG* against *a-b.* The version of *d* is here, as often, in a class by itself, agreeing frequently with *a-b,* but

[30] Cf. analysis of *d* variants below, pp. 89 ff. and ch. VII.

quite often presenting a text peculiar to itself. For a comparison with the *Itinerarium* it is the main text of the *Recueil,* the version of *a-b,* which is much the most interesting. This version does sometimes agree with the abrégé, *cJ,* and *gG* on points of fact, but there is never the same textual similarity as there is between these three texts among themselves. For example, there is the account of Richard Coeur-de-Lion's meeting with his future wife, Berengaria of Navarre.[31] According to the *Itinerarium,* Richard went to Reggio to meet his mother Eleanor, his sister Joanna of Sicily, and Berengaria, and sent Joanna and Berengaria on ahead of him in their own ship. All the versions of the continuations and the abrégé agree, though they tell the story differently, that Eleanor and Berengaria arrived at Messina when Richard had already left, but found Joanna's ship about to sail, and Berengaria joined her. When the queens arrive off the coast of Cyprus, all the texts have some account of trouble with Isaac Comnenus, but the details differ. In the *Itinerarium,* Isaac sends gifts to the queens, who temporize, agreeing to disembark the next day, but before this becomes necessary, Richard arrives. In the *Eracles,* versions *a-b* and *d,* Isaac refuses the queens' request for a renewal of their water supplies, and sends ships to pursue them. They raise anchor and flee, and meet Richard's fleet on the high sea next day. In the abrégé, and in the *Eracles cJ* and *gG,* which are here once again in complete agreement, Isaac orders Joanna to disembark, she refuses, and is pursued by his ships, but meets Richard's ship almost immediately. A footnote in the *Recueil* claims, somewhat rashly, that the accounts of *a-b, d,* and the *Itinerarium* are similar, 'à quelques différences près'.[32] But in reality the differences are quite large, and almost as great as those that separate the *Itinerarium* from the other versions of the continuations, and from the abrégé.

It is with the arrival of Richard's army in Palestine that the similarity between *a-b* and the *Itinerarium* and *Estoire* first becomes really clear. The episode of the dromond for example agrees in detail:[33] the ship contained reinforcements of troops,

[31] *Itinerarium,* pp. 175-6, and see also pp. 186-8 and 195-6. *RHC* ii. 157 ff. Cf. also M-L pp. 270 ff.

[32] *RHC* ii. 160, note *b.* The *Itinerarium* is here referred·to as 'Vinisauf,' who was then erroneously believed to be the author.

[33] *Eracles* xxv. 27; *RHC* ii. 169. *Itinerarium* ii. 42; pp. 204 ff.

arms, serpents, and phials of Greek fire, not an inventory that could easily be hit on by accident by an author inventing his own fictitious details as required, and the ship is said in both chronicles to have been sunk off Acre, after an engagement with Richard's galleys. The only small difference is in the fate of the crew: in the *Eracles* all are drowned, while in the *Itinerarium* some are taken prisoner. There is no question of direct dependence of one account on the other, for each gives details that the other omits. For example, the captain is named in the *Eracles* but not in the *Itinerarium,* while the latter has more details on the actual skirmish. But the agreements here cannot possibly be explained as chance.

The taking of Acre, on the other hand, is not identical in the two texts, though the differences are not so great as to preclude the possibility of two very different adaptations of the same text.[34] The main difference is that in the *Eracles* story the French and English kings attack together, then Richard alone, then the two together again, whereas in the *Itinerarium* Richard is ill, and it is Philippe-Auguste who attacks alone. The terms of the treaty are also rather differently given, but in this case the the difference is very much one of emphasis, rather than fact. The *Itinerarium* is very precise about the numbers of prisoners involved, and gives first the propositions made by the Saracen leaders (*majores*) and then the terms finally agreed after negotiation. The *Eracles* has the whole surrender conducted by one Saracen leader, Caracoush, who was commander of Acre in Salahadin's absence, and mentions the release of all the Christian prisoners, not merely a certain number. These two versions could conceivably have been differently, and possibly rather carelessly, adapted from the same source, or they could represent two different sources; it is hard in this case to say that one is definitely the case rather than the other. But it is worth noticing that the account of the surrender given by *cJ, gG,* and the abrégé is much further from the *Eracles* and the *Itinerarium* than they are from each other, giving the terms quite differently: a one-for-one exchange of prisoners, agreed ransom for those of rank, and no mention of safe conduct for the citizens of Acre.[35] Once

---

[34] *Itinerarium,* pp. 214-15 and 231-4.
[35] M-L pp. 274 ff. Cf. *RHC* ii. 171 ff. variant readings.

again, we are back to the situation where, though none of the *Eracles* texts agrees exactly with the *Itinerarium,* the version of *a-b* does bear some resemblance to it, and when compared to that of *cJ, gG,* and the abrégé, seems in fact nearer to the *Itinerarium.*

On the assassination of Conrad of Montferrat, however, the several versions of the *Eracles* agree factually with the abrégé against the *Itinerarium.*[36] All the texts are agreed on one point, that the Assassins were somehow involved. The *Eracles* and the abrégé agree in mentioning Conrad's capturing an Assassin ship, and making this out to be the motive for his murder. But the *Itinerarium* is much vaguer, treating it rather as a caprice of the Old Man of the Mountain, 'qui Marchisum morte dignum judicabat, et infra certum illius temporis trucidari mandaverat'.[37] But here we are really up against national prejudice. It was very much in the English interest to be as vague as possible about the death of Conrad, since not a little suspicion fell on the English hero, Richard himself. The French chronicles are at pains to point this out, reminding us that Conrad died on Tuesday, and on Thursday Richard married off the widow Isabel to his own nephew, Henri de Champagne. The *Itinerarium* on the contrary goes to considerable, indeed imaginative, lengths to put Richard in a good light, providing us with a dramatic but unlikely scene in which the dying Conrad instructs Isabel to hand over Tyre to Richard, and to no one else, and the author accuses the French directly of spreading slanderous rumours about Richard. This episode is therefore even more difficult to evaluate than the surrender of Acre, for here we can be quite certain that deliberate falsification is operating in at least one text, and very possibly in both. But while it is impossible to ascertain that both accounts did have a common source, it is equally impossible to demonstrate that they did not.

But one last episode which offers possibilities of a comparison between the various texts provides us with very clear evidence indeed. It is the story of a present of horses made to Richard during the siege of Jaffa by Salahadin (or in some versions by his brother Saphadin), and it occurs in all the texts except the *cJ* and *gG* versions of the *Eracles*. In this

[36] *Itinerarium,* pp. 338-41. *RHC* ii. 192 ff.   [37] *Itinerarium,* p. 339.

episode *a-b* is in clear agreement with the *Itinerarium*: in both texts Saphadin makes a present of two horses to Richard, and he is able to make good use of them. 'Quant li rois les ot receus, si fist monter sus et les fist assaer et eschaufer; si trova que il estoient moult bien en frain. Si monta sur l'un et fist monter Guillaume de Preaus sur l'autre et establi ses gens et issi hors dou chastel et se feri es Turs qui estoient ou borc, et les mist a desconfiture.'[38]

A very different light altogether is cast on the incident by the abrégé.[39] Here we read that during the siege, Salahadin saw Richard fighting on foot with his men, and finding this a pitiful state for a king, sent him a horse. Richard made a servant mount, and the horse immediately carried him back to the Saracen camp. Salahadin, says this text, 'en fu mout honteus de ce que li cevaus estoit retornés. Si en fist .i. autre apparellier, et se li renvoia.' From being a simple and well-intentioned gift, the horse here becomes a wily trick apparently designed to take Richard captive. The remaining version of the story, that given by the *d* version of the *Eracles*,[40] is much the most interesting, and the most convincing, in that it paints the episode neither all black nor all white, but puts a much subtler interpretation on it altogether. The story occurs in this text in the course of a very lengthy variant, which gives much more detail about the siege of Jaffa than do any of the other texts at all. The incident of the horses is related thus. Richard disembarks at Jaffa just at the Saracens are about to take the castle, and himself leads, on foot, the counter-attack, displaying considerable personal bravery in doing so, and preventing the Saracens not only from capturing the castle, but also from taking a single prisoner. The defeated Saracens return to their commander, Salahadin's brother Seif Eddin, who is much astonished at their failure, and demands to be shown Richard, whom they point out standing with his men on a hillock. It is at this point that Seif Eddin has the idea of sending him a horse; but the motives the author attributes to the defeated Saracen in behaving thus towards the victor

[38] *RHC* ii. 197, main text. Cf. *Itinerarium*, p. 419.
[39] M-L pp. 281-2.   [40] *RHC* ii. 195-6, *d* variant.

are much subtler than either the plain treachery or simple generosity of the other versions.

> Seif Eddin, le frere Salahadin, demanda ou estoit le rei. L'en li mostra ou il estoit aveques ses homes sur un toron. Il s'entremist de bien et d'onor, si li envoia un cheval tirant, qui estoit mult mesaisié de la bouche, par un sien memeloc, et li encharja que il deist au rei que n'en esteit mie avenant chose que rei se combatist as Sarasins a pié.[41]

The suggestion of this passage is that Seif Eddin's intention was not that Richard should be brought back to the Saracen camp by the horse, and taken prisoner, but that his skill as a knight should be tested, and perhaps found wanting when the horse threw him, and that Seif Eddin's own face should thus be saved. In fact Richard realizes that the horse is not the simple present it appears, and makes the mameluke gallop it. Seeing it is pulling at the mouth he then says, 'Mercie ton seignor et li meine son cheval, et li di que ce n'est mie l'amor qui entre lui et moi estoit qu'il me mande cheval tirant por mei prendre.'[42]

The mameluke rides the horse back to Seif Eddin, who is *hontous* and sends Richard a good horse, which Richard has tried by a servant, finds satisfactory, and rides in battle.

This version given by *d* is illuminating from several points of view. It is another illustration of Richard's character as seen through the eyes of the Saracens, and of the Syrian Franks. As we shall see later,[43] the author of *d* has not much time on the whole for European crusaders, a rule to which Richard is the striking exception, and there is also evidence that Richard was equally admired by his Saracen enemies both for his courage in battle and for his intelligence and cunning. Bearing all these facts in mind, and remembering also that *d* is the most pro-Saracen of writers,[44] and would tend if anything to whitewash Seif Eddin's motives, we can see that the story is told as an instance of Richard's bravery

---

[41] Ibid., p. 195, *d* variant.   [42] Ibid.,   [43] Below, pp. 99 ff.
[44] This is true to a certain extent of all the versions of the *Eracles* and of the abrégé, *pace* Mayer. His statements that Ernoul (by which he means the abrégé) portrays Salahadin in a bad light, and that this is common in Oriental chronicles, seem incapable of explanation. Certainly they are untenable. See Mayer, *Das Itinerarium Peregrinorum*, Introduction, p. 84.

and his cunning. The gift of the *cheval tirant* is a ploy to put both qualities to the test, and Richard's words, *por mei prendre*, evidently mean, in the context, not 'to capture me' but 'to trick me'.

From a textual point of view, the details of this version would seem to explain the conflicting details of the others. If we suppose this to be the original story, it is easy to see how the others have arisen from it. The *Itinerarium* and *Eracles a-b* mention two horses, as in the original story, but omit the element of trickery, and start as it were at the point at which Richard tries out the second horse, and rides it successfully. The abrégé on the contrary emphasizes the first part of the story, adding its own interpretation of the servant returning to the Saracen camp on the horse, namely that it was trained to return with its rider, and only mentions the gift of the second horse briefly. This emphasis squares with the desire to put Richard in a particularly good light and the Saracens in a particularly bad one, but might also simply spring from a misinterpretation of the phrase *por mei prendre*. The *d* version contains all the details of the other two versions of the incident, and some more besides.

To sum up, in this episode we clearly have three versions of a single story, all evidently derived from one original version, to which *d* is closest. Given that this is so, we can see which of the other texts are closest to each other by seeing which agree in their adaptation of the original, and we find that without any doubt at all the *Itinerarium* and *a-b* agree exactly with each other in giving an adaptation unlike that of any of the other texts. This is the clearest though not the only illustration we have of the relationship of these two texts.

So the picture that emerges from the examination of the *Estoire* and *Itinerarium* in relation to the continuations of William of Tyre and to the abrégé is this. What resemblances there are between the two groups of texts are invariably to be found in the *Itinerarium* and the *a-b* version of the *Eracles*. These are strong enough to suggest some slight and tenuous connection between the two, but nothing more; in fact Mas-Latrie's suggestion that the *Itinerarium* was a translation of the original text of Ernoul, of which the abrégé is an adaptation, can be definitely discounted. The resemblance

that there is between *a-b* and the *Itinerarium* can be best expressed by saying that although *a-b* drew on the materials used
by the compilers of the other versions of the *Eracles, cJ, gG,*
and *d*, and by the compiler of the abrégé, he also had to hand
another source, or sources, belonging to a tradition not known
to these other compilers, but known to Richard of Holy
Trinity, the author of the *Itinerarium,* in the version Mayer
calls IP2. Thus *a-b* is the only one of the *Eracles* texts to
bear any relationship at all to the *Itinerarium,* and that but
a slight one. This conclusion throws no more light on the
sources of the *Itinerarium* and the *Estoires,* and is disap-
pointing in that the contrary conclusion, that is a confirmation of Mas-Latrie's notion, would have set us well on the
way to reconstructing the original work of Ernoul. But this
examination of the continuations and the *Itinerarium* has
provided some small unlooked-for but useful results in
demonstrating certain things about the continuations themselves. It has shown that there is, in this period of the
continuations at least, a clear and strong link between the
Eracles versions *cJ* and *gG* and the abrégé; that *a-b* is
somewhat separate from these, often in agreement with
them, but containing also material of its own differing from
theirs; and that the text of *d* is the most complex of all in
construction, agreeing now with *a-b* against *cJ* and *gG,* now
with *cJ* and *gG* against *a-b*, and very often giving a text
totally different from all the others which in one case at
least has already provided us with the key to a textual
riddle. All this does not answer the original question about
the *Itinerarium,* but it does answer a more important
question about the grouping of the various continuations
among themselves. And though the path it sets us on is
more devious than that envisaged by Mas-Latrie, it may
eventually lead to the same place, and to the rediscovery of
the original chronicle of Ernoul.

VI

THE WORK OF ERNOUL. ii:
THE STRUCTURE OF THE CONTINUATIONS

IT IS CLEAR then that Mas-Latrie's hypothesis about Ralph of Coggeshalle cannot stand, and that the clue lies rather in his more general proposition[1] that the chronicle of Ernoul is not now extant, but served as source material for both the continuations and the abrégé which, though it is not by any means the most faithful representation of Ernoul's text, has by chance preserved the name of the author. This is as yet only a hypothesis, but it is one which fits all the known facts about the texts, and which should be capable of proof or disproof, by comparing the texts with each other.

Assuming then that the work of Ernoul belongs to a quite different stratum in the formation of the corpus from that of Bernard, to an earlier and altogether more obscure phase, the problem is to trace what remains of his work, incorporated into the various texts now extant. It is necessary therefore to sift through this mass of accumulated material, attempting to distinguish fragment from fragment, to separate out the many elements in its composition, in the hope of recognizing what came from the hand of Ernoul. His work was evidently a popular source with compilers: the key section in which he is named in four manuscripts[2] appears again, though in every-varying forms, in every single version of the continuations, and that is merely an indication, not a definition, of the frequency with which his account was drawn on.

The problem of establishing the archetypal form of that account is in some ways akin to the problem presented by the Tristan romances. In each case the different versions present the same mixture of agreement, contradiction, and revision. The two questions differ, however, in two important ways. In the case of the Tristan legend, however great the weight of evidence in favour of postulating one fixed, written form from which all the other versions ultimately derive, its

---

[1] See the general argument of his *Avertissement,* and especially p. xxiii, for the sources of the first period of the continuations.
[2] Cf. above, p. 41.

existence is still not a total certainty, its form is a matter
for speculation, and the criteria for establishing its content
are, as Bédier's account of his own method shows, at least
largely subjective.[3] Even after Gertrude Schoepperle's
revisions, the *estoire* remains a rather nebulous entity, of
questionable date, unknown authorship, and disputed regional
provenance. Our knowledge of Ernoul, thin though it is, gives
us a quite different starting-point. We know that he did have
something written—'cest conte fist metre en escrit'—and we
have certain criteria by which to judge what that *conte* could
have contained and to a certain extent what it could not—
namely Ernoul's political sympathies, his geographical location,
and his social status. True, his work is quite certainly lost, and
he himself but little known to us. But what we are looking
for did once exist as a written document, and those few
features of its author's life which are clear put him in an
entirely different category from the hypothetical author of
the hypothetical *Ur-Tristan*.

But the second major difference between the two problems
weighs on the other side. The Tristan tradition is a fiction.
If therefore identical episodes appear in two versions, it is to
all intents certain that those versions are derived either one
from the other, or both ultimately from a common source,
for the likelihood of two authors inventing independently
precisely the same fiction is negligible. With chronicles, on
the other hand, there is always the possibility that both are
independently telling the truth, and seeing it, for once, in
the same light. In other words, there is in a sense always a
common pool of material, namely the events as they actually
happened. The similarities between two written accounts
must be extensive and detailed beyond the basic similarity
of the subject-matter, before we are justified in assuming a
textual relationship between the two.

How are we to decide, among the many sources of which
each compiler seems to have made often very free use,
exactly what is to be attributed to Ernoul? The only possible point of departure is the quite fortuitous preservation
of his name in the four so-called Ernoul manuscripts,

---

[3] *Le Roman de Tristan par Thomas*, ed. J. Bédier (Paris, 1905). For the description of the method he adopted see vol. ii, pp. 188 ff.

fortuitous in the sense that they are in general very far
from being the most detailed version of the text. But they
provide us with a starting-point, a single episode to which
the name of Ernoul is firmly attached as that of its narrator,
and from which it is possible to work in each direction in
turn, trying to discover how far before and how far after
this point the narration of Ernoul extended. The obvious
method that presents itself is to examine all the versions,
both of the abrégé and of the *Eracles,* and to attempt to
mark off the limits of this part of their text. Of course there
is nothing to prevent a compiler breaking off before he
reaches the end of a particular source, or beginning part way
through one. But if several versions turn out to agree on the
point of change from one source to another, then the evidence is strongly in favour of supposing that to have been
the end of their common source.

How is such a change to be perceived in any one chronicle?
As we have seen, the details of Ernoul's biography are not
known to us. But two things are certain: he was a layman,
and he was an Ibelin partisan. It would be unwise to attach
too much significance to the first fact, for Ernoul as a *grand
seigneur* in Outremer would have had plenty of clerkly help
at his disposal. Thus written Latin sources which he himself
might not have been able to read would nevertheless be
accessible to him, and the long Biblical passages which
appear so frequently in certain parts of the compilations,
and which imply a more detailed and exact knowledge of
the Vulgate than an ordinary layman could be expected to
have, cannot be dismissed out of hand as later clerkly interpolations in Ernoul's work. Ernoul's other distinguishing
mark, his loyalty to the Ibelin cause, is much more reliable,
though here again there are certain limitations to be recognized. The Ibelins, being as they were one of the most
important families in Outremer, were bound to figure in any
contemporary chronicle, and their doings were to some
extent a matter of common knowledge. It would not be
possible to write a history of Frankish Outremer at this
period without mentioning them a good deal. But not all
writers present them favourably by any means, or even impartially, as we have already seen, particularly around the
time of the fall of Jerusalem, when their behaviour was even

more than usually ambiguous. What one is looking for in tracing Ernoul's work, therefore, are passages unwaveringly favourable to the Ibelins, and preferably those containing information about them which would be not readily available, or of no interest, to anyone not closely connected with the family.

The abrégé has already been examined in this light by Mas-Latrie, who observed that there was probably a break in redaction about 1192 or 1194.[4] This is not to prejudge the issue of the date of compilation of the earliest version of the abrégé, which early references to the fall of Constantinople in any case fix after 1204; nor does it exclude the possibility of interpolation of material from other sources before that point. But it is here that all mention of the Ibelins ceases abruptly and for good. Balian d'Ibelin, who has been the central figure of the history up to this point, and who now disappears abruptly, may well have died then. The chronicle mentions him for the last time in the terms of the treaty made between Salahadin and Richard Lionheart in 1192,[5] and 1193 is the date when he is last heard of definitely. But the rest of the large Ibelin family continued the family tradition of political eminence with perhaps even more distinction; in the remainder of the abrégé, however, they are mentioned merely in passing occasionally, as if of little importance and no interest at all. The conclusion is inescapable: at or about this point the compiler of the abrégé changes sources, and begins to use a non-Ibelin source. This applies of course to all three versions of the abrégé— z, A (Bii), and the lost Bi—since they are all in agreement on this.

In the case of the *Estoires d'Oultremer,* it is much more difficult to say where a break occurs, for two reasons. First, the compiler of this farrago is minimally concerned with the historical interest of the book as we understand the term, or even as his contemporaries appear to have understood it, so it would be rash to assume that a change in his source indicates anything more than a whim on his part. Secondly, the whole thing is such a patchwork in any case that abrupt changes from one subject to another and back again are the

---

[4] M-L pp. 498-9.   [5] M-L p. 293.

rule rather than the exception. By the same tokens, the extant manuscripts of the *Estoires* cannot provide evidence for our present purpose. But it is necessary to mention again in this connection the translation of Citry de La Guette.[6] If it is as accurate a rendering of its original in all parts as it is in those parts we can check on, then that original differed from the extant manuscripts in one vital respect. Citry de la Guette's narrative is very detailed up to and including the fall of Jerusalem, then slightly less so until a point just after the division we have noted in the abrégé, to be precise, the death of Henri de Champagne in 1197. After this incident there is no detailed narrative at all, merely a list of the major events from then to the time of writing, which is evidently between December 1239 and the autumn of 1243. The text also contains an account of Salahadin's death amounting almost to a panegyric. There is no perceptible break at all in the narrative before Henri's death. For what the evidence of Citry de la Guette is worth then, it seems that his manu- script was based on a chronicle in which the compiler made fictitious interpolations (as described in the review of texts)[7] and that this chronicle ended in the year 1197, with the death of Henri de Champagne.

We now turn to the continuations proper.[8] These present in general a rather different pattern from the short chronicles the abrégé and the *Estoires*—and they also differ considerably among themselves, as can be seen from the table on p. 10-11. On the whole the constituent elements are matched together in a much more sophisticated way than is the case in the *Estoires* or the abrégé, and this makes it more difficult to discern the structure. But there are some striking exceptions to this rule (notably in *d*) and there is also the advantage that, with several texts covering basically the same ground and drawing to a large extent on the same sources, close comparisons between them are possible in a way in which they are not for the relatively isolated *Estoires* and abrégé. Leaving aside verbal differences between manuscripts of the same family, the variants between family and family are of two kinds: those where one version gives what is obviously

---

[6] Cf. the description of his book above, p. 16.
[7] See above, pp. 13-15.   [8] i.e. the texts of *a, b, cJ, d*, and *gG*.

merely a fuller or more abbreviated version of the same material as the others, and those where the compiler has evidently used a new source, not used by the other compilers, or has added original material of his own. While the first are significant for establishing the relationships of the texts in so far as they are dependent on each other, the second indicate where that dependence begins and ends.

The five main versions of the continuations listed above can be divided for the period in question, i.e. up to 1232, into three groups: a and b (the Colbert-Fontainebleau continuation as Mas-Latrie calls it), cJ and gG, and d alone. The middle pair, cJ and gG, correspond quite closely to the abrégé, and differ hardly at all from each other materially in this period, while the last, d, is so idiosyncratic that it demands to be considered quite separately. Versions a and b present no material differences from each other in this period, and though minor differences of reading between them will occasionally be referred to, they may generally be taken as a single version. The relationship of this version to that of cJ and gG changes radically at the end of Book xxx, chapter 10, so that two separate comparisons of these versions are required, first up to that point, and then from there to the end of the period in question.

Let us first consider therefore the relationship between a and b on the one hand and cJ and gG on the other, from the beginning of the continuations, that is xxiii. 1 of the *Eracles,* up to xxx. 10 inclusive, classifying the variants not in the order in which they occur, but according to kind, and to their significance for the present question.

Some of the differences between these two versions may be quickly seen to give no indication at all of a difference in source. In xxvii. 14-16, for example, cJ and gG give a much abbreviated account of the succession quarrels which followed the death of Tancred. The fact that they (and also d) give here the same text as Bernard is itself interesting, and will be considered further later, but there is nothing in this account that could not have been drawn from that of a-b, or from a common source. So as far as the question of source goes, this variant is immaterial. The same is true of xxvii. 6-11, which treat of the attempted assassination of Amalric in 1198, and the taking of Beyrouth in the same year: *cJ* agrees with Bernard exactly, while *gG* and *d* differ merely in saying that it was Huon de Tabarie who was suspected of instigating the assassination attempt, and consequently banished from the Kingdom, whereas *cJ* and Bernard simply say it was *ciaus de Tabarie*. The account of *a-b* gives the events in a different order, Beyrouth first and the assassination attempt second, and says that Raoul de Tabarie was accused and banished. But again, apart from the names of the brothers, who are quite often confused with one another anyway, partly because of the practice of writing initials only, partly because they so frequently acted together, there is no material in any version which is not also found in the others.

Two other similar instances are xxiii. 22, in which *gG* has the Bernard text while *cJ*, *d*, and *a-b*, though not disagreeing on what happened, give slightly different details of Baudouin de Rames's refusal to do homage to Guy, and xxxiv. 23, where *cJ*, *gG*, and Bernard omit the death of the German Emperor and give a briefer account of Margaret of Hungary's arrival in the Holy Land. Lastly there is the variant in xxiii. 1 concerning the deaths of Langosse and Andronicus, and the accession of Isaac Angelus. Here, as in xxiii. 22, Bernard and *gG* agree against the other texts, the differences being in this variant a little more marked than in those observed up to now. For example in *gG* and Bernard, Isaac takes the advice of his brothers; in *a-b*, *cJ*, and *d* he is helped by his mother.[9] But the narratives are still of the same order, and again suggest a revision rather than a new source.

All five of these variants, in short, point to the same conclusion. They resemble each other to a degree that indicates a common source, and where they split into two groups the groups tend to suggest two intermediate versions, from one of which derive *cJ*, *gG* and Bernard, from the other *a-b*.

There remain three sections in which occur significant differences in redaction between *a-b* and *cJ* and *gG*. These concern, again in order of importance and not of occurrence, the Third Crusade and the truce of 1192, the death of Henri de Champagne, and the battle of Hattin.

---

[9] A confusion between *mere* and *frere* perhaps?

The narratives of the Third Crusade have already been compared in detail in a previous chapter.[10] To summarize the conclusions of that discussion: differences are observable between the two accounts (the *a-b* version on the one hand and that of *cJ* and *gG* on the other) not only in the interpretation of the facts, but, more significantly, in the statement of what the facts were. From these differences it appears that for the history of the Third Crusade, these two versions had a common source, but that the compiler of *a-b* used an extra source as well, not known to the compiler of the version of *cJ* and *gG*. To use an extra source for this section of the narrative is not a surprising thing to do, for the texts which do not do so (*cJ* and *gG*) are thin at this point.

This divergence between *a-b* and *cJ* and *gG* ends with the departure of Richard Coeur-de-Lion from the Holy Land, and the truce of 1192, that is, at the very point in the abrégé where the pro-Ibelin bias ends. As we should by now expect, *gG* and (less accurately this time) *cJ* agree exactly with Bernard in enumerating not only the terms of the treaty but also the various restitutions of property Salahadin made to particular individuals, namely Caiphas, Caesarea, Arsur, and Jaffa to their respective lords, and the gifts of Sarfent to Reynaud of Sidon, and Caymon to Balian d'Ibelin.[11] In place of all these details, the *a-b* version says of Reynaud that he was given not only Sarfent but also half of all the territory of Sidon, and specifies that this was to make amends for the occasion on which Salahadin had broken his word by taking Reynaud prisoner after granting him a safe conduct.[12] For the rest this version merely says 'Li Crestien orent Japhe et Arsur et Cesaire et Cayphas et Acre et Sur.'[13]

The last two towns named were in Christian hands at the time of the truce anyway, and we are left to deduce that the first four were handed over as part of the treaty. Again we observe general material agreement between *a-b* and the version of *cJ* and *gG*, with differences of detail and emphasis. Again the inference is of one original source, with *cJ* and *gG*

[10] Cf. above, ch. V, especially pp. 65 ff.
[11] *RHC* ii. 199 n. 4 *g* variant, 197-9 *c* variant. Cf. M-L pp. 293-4.
[12] See *Eracles* xxvi. 9. *RHC* ii. 187-8.   [13] *RHC* ii. 199.

drawing on a different intermediary from *a-b*. A new point is that the ending of this long and important variant in this particular place must be borne in mind as corroborative evidence for placing a change in the redaction of the continuations here.

The second major divergence between these two versions of the continuations is in their accounts of the death of Henri de Champagne. Here the version of *d* may conveniently be included in the comparison with the others. The story occurs in xxvii. 3-4,[14] and there are three versions of it: one in *a-b*, another in *cJ, gG,* and Bernard, and the third in *d*.

In the story as recounted by *a-b*, Henri is leaning on a barred window, goes forward to receive a delegation of Pisans, returns by mistake to a different window with no bars, and falls backwards through it. His dwarf, attempting to catch at his clothing, falls with him, and both are killed. Henri is buried in the Church of the Holy Cross, with the dwarf at his foot.

In *d*, Henri is at Acre for the muster of the army to raise the siege of Jaffa, and as he leans on a barred window, this time looking out, the bars (*'treillis'*) give way. The dwarf throws himself after Henri in grief, and is killed. The author of the *d* version also comments that some alleged that, but for the dwarf's falling on top of Henri, Henri would not have died immediately, and he adds to this a short eulogy of the count.

In *cJ, gG,* and the abrégé (all versions), the dwarf is a *vaslet* and he is holding the towel while Henri washes his hands before supper, when Henri falls out of the unbarred window. The servant jumps after him 'por ce qu'il ne voloit mie que l'en deist qu'il l'eust bouté'. Again the narrator says that if he had not done so, Henri would not have died at all. The servant is not killed, but escapes with a broken thigh-bone and raises the alarm, which is at first mistaken for a warning of approaching Saracens. This account adds that Henri had several times ordered the window to be

---

[14] *RHC* ii. 219-221, main text and *c* and *g* variants, and p. 220, *d* variant. M-L pp. 306-7.

barred 'por les enfans', and *cJ* and the abrégé add further
that this was in fact done after his death.

The basic facts that emerge are these: Henri fell out of a
window and a servant of some kind fell with him. The differences between the versions may be summarized thus: What
was Henri doing before he fell? Were there two windows, or
one? Was the servant a dwarf or not? Was he dragged after
Henri or did he throw himself down? Was he killed, or only
injured? Some of these differences are clearly attributable to
attempts to make sense of an incident after it has happened,
for example, none of the narrators can really know what
went through the dwarf's mind at the time. His motives can
be speculated on *ad infinitum,* and what easier than to
substitute for one speculation another more to the taste of
the compiler?[15]

It is evident that of these three versions of Henri's death,
none could have given rise, even with much adaptation, to
the other two. Must we postulate one common source,
variously adapted, or several different sources?

As far as the question of the windows goes, an original
narrative mentioning two, one barred and one unbarred,
could give rise to all three existing versions, *a-b* preserving
both, *d* omitting the second, and *cJ-gG* omitting the first.
Similarly the differing reasons for Henri's being at Acre and
his occupation at that moment are not mutually exclusive.
We can easily suppose that the three versions chose three
different details—the visit of the Pisan delegation, the muster
of the army, and the hand-washing—from a much longer
and more elaborate source offering all three.

On the other hand, there is direct contradiction between
the versions on the subject of the servant. A dead dwarf, or
a *vaslet* with a broken leg? Here we must simply opt for
a-b and *d* in preference to *cJ-gG*, on the grounds that they are

---

[15] A curiously similar instance is provided by the death in 1366 of the Infante
of Spain: ' . . . Sus hijos fuessen traidos à la seguridad de nuestra Ciudad y
Alcaçar donde murio el Infante Don Pedro. Dizen algunos que de una ventana
mui alta se cayò de los braços al ama que le tenia; la qual arrebatada del
dolor se arrojó tras el. Cierto es que nuestra Ciudad celebró sus funerales con
aparato y sentimiento conveniente . . .' Diego de Colmenares, *Historia de la
Insigne Ciudad de Segovia, y conpendio de las Historias de Castilla* (Segovia,
1637), p. 283. I am grateful to Dr. J.P. Croft of Royal Holloway College,
London, for drawing my attention to this passage.

at once less elaborate and more precise, particularly in *a-b*'s
account of the place and nature of the burial, details which
could moreover have been verified at the time, and would
probably have been a matter of fairly common knowledge.
As for the broken leg and the alarm, it is perfectly possible
that the dwarf did break a leg in falling, but he must have
died fairly quickly to be buried with Henri the next day, as
the climate necessitated, and the alarm could well have been
his cries as he saw Henri fall, and fell himself. The survival
of the dwarf and the raising of the alarm after the fall thus
appear as unnecessary elaborations, the first invented to
explain the second. If these two traits—the alarm mistaken
for a warning of an approaching army, and the injuries of
the dead dwarf—were mentioned in passing by the original,
their omission in *a-b* and *d* and their elaboration in *cJ-gG*
is a credible and sufficient explanation of the present versions.

It thus becomes clear that all these versions could indeed
have come from one ultimate source, and that there is no
need to postulate more than one. It is also clear however
that there were two intermediate versions of that source, as
the earlier more minor variations between the texts had
suggested, *cJ-gG* and the abrégé deriving from the one, *a-b*
and (with reservations) *d* from the other. We should here
add, however, a further qualification to this hypothesis,
namely that in the chronicle as a whole, as in the example
of Henri's death analysed above, *a-b* and *d* consistently give
a simpler account, while *cJ, gG,* and the abrégé generally
have a more artistic story with more dramatic appeal. Such
a judgement is of course, like Bédier's on the *Tristan,* at least
party subjective.[16] But on the credit side of the argument
it must be added that in the case of chronicles there is a
great deal to be said for preferring the least ornate and
'literary' version, as having less popular appeal, and therefore
being most liable to revision in the interest of increased
suspense and excitement. If one has to choose one version
as being closer to the original, this is the one to opt for. The
possibility therefore presents itself that *a-b* and *d* drew
directly on the original, while *cJ-gG* and the abrégé are

---

[16] *Le Roman de Tristan par Thomas,* ed. J. Bédier (Paris, 1905), ii 192: 'Chacun
sait combien de telles déterminations sont sujettes à caution et précaires', etc.

drawing on an adaptation of that original, and are at one remove more from it than are *a-b* and *d*. This would also account for the fact that whereas *cJ, gG,* and the abrégé are in total, usually verbatim, agreement with each other, the agreement between *a-b* and *d* is very variable and intermittent. Sometimes they too agree verbatim, at other times not even the substance of their narrative is the same. In other words, while the first group of texts are, in this section (up to xxx. 10) anyway, simply copies of one text, the second group are rather adaptations of their common source. These relationships may be represented by a provisional stemma, thus:

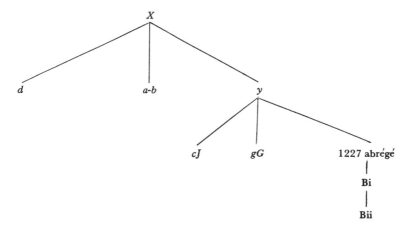

It must be emphasized that this stemma is valid only for the continuations up to the end of xxx. 10 and not at all after that point, when the relationship of the texts becomes completely different. Moreover the place assigned to *d* is very provisional.

It remains to consider the variants of *d* in this section, again confining ourselves to material differences, and leaving aside for the present variant readings which indicate only the relationships between several manuscripts of one continuation, and not between one continuation and another. In fact *d* contains much factual information not found in any other text at all; a brief review of these peculiarities will enable us to consider what they indicate about the sources of *d,* and since to categorize them *ab initio* would be to beg the question, we shall in this case enumerate them in the order in which they occur in the text. Comparing the text of *d* with the other continuations is not easy, because even a cursory comparison shows that this is very much a contaminated text, which stands in no simple relationship to any of the others. So it is difficult to describe its vagaries without setting up a standard of comparison which may prove in the end misleading, that is, without describing it in relation to other texts, to which it may seem to be comparable, but with which it is in fact but little connected. However, some comparison must be made for the sake of clarity, and since in the section of text in question, i.e. up to xxx. 10, the text of *d* is for much of the narrative in agreement with that of *a-b*, as had already become apparent in the discussion of *a-b*, it is to that text that we shall now compare it. But it must be stressed that the method adopted is no more than one of expediency, and does not by any means imply that *d* is in any way dependent on *a-b*, or even that it is necessarily another adaptation of precisely the same sources.

The first divergence between the texts of *d* and *a-b* comes just after the beginning of xxiii. 40, part of the way through the narrative of Hattin.[17] This variant continues for ten chapters, covering the surrenders of Tiberiade and of Acre, Balian d'Ibelin's journey to Jerusalem, the history of Johan Gale, and Conrad of Montferrat's sojourn in Constantinople, his arrival in Palestine, and his organization of the defence of Tyre. All these topics are also treated in the corresponding section of *a-b*, with the exception of Johan Gale, who appears later (xxiv. 12).[18] On each subject, *d* gives a much more detailed narrative, but one which is never in contradiction with that of *a-b*. In all these ten chapters there is but one small difference of fact between the two texts: Conrad arriving incognito off Acre is in *d* recognized as a Christian by an apostate Saracen, while in *a-b* the Saracens of whom he inquires the political situation assume him to be friendly to Salahadin.[19] Otherwise *d* is in each case simply a fuller version of the same story, thus tending, in this case, to confirm the stemma above, and to suggest that *d* is drawing on the same source as *a-b*, giving in parts a fuller rendering of it. Sometimes

[17] *RHC* ii. 62 ff.   [18] Ibid., pp. 121-3.
[19] Ibid., p. 75 main text, p. 76 *d* variant.

we can even see from *d* exactly what sort of telescoping has been effected in *a-b*'s adaptation. For example, according to *a-b*, Renaud de Châtillon, taken prisoner at Hattin, is beheaded by Salahadin. But *d* specifies that Salahadin himself ran Renaud through with his sword, and that the mamelukes standing by then rushed forward and beheaded him.[20]

The next three variant passages of *d*, in chapters 52, 62, and 64 of this same book xxiii, are all anecdotes connected with the events being described. They occur in a narrative identical, apart from their presence, to the corresponding sections of *a-b*, and fit smoothly into the story as illustrations or reinforcements of the point being made. The first two of these anecdotes relate to the siege of Jerusalem—how Salahadin sent for Thomassin d'Ibelin and Guillemin de Gibelet, and wept over these Christian children whom his imminent victory was to disinherit,[21] and how an apparently poor man was discovered attempting to defy the surrender terms by taking money out of Jerusalem with him.[22] The third anecdote describes an incident during the march of the Christians escaped from Jerusalem, when the men of the Lord of Nefin ambushed and robbed them, treating their own countrymen, as the chronicler is quick to point out, worse than the Saracen enemy had done.[23] What the source and significance of these anecdotes is, we shall see.

Book xxiv covers the events succeeding the fall of Jerusalem, and contains seven variants in *d*. The first of these is in chapter

---

[20] Ibid., p. 67 main text, p. 69 *d* variant. This precision in *d* may throw an interesting light on another text, the Latin continuation of the *Historia* which is found in the British Museum MS Royal 14.C.x, in which a curious discrepancy occurs, Renaud being killed twice. See M. Salloch, *Die lateinische Fortsetzung Willelms von Tyrus* (Leipzig, 1934), p. 12 of the Introduction and pp. 79 and 80 of the text. It seems that there is here a confusion between the two actions described in *d* and the single one of all the other chronicles. The Latin continuator has the idea of two attacks, but in his version they have become completely separate incidents and thus produce, nonsensically, two deaths. It is also possible that he has confused two people—Renaud of Châtillon and Renaud of Sidon—but in any case there is something wrong with his text, for we know that Renaud of Sidon was not killed by Salahadin, either at the seige of Mont Royal or elsewhere; on the contrary we find him still alive in 1192, and receiving from Salahadin half the territory of Sidon, and the town of Sarfent, to make amends for the treatment he had received at the siege of Mont Royal. See *RHC* ii, 110-11 *d* variant, and 199 main text.
[21] *RHC* ii, *d* variant pp. 84-5.
[22] Ibid., pp. 97-8. [23] Ibid., pp. 100-1.

two;[24] it concerns Salahadin's purification of the Temple, and except that it contains some brief explanatory details on the Saracens' religious beliefs, it is trivial. Again, it is explicable simply as a fuller adaptation of the same source used by a-b. The second variant passage similarly contains insignificant differences of detail in the accounts of the taking of Beauvoir and the siege of Tyre, but also adds a unique account of the siege of Mont Royal.[25] The third, in the following chapter, is totally insignificant, being simply a differently worded version of exactly the story contained in a-b.[26] It is in chapter four that we first meet a really major variant in book xxiv, a long and detailed account of the ruse Salahadin employed to take Beaufort.[27] It is most interesting to find d placing the capture of Beaufort at this point, for it agrees with the chronology of the Arabic chronicles, in dating this event in the same year as the fall of Crac and Beauvoir, 1189.[28] The text of a-b completely misplaces all these events in 1192, during the Third Crusade.[29] That this is erroneous is clear from the fact that a-b says they had all been besieged two years, which agrees with the other sources (cf. above), but disagrees with them in that they all situate the investing of the castles in the year of the fall of Jerusalem, 1187, when Salahadin was consolidating his territorial position, and thus put the whole thing three years earlier. We are forced to conclude that the account of these sieges was contained in X of the stemma above (p. 89), and that the compiler of a-b at first omitted it, and later reversed the decision, probably because he had realized that the terms of the 1192 treaty made reference to the incident at Beauvoir.

No less illuminating is the next variant of d, in chapters eight and nine of the same book. The additional passing references made in d to the wars between France and England are of little importance; the salient feature is d's omission of the death of Barbarossa, which every other text of the continuations gives at this point. This omission on the part of the d compiler is interesting because Barbarossa's death will

[24] Ibid., pp. 103-4.   [25] Ibid., pp. 104-5.
[26] Ibid., pp. 108-9.   [27] Ibid., pp. 110-11.
[28] Ibid., p. 122: 'Cil des chastiaus [sc. Crac and Beauvoir] se furent tenus deus ans et demi apres la terre perdue.'
[29] RHC main text, pp. 187-8.

be recounted later, in chapter twenty-six of this same book,[30] by *d* and also by *a-b*. Thus *d* avoids giving two narratives of this same event, and does it by omitting not the second of them, but the first. What is more the two, as given by *a-b*, contradict each other:

> Un jor se estoit li empereres herbergez en Ermenie, sur une riviere. Si li prist talent de baignier soi. Si entra ens, en tel maniere que il fu noiés.[31]
>
> ... et l'empereres se mist a passer le flum, et li dui chevalier devant lui, et de ses homes devant et derriers lui a grant plenté. Si come il fu el mi luec dou flum, li chevauz sus cui il chevaucheit trabucha et il chei ou flum. Par la force de la chalor que il avoit sofferte et par la froidure de l'eve ou il chai, il perdi sa vertu, que il ne se post aider. Les veines de son cors s'ovrirent, si que il nea.[32]

The first account, which is found in *a-b, cJ*, and *gG*, is premature. It is evident that the second, detailed account, found in *a-b* and *d*[33] in its chronological place, is that of the archetype, while the allusion of xxiv. 9 (the first passage quoted above) is an interpolation. The compiler of *d* has avoided, somehow, the errors of duplication and contradiction.

If further proof of the theory that *d* and *a-b* are differently adapting one source is still needed, it is provided by the next variant passage, in the same chapter. It is the story of the martyrdom of a number of Templars taken prisoner by Salahadin, whom he offers to take into his own service, on condition that they apostasize. They refuse, and are all put to death. The emir Boha-Eddin Caracoush, warning Salahadin that this action is unwise because it invites vengeance, expresses himself in a quite particular metaphor: 'Je vos fas assavoir que les Templiers naistront o toutes lor barbes.'[34]

This whole incident is found only in *d*, but a little later, in *d* and this time also in *a-b*, Caracoush makes this comment on the arrival in Outremer of Jacques d'Avesnes: 'Sire, dist Caracois, ce est le secors qui vient as Francs. Je vos di(s) bien, quant vos comandastes a occirre les Templiers, que il Templier naistreent o toutes les barbes.'[35]

As in the case of the taking of Beaufort, it is clear that here again the compiler of *a-b* has omitted an incident to which,

[30] Ibid., pp. 137-8. [31] Ibid., p. 117.
[32] Ibid., p. 138.
[33] The abrégé, *cJ* and *gG* do not contain xxiv. 16-xxv. 5 at all.
[34] *RHC* ii. 124, *d* variant. [35] *RHC* ii main text, 128.

though he does not know it, his source will later refer back.
In the first example, he remedies this by an afterthought and
adds the episode just before the reference to it. Here he leaves
in the reference, but it has nothing to refer to.

Apart from the narrative of the Third Crusade, which is a
question apart, and has been dealt with elsewhere,[36] there are
three more variant passages in *d* between here and the end of
the section under consideration, xxx. 10. The first is very long,
from xxvi. 7 to xxvii. 5, and like those already examined, consists of basically the same narrative as in *a-b* with a good deal
of extra material added. Some of this is extra details about
events covered in both versions, and some touches on matters
not dealt with in *a-b,* or indeed in any version except *d.* Yet
a third category of these variant passages is material not found
in *a-b,* but found in *cJ, gG,* or the abrégé, or all three, at a later
point, which re-emphasizes the relatedness of *d* to these three
texts, albeit at some distance in this section. Like all the variants
up to now, this one does not contradict *a-b,* the only slight
exception being in the matter of the death of Henri de
Champagne examined above with which this lengthy variant
comes to an end.

After this point, *d* offers no more information peculiar to
itself, nor even any revisions of material found elsewhere but
expressed in a different way. Wherever *d* differs from *a-b* from
now on, it is in agreement with *cJ* and *gG.*[37] How does this
agreement come about? The direct dependence of *d* on *gG*
can be ruled out, because of their dates of composition, while
the inverse relationship must also be eliminated as a straightforward solution, since it would not account for the strong
similarity of *cJ* and *gG,* especially in other parts of the text,
where *d* is not in agreement with them. The only possible
explanation is that we have here a quite different relationship from that illustrated by the stemma on p. 89: *d, cJ,* and
gG are now drawing on a common source, not used by *a-b*
which is here in a class by itself. It is apposite to mention here
that from 1205 to 1231 this is consistently the situation;
indeed it is true to say that for that period, *cJ, gG,* and *d* are
one same version, with *a-b* completely unrelated to them.

---

[36] In ch. V above.
[37] There are two passages which come before xxx. 10 for which this is also true
namely xxvii. 6-11 and 14-16.

For the intervening section, from xxx. 10 to the year 1205, all the versions agree with each other.

So it is clear that the relationship of the continuations one to another undergoes a radical change at the death of Henri de Champagne. After that matters are simple enough—agreement between all the versions up to 1205 (death of Amalric of Lusignan), then two narratives only up to 1231, one in *a-b*, and the other in *d, cJ, gG,* and the abrégé. It is to the period 1186-97 that we can reduce the most complicated section of the continuations. The stemma on p. 89 has been suggested as representing the texts in this period, but there are some modifications we must now make.

First, the stemma as it stands shows one source, *X,* with three texts deriving from it: *d, a-b,* and the lost *y,* the common intermediate source of *cJ, gG,* and the abrégé. But it has become evident that *a-b* and *y* have a certain common consistency in their adaptations of that source, not shared by *d.* In other words, if the stemma were exact as it stands, one would expect that between these three—*a-b, d,* and *y*—there would be a fairly random distribution of the material originally to be found in *X.* But as we have seen, though this is the case very often, there is a very large body of material found only in *d,* much more than can be accounted for at chance level, and which is consistently absent from *a-b* or any of the texts dependent on *y.* But on the other hand there is really nothing in *a-b* or the *y* texts which allows us to postulate any kind of dependence of one on the other, to see *y,* for example, as based on *X,* but influenced by *a-b,* or vice versa. What then accounts for this common elimination of a large body of material by these two texts?

A possibility which suggests itself is of course that the material peculiar to *d* was not in *X* at all, but was drawn by the compiler of *d* from another source known only to him and not to the other two compilers. The objections to this are that first, the 'additions' of *d,* if such they are, fit into the narrative so smoothly that were it not for the existence of the other texts which omit them, one would not have any notion that they were additions. It seems scarcely credible that there was another chronicle besides *X* which covered the same ground for the period 1186-97 so exactly that the compiler of *d* could fill out *X* from it with so little trouble and so much conviction.

Secondly, and more serious, we have already seen two certain instances, the taking of Beaufort and the martyrdom of the Templars, where there is no doubt at all that, far from *d* adding extra material to what was in *X*, *a-b* has omitted information that was in that source. It is highly probable therefore that the same thing has occurred in other instances too, which are not so easily detectable, and that where *d* has, in an otherwise similar narrative, extra material, it is material that was in *X* and has been eliminated by the *a-b* compiler.

The possibility of *d* having access to an extra source quite separate from *X*, and yet resembling it so extraordinarily closely, seems in fact unlikely; yet his version is more different from the other two than can be explained by mere chance selection of material from *X*, especially as the passages preserved by *d* alone have, as we shall see, a number of characteristics in common. We are forced to conclude that the elimination of this material was made at a stage between *X* and *y*, by some adapter whose work was then further adapted by the compilers of *a-b* and *y*. Thus the *d* compiler would use *X*, while the compilers of *a-b* and *y* both used an adaptation of *X*, which we may conveniently designate *Xi*. What is found in *a-b*, *d*, and the derivatives of *y*, must have been in *X*, and been preserved both by *d* and by *Xi*, while the passages found only in *d* were in *X*, but were eliminated by *Xi*, and hence were all unavailable to *a-b* and *y*.

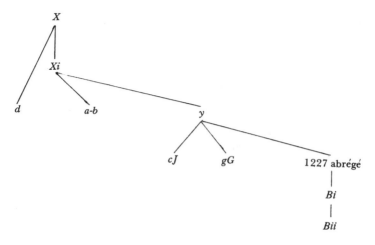

It is of course possible that the *d* compiler did have access to *Xi* and that he followed it for much of the narrative, only turning to *X* when he realized that it had some advantage— more information, a diverting anecdote, an intriguing detail to offer. It is impossible to calculate sufficiently precisely the degree of agreement and disagreement between *d* and the texts derived from *Xi* to say whether this is the case or not, nor does it greatly matter.

What does matter, as far as the problem of tracing the work of Ernoul is concerned, is that it is certain that all the continuations had in common, ultimately, one source, which, to judge from the complete change in the relationships of the continuations to each other after the death of Henri de Champagne, ended then. This strongly supports Mas-Latrie's hypothesis: 'Peut-être faudrait-il alors réduire aux années antérieures à 1197, si ce n'est la chronique primitive d'Ernoul, du moins une chronique antérieure employée par Ernoul.'[38]

The question now is, is it indeed 'la chronique primitive d'Ernoul' which ends here? The variants of *d* now appear as fresh evidence of the nature of this source chronicle, *X*, and though we must allow for the tastes of the compiler of *d* operating in the selection of material from *X*, and conceivably embellishing a little too, we may at least find in these variants some clear indications of those characteristics of *X* which the compiler of *Xi*, on which all the continuations except *d* depend, thought fit to eliminate. Did *Xi* select purely capriciously, or can those of his omissions which are fossilized in *d* be characterized? And if so, do they allow us to identify *X* as 'la chronique primitive d'Ernoul'?

[38] M-L p. 499.

VII

'LA CHRONIQUE PRIMITIVE D'ERNOUL'

WHEN WE come to consider the characteristics of X, as manifest in the variants of the only continuation derived directly from it, d, one thing immediately becomes apparent: the author of X was a native of the Latin Kingdom of Jerusalem. There is, to begin with, his use of the term *Outremer*. The normal usage of this term by European chroniclers, and by the compilers of all the other continuations, is that by it they indicate Palestine or the Near East in general; in fact the lands over the sea from Europe. But X always uses it to mean Europe, the land over the sea from Palestine. For example, at the end of xxiii, 64, the Christians escaped from Jerusalem are wintering at Alexandria:

b	*cJ* (*gG* similarly)	*d*
. . . et demorerent ilec jusques au mars.	. . . jusques au mars qu'il entrerent en nes pour passer en terre de Crestiens.	La furent jusques au marz que il entrerent es nez por aler Outre mer en terre des Crestiens.[1]

Again, when Salahadin hears of the preparations for the Third Crusade, the same difference of viewpoint is clearly evident in d:

a-b (*cJ*, *gG* similarly)	*d*
Noveles li vindrent que li empereres d'Alemaigne estoit croisez, et li rois de France et li rois d'Engleterre et tuit li haut home *de Crestienté*. . . *por aler* sur lui.	Noveles li vindrent que l'empereor d'Alemaigne et le rei de France et le rei d'Engleterre, et tuit li haut baron *d'Outre mer* estoient croisié *por venir* sur lui.[2]

In this example the term *Outremer* might of course be an addition, a gloss by the compiler of d, if he himself, and not the author of X, worked in Palestine. That this is not the case is clear from the whole cast of mind evident throughout the variants of d, which is that of a colonial Frank, a *Polain*[3] as the European crusaders called them. This Palestinian

---

[1] *RHC* ii. 101, main text, note 30, and d variant.
[2] Ibid., p. 118, main text and d variant. My italics.
[3] For the term *Polain*, see Appendix II.

orientation of X is often implicit in the very manner in which he reports an event. Compare for example in xxvi. 23:

a-b	d
Quant li empereres ot tout apresté et il dut mover, si le prist une maladie de quoi il fu morz a Brandis, ou l'assemblée estoit, si que l'en dist que sa feme l'empereris Costance l'avoit enpoisoné.[4]	Dedens ce que les Alemans atendoient a avoir le chastel dou Toron, novele lor vint que l'emperere Henri lor seignor estoit mort, et que le secors de Babiloine venoit a ciaus dou chastel. Et enssi com il aparsurent le secors il orent conseil entr'iaus; si se departirent come ciaus qui avoient perdu les cuers et la volenté por la mort de lor seignor.[5]

Another trait of X which is here and everywhere apparent is his dislike of European crusaders, whom he regards as inept meddlers, and especially Germans. The whole variant from which the above passage comes is one long discourse on the various deplorable features of the German character, beginning with their military inferiority: 'Ensi come les Alemans virent le poeir des Sarasins qui estoit si grant, il furent esmaié.'[6] Only the courage and wisdom of a Syrian baron, Hugh of Tiberiade, prevents the total defeat which the Germans' panic very nearly causes. The Germans moreover fail to understand anything about the mentality of the *gens de la terre,* whom they treat in a high-handed and patronizing manner, or that of the Saracens, whom they consistently underestimate, and with whom they refuse to deal on equal terms. X puts into the mouths of the Saracens one of his own criticisms, saying that the Saracens feared the cruelty of the Germans;[7] elsewhere he simply makes criticisms explicitly and categorically of the German character and its nefarious effects on German diplomacy:

Les Alemans se fient moult en lor force et en lor fausse vertu, ne n'orent pitié des esclas Crestiens que l'on lor devoit rendre, ne ne conurent le bien et l'onor qui lor avenoit. Car se il eussent receu le chastel en la maniere que li Sarasin le voloient rendre, les Sarasins lor eussent des puis rendu le chastel de Biaufort, qui est en la terre de Sayete, et les autres chastiaus.[8]

---

[4] *RHC* ii. 210. [5] *RHC* ii, *d* variant, 222. [6] Ibid., p. 217.
[7] Ibid., p. 222. [8] Ibid., p. 221.

One might think these criticisms typical of any French
writer, whether Syrian or not. But X's marked hatred of
Poitevins defines his allegiance much more closely. Only in
the variant of d do we find preserved the political song composed by the Poitevins against *ciaus de cest pais*: 'Maugré li
Polein avrons nous roi Poitevin.' Ceste haine et cest despit
firent perdre le roiaume de Jerusalem.'[9]

Again the author does not hesitate to generalize. Guillaume
Barlais is taken as being typically Poitevin: 'A tant s'en parti
dou conte Guillaume Barlais, et si s'en ala por saisir Japhe.
Mais il fist come Peitevins, que dou conseill et dou comande-
ment dou conte il ne fist mie le disme. Car il euvrent de lor sens
et s'aseurent en lor poeir.'[10]

The variants of d, in these and in many other instances, consistently display an attitude which can only come from a
Syrian Frank, opposed to Guy, the *roi Poitevin,* and belonging
to the faction of which Raymond of Tripoli was the unofficial
leader.

Again, X is conscious that the customs of the Kingdom of
Jerusalem are particular, and is often at pains to explain them
to his readers. For example, the account of the procedure for
electing the Patriarch of Jerusalem appears in all the continuations (xxiii. 38) but only d also relates the scandal which
later broke out and which resulted in the procedure's being
changed.[11]

Similarly, d explains more precisely than the other texts
why Raymond of Tripoli led the vanguard at Hattin: 'Ce est
le droit des barons dou roiaume. Quant il i a ost banie en lor
seignorie, li baron en cui terre se doit faire le bataille, il a la
premiere eschiele et la premeraine pointe, et a l'entrer de sa
terre fait il l'avant garde, et au retorner l'ariere garde. Por ce
ot le conte de Triple la premiere pointe, que Thabarie estoit
soue.'[12]

When Conrad of Montferrat and his men arrived off Acre,
a-b, cJ and gG merely say that they heard no bells sound, and
saw no boat coming to meet them, ' . . . si en furent moult
corrocez, ne n'oserent ancrer, ains se traistrent arriere'.[13] In
d we find this reaction elucidated:

[9] *RHC* ii, d variant, 63.   [10] Ibid., p. 219.   [11] Ibid., pp. 203-5.
[12] Ibid., pp. 64-5.   [13] *RHC* ii, main text, 75.

En le tens que il furent arivés devant la cité d'Accre, il estoit costume en la devant dite cité que on sonoit une campane quant aucune nave ariveit d'Outre mer, et une gamele aloit a la nave, et grant piece avoit que nave n'en estoit venue. Quant le marquis ariva, il n'en oi poinct de campane soner, si fist geter une barche en mer, et mist des plus sages homes de sa nave et les envoia en la cité por savoir que ce devoit que il n'avoient point oie la campane soner, et quels noveles il i avoit ou pays.[14]

Inevitably, X displays a particular interest in local politics. This interest is to a certain extent evident in all the continuations, but examination of the d variants shows that there was much more of this kind of information in X than the compilers of Xi thought worth preserving. Just as the author of X regarded Europeans as outsiders, and their exploits as less useful than operations directed by Syrians, so European chroniclers tend to look chiefly on the broad outlines of the Holy War as of most interest, the rest being petty squabbles between local warlords. Only when such quarrels seriously affect the larger issue, as in the case of Raymond of Tripoli's refusal to recognize Guy as his sovereign, do they stop to give details, and then in a perfunctory fashion very different from that of X, as we have already seen in several of the variants of d examined above. So in the other continuations, the Polain-Poitevin rivalry is completely passed over, the misdeeds of the lords of Nefin are of no interest to those who did not know them, and possibly did not even know of them, and even an event as interesting to the historian as the founding of the first commune at Antioch is left aside.[15] Perhaps the most surprising omission of this kind is the account, preserved only in d, of the quarrel between Henri de Champagne and Amauri de Lusignan, which resulted in Amauri's resignation as Constable of the Kingdom of Jerusalem and his departure for Cyprus.[16] This information is absolutely necessary if we are to understand how Amauri came to be in Cyprus at the time of his brother Guy's death, and was therefore elected King chiefly on account of his being immediately available. Similarly, apropos of Richard's capture by the Duke of Austria, d adds an anecdote concerning Richard's behaviour towards the Duke in the Holy Land after the siege of Acre, which he rightly or wrongly, but certainly convincingly, offers as the cause of the Duke's ill feeling towards Richard. He also

[14] *RHC* ii, *d* variant, 76.   [15] Ibid., p. 209.   [16] Ibid., pp. 202-3.

has more detail on the raising of Richard's ransom, but recounts it as something known to him only at second hand, as
hearsay, with at one point four out of six consecutive sentences
beginning with the words 'l'en dist que.'[17]

Curiously enough, another manifestation of X's parochialism
is quite the opposite of these useful explanations, namely an
assumption of knowledge on the part of his readers, in the
form of allusions, made in passing, to what is assumed to be
a body of common information. This assumption was doubtless justified at the time and in the place in which X wrote,
but he often leaves us guessing. For example, on the Jerusalem
succession agreement made at the marriage of Isabelle and
Henri he says: 'L'on dit que la greignor partie et le miaus des
gens dou reiaume jurerent au conte Henri que il fereient de
ses heirs seignors et reis de Jerusalem. Car ciaus qui jurerent
au conte Henri n'en esteient neent tenus au marquis ne a ses
heirs; se il l'ont d'autre maniere fait, il est bien seu.'[18]

One of the more awkward aspects of this local element in
X, which often explains Xi's omissions or adaptations, is his
attitude towards the Saracens in general and Salahadin in
particular. Salahadin was every European chronicler's problem: the good pagan. He failed completely to fit into any of
the usual categories, and often the despairing authors took
refuge in convenient, if arbitrary, fictions. Thus, as we have
seen in the review of extant texts,[19] the compiler of the
Estoires d'Oultremer makes two interpolations designed to
demonstrate in the one case that Salahadin had been dubbed
a knight in the proper manner by a captive Christian baron
who could not ransom himself in any other way, and in the
other, that Salahadin's grandmother was French. Thus also another
pseudo-historian, the Menestrel de Reims, asserts that Salahadin
was in fact a crypto-Christian, and baptized himself on his
death-bed.[20] But X, far from indulging in these fantasies, is
not even aware of the problem. To him, Salahadin is a military opponent, but that does not mean he must be painted
as a complete villain. Twice d includes accounts of internal
Saracen politics, and three times he recounts episodes which
shed a totally different light on the relations between Saracens
and Christians from that carefully cast by the other continuators.

[17] Ibid., pp. 201-2.   [18] Ibid., p. 193.   [19] Cf. above, p. 15.   [20] Cf. above, p. 15.

They mention briefly, though with reasonable clarity and accuracy, some of the dispositions Salahadin made of his land at his death, and also the death in a hunting accident of his son Malek-Aziz.[21] But they are not interested in the in-fighting among the Saracens which filled the interval between these two events, and which *d* recounts in some detail. This variant of *d* also illustrates the kind of parallel *X* so often draws between Saracen and Christian customs, to elucidate the former in terms of the latter, and so make them readily understandable to a Christian audience: 'Ensi come le patriarche corone le rei de Jerusalem de corone d'or et l'enoint, en itel maniere (chez) les Sarasins le plus grant home, qui est en icele seignorie porte devant celui qui deit estre soutan une housse devant lui, mostrant la et disant au pueple: Vees ci nostre seignor.'[22]

Moreover *d* alone of all the continuators mentions the quarrels between Salahadin and his brother Saphadin, the defection of a large number of discontented mamelukes to Richard's service, and the employment of Bedouin Arabs as spies,[23] though all these are directly relevant to a clear understanding of Richard's policies, and are evidently put in by *X* for that purpose. In this case the *d* compiler is not only a better historian, but produces a better narrative, in the sense of a more easily understandable one. His interest in the Saracens for their own sakes, and not merely as an adjunct of the main characters, the Franks, prevents the imbalance, and the frequently ensuing incomprehensibility, commonly found among chroniclers of the crusades, and from which another more famous native of Outremer, William of Tyre, is so notably exempt. The relative impartiality of *d* is clear from three other episodes included only in his version. There is first the curious tale mentioned earlier,[24] of Salahadin's treatment of two Christian children, Thomassin d'Ibelin and Guillemin de Gibelet, which shows Salahadin as a man of honour—he is answering a request from Balian d'Ibelin that he should take the children under his protection—and capable of fine feeling as well as military prowess. He is at once sure of imminent victory, and aware of the implications of defeat for the children

[21] *RHC* ii, main text, 222; cf. *d* variant, 212.   [22] *RHC* ii, *d* variant, 211.
[23] Ibid., pp. 196-7. Cf. also Salahadin's remarks about his brother, ibid., p. 85.
[24] Ibid., pp. 84-5, Cf. above p. 91.

of his enemies. The whole story brings to light moreover a much closer and more trusting relationship between Saracens and Christians than is usually allowed for, though admittedly the family concerned is one which was known to be, for good or ill, hand in glove with Salahadin. The Ibelins are not, however, involved in the other two variants of this kind. When Guy de Lusignan became King of Cyprus he sent to Salahadin, says *d*, for advice on how to administer his new kingdom. And once again Salahadin behaved in the best traditions of chivalry, even enunciating one of the tenets of knightly conduct explicitly in the process: 'Salahadin respondi as messages que il n'ameit gaires le rei Guy, mais depuis que il li requereit de conseill, il le conseillereit au miaus que il savreit. Car puis que l'on demande conseill a autrui, soit ami, soit henemi, leiaument li doit conseillier.'[25]

This does not necessarily tell us anything about Salahadin, who may or may not have ever expressed such a sentiment, but it tells us quite a lot about the compiler of *d*, who thought it worth including, and about *X*, who credited Salahadin with the saying in the first place.

The last of *d*'s exclusive sidelights on Salahadin is also the most important historically, and the most embarrassing to the traditional view of all Christians as the sworn and implacable enemies of all Saracens. It concerns the marriage proposed, though never contracted, between Salahadin's brother Saphadin and Joanna of Sicily, Richard Coeur-de-Lion's widowed sister. The possible effects of this marriage, and the alliance it implied between Richard and Salahadin's own brother, were wide indeed, and could well have spelled the end of Salahadin's domination in the East: '. . . et se icelui mariage se feisoit, il [Salahadin] doutoit que il ne perdist toute sa conqueste.'[26]

This fear was so real that it led Salahadin to offer Richard a truce on terms extremely favourable to the Christians, including the return to them of part of the Kingdom of Jerusalem. But Richard replied that he would have all the Kingdom, as Amalric I had held it before Nureddin's conquest, or nothing at all; a rash refusal he was soon to regret when affairs in England compelled him to accept an unfavourable treaty, that of 1192, before leaving Outremer. The enormous gains Richard

[25] Ibid., p. 188.   [26] Ibid., p. 198.

might have achieved for the Christians' cause had he accepted the offer are a measure of his lack of acuteness, and probably of his over-confidence, in refusing, and the incident is consigned to silence by everyone except the *d* compiler.

It would be misleading, however, to represent *X* as pro-Salahadin on principle, and his so-called objectivity as merely a pendulum swing between that and the other extreme. He is quite as capable of criticizing Salahadin as of praising him, as the occasion demands, as witness the story of the massacre of the Templars, which, as we have already seen, was in *X*, but is preserved only in *d*.[27] It is a first-class illustration of *X*'s attitude. He begins by stating his judgement of Salahadin's action clearly: 'Quant Salahadin fu en la cité de Domas il ot en sei un mauvais apenssement. Car il fist ocire tous les Templiers, qu'il avoit pris en la bataille.'[28]

The Templars refuse to save themselves by apostasizing, and are put to death. But *X*, despite his stated opinion of Salahadin's action—'un mauvais apenssement'—now displays his rather out of the ordinary comprehension of Salahadin's motivation: 'Mult fu grans la doulor et la mortalité et la confusion de sanc. Car il cuida faire grant sacrefice a Deu en ce que il faiseit ocire les Crestiens. Car ensi le dist Nostre Seignor en l'Evangile a ses deciples: "Encore venra l'ore que cil qui vos tueront me cuideront avoit fait grant sacrefice." '[29]

Now *X* is far from being politically naïve, and we can safely assume that he realized full well what Salahadin's real motive must have been, namely the desire to eliminate one of the most important elements in the Frankish army. But *X* is subtle enough to be able to criticize Salahadin without feeling it necessary to blacken his character entirely: though he had acted on 'un mauvais apenssement' he must still be credited with some religious sincerity. Unlike Marsile, 'qui Deu nen aimet',[30] Salahadin is here seen not as a God-hater, but precisely as thinking that his deed is pleasing to God, misled by his false religion, but for all that in good faith. The

[27] Cf. above, p. 93.
[28] *RHC* ii, *d* variant, 122.
[29] Ibid., p. 123.
[30] *La Chanson de Roland,* ed. Whitehead (Oxford, 1957), v. 6; and the same sentiment throughout.

perspicacity of *X* in this and other instances is matched, though in a rather different way, only by that of William himself.

Another of the peculiarities of the variants of *d*, though connected with the author's interest in Palestine and Outremer in general, merits particular mention. All the continuations have quite a lot of material on Cyprus, inevitably, but *d* has more than the rest. After the request from Guy to Salahadin, for example, quoted above, he goes on to tell us what the advice was, and how Guy implemented it by giving large fiefs to those who were willing to come from Palestine and settle there, '. . . ensi que, la Deu merci, sont devenus chevaliers et grant vavassors de l'isle de Chypre.'[31]

Is there a note of personal interest here? It seems difficult to account fully in any other way for this sudden change of heart towards Guy, hitherto the villain, one of those 'par cui la terre fu perdue', and now suddenly transformed into the good and wise ruler. Was *X* himself one of those who had benefited by Guy's policy, who had become a 'grant vavassor de l'isle de Chypre'? Was he in fact none other than Ernoul de Gibelet? All the evidence of the variants of *d* so far examined points to that conclusion—the close interest in local affairs in Outremer, the exact information about Saracen customs, and the very un-European attitude towards them, the identification with the anti-Guy faction in Palestine. It is now time to examine the variants in the light of those more precise criteria we have already established[32] —Ernoul's status of layman, his commitment to the Ibelin cause, and his inside information on the family.

To begin with the first, there are in the variants many traits which tend at first sight to suggest clerkly authorship. In general terms, the text of *d* has a much more professional appearance than any of the others. For example, it offers a scattering of year dates in the section in question, whereas the abrégé has not one, and of the continuations, in the period up to 1232, *a-b* has two, *gG* has one, and the others none at all. Similarly, the style of *d* is far superior to that of the other texts, and will be discussed more fully elsewhere.[33]

---

[31] *RHC* ii, *d* variant, 189.   [32] Cf. above, p. 80.
[33] See below, ch. IX, especially pp. 163-8.

Briefly, it displays a vocabulary infinitely richer, with oc-
casional learned forms (e.g. *pecunie, nave*) and a love of striking aphorisms, proverbial locutions, and metaphors. There are
also Biblical quotations—for example that added as a comment
on the martyrdom of the Templars[34] and the lament over
Jerusalem inserted into the cautionary tale of the lords of
Nefin.[35] Elsewhere we find evidence of an interest in ecclesiastical affairs, and accurate information about them,[36] which,
though not extraordinary by the standards of medieval Latin
chroniclers, does stand out in comparison with the general run
of vernacular chronicles, and with the other continuations in
particular. Two questions present themselves: are these features
necessarily the work of a clerk? and to what stage of the work
do they belong—to the author of *X* or to the compiler of *d*?

As for the general style, it suggests the hand of a professional
writer, but it does not do more than suggest. It is quite unlike
the work of that impressionable but incoherent layman, Robert
de Clari, whose ultimate description is to say he cannot describe. But an intelligent layman could do better than that, as
the chronicle of Villehardouin demonstrates, and though the
style of *d*, so much livelier and easier to read, so much more
varied in the devices it employs, is more skilful still than that
of Villehardouin, it is not beyond the bounds of possibility
for such a layman. Also we must remember, if it is the work
of Ernoul we are looking for, that Philippe de Novare describes him as a *grant plaideor*;[37] he had presumably acquired
in court an eloquence which would stand him in good stead
when he turned his hand to writing his memoirs.

Knowledge of Latin is another matter, however, and that
is implied in the sentence, 'Car ensi le dit Nostre Seignor' etc.[38]
The quotation is a translation of John 16:2, and though not
absolutely precise—it renders the singular 'omnis qui interficit
vos' by the plural 'cil qui vos tueront', and adds the adjective
grant where the original has only *obsequium*—it still seems too
close to be merely a rendering from memory by a layman who
had heard the saying. (The verse was part of the Gospel for the

---

[34] *RHC* ii, *d* variant, 123. Cf. John 16:2.
[35] Ibid., p. 100. Cf. Lamentations 1:1.
[36] Ibid., pp. 203-5. Cf. above, p. 100.
[37] Cf. above, p. 45.   [38] Cf. above, p. 105.

Sunday after Ascension Day.) It expresses not merely the idea of the verse but the actual wording, and so we must conclude that it was drawn direct from the Latin, and indicates the hand of a clerk at work on the text at some point. The lament over Jerusalem is imitated, rather freely, from the opening verse of the Lamentations of Jeremiah:

> Quomodo sedet sola civitas plena populo! Facta est quasi vidua domina gentium; princeps provinciarum facta est sub tributo.

> Qui vos porreit conter le plor et la doulor de si grant mesaventure qui avint a la sainte cité de Jerusalem? Cele qui esteit nomée dame des autres citez devint serve et ancelle; cele qui deveit regner en franchise fu puis tributaire.[39]

Though this is free in comparison with the first example, it is still undobtedly a Biblical quotation, and has the added complication that the Book of Lamentations, unlike the Gospels, is not in the liturgy one of the more frequently read parts of the Bible.

The dates do not of course necessarily have to come from a written source, or be put in by a clerk. They are all fairly memorable, and in any case are only approximately accurate, with the exception of Hattin, which is given with its day, date, month, and year.[40] Otherwise there are instances like Guy's death not only being a year out, but being said to have occurred in the same year as that of Salahadin,[41] whereas in fact they were fourteen months apart, in May 1194 and on 3 March 1193 respectively. It is the size of error that might easily be made by a slip of memory. The list of events given all together under 1196[42] appears at first sight simply wrong, but in view of the fact that they did all occur as nearly together as for example the deaths of Guy and Salahadin, and are to a certain extent causally related also, it would seem that the date has been wrongly remembered, or even wrongly copied (xv for xi) rather than the train of events totally misunderstood. Clement III died, and was succeeded by Celestine III, in March 1191, Henry VI was crowned Holy Roman Emperor by the new, and more amenable, Pope on 15 April following, and Richard was captured at Vienna in December 1192, and handed over to Henry three months later. But in general we may say that all these could easily have been remembered with

---

[39] Ibid., p. 100.   [40] *RHC* ii, *d* variant, 66.   [41] Ibid., p. 211.   [42] Ibid., p. 213.

this degree of accuracy by any well-informed person writing only a few years after the events.

The several instances of interest in ecclesiastical affairs vary in kind. In the account of the conquest of Cyprus we find these asides:

> (1) Mais le Rei de Gloire, qui aveit conduit le rei Richart jusques la et voleit planter iqui la bone plante, ce est assaveir Sainte Yglise et la Crestienté de la loi de Rome en la devant dite isle, et arachier la mauvaise racine des felons Griffons, il manda son bon conseill au rei Richart . . .

> (2) Mais la porveance et l'aie dou Rei de Gloire, qui ne deguerpist pas les siens, dona force et victoire au devant dit rei.

> (3) Et ensi par l'aie de Dieu sousmist le rei toute la seignorie de Chypre a son pooir et la torna a la lei des Latins, et fu fait arcevesques de Nicossie Salein, qui estoit arcediaque de Saint Jorges de Rames.[43]

These are strongly partisan statements; and only in *d* is the conquest of Cyprus depicted in this light. But it could as well be the virulence of feeling of a knight as of a clerk. One of the duties of a knight was to defend Holy Church and the true faith against unbelievers, which to the Franks in Outremer meant not only the Saracens but also the *felons Griffons.* 'Rei de Gloire' is a very common title not only in the Psalms, but in religious parlance in general, and the planting metaphor, though commonly found in Scripture, is not exclusively a scriptural turn of phrase. What is more, all these comments relate to Cyprus. What more natural than that a 'grant vavassor de l'isle de Chypre' should feel particularly strongly about the conquest of the island where he had made his home, and the replacement of the 'mauvaise racine des felons Griffons' by the *loi de Rome*; or that he should know the name of the Archbishop of Nicosia, and where he had come from?

Rather different, however, is the long digression on the Church and State quarrel offered by way of elucidation of the change in the election procedure for the Patriarchate of Jerusalem. The form of election is explained of course in the abrégé and in *gG*, whose compiler believes that it is still followed.[44] But *d*, after an account of the procedure couched in much the same terms as that of the other two versions, goes off into a long excursus on the revision of the procedure effected by Celestine III in 1194, after the quarrel between

---

[43] Ibid., pp. 165, 166 and 167.   [44] *RHC* ii. 59, *g* variant.

Henri de Champagne and the Canons, and the subsequent scandal. A specific reference is given to Celestine's decretal on the subject: 'Dont le Pape Celestin reprist le conte Henri, et fit une decretale, si comence enssi: Com la terre, qui est commeue et apelée l'eritage et la partie de Deu. Des adonques en ça le rei de Jerusalem n'en est pas sort.'[45]

There follows a short sketch of the difficulties between Pope and Emperor over the preceding hundred years, which is distinctly biased in favour of the Church. Now this is quite unlike the three extracts from the conquest of Cyprus quoted above, in that while they can easily be seen as the work of a layman this passage really cannot have come from a layman's pen. Someone attached to the court would have known as much as is said about the elimination of the king's role in the election, but it is stretching a point rather too far to imagine a layman knowing the title of the relevant decretal, and the history, however briefly, of the disagreements of Church and State during the whole period of the existence of the Latin Kingdom of Jerusalem. The information in this case is altogether too technical and precise, and covers too long a period, for it to be accounted for as first-hand knowledge, or as the evidence of an oral source. It betrays beyond doubt the hand of an ecclesiastic.

Who was this clerk? to what stratum in the cumulative formation of the text does his work belong? to X, or to the compilation of d from X? It is now necessary to look closely not at the content of the passages we have indicated as being beyond doubt clerkly in origin, but at their context. The most obvious case, which may therefore be disposed of first, is the lament for Jerusalem:

Ensi come il orent passé le Pui dou Conestable, et entrerent en la terre dou seigneur dou Botron et de Nefin, Renaut, qui sires estoit de Nefin, fist metre ses serjanz en un destreit de sa terre et lor comanda que il deussent rober et tolir as genz de Jerusalem quant que il poreient aveir, ensi que il pristrent le remanant que Salahadin aveit laissié a ciaus de Jerusalem. Qui vos porreit conter le plor et la doulor de si grant mesaventure qui avint a la sainte cité de Jerusalem? Cele qui esteit nomée dame des autres citez, devint serve et ancelle; cele qui deveit regner en franchise, fu puis tributaire. Cil qui eschaperent de la maisnée dou seignor de Nefin alerent envers Triple et cuiderent avoir recet dedens Triple.[46]

[45] *RHC* ii, *d* variant, 204.   [46] Ibid., p. 100.

Quoting the lament and the surrounding text *in extenso* shows just how irrelevant it is to its context, how badly it is placed, and how blatantly it breaks the train of the narrative. Clearly this is an interpolation at some point; it does not belong to X.

In the other instances we cannot hope for such a piece of excessively clumsy compilation (even by the standards of the d compiler, which are fairly low in this respect) to enable us to assert so definitely that an interpolation has been made. In the case of the Templars for example, all we can say is that the quotation from John [47] could be removed without prejudice to the sense, and so may possibly be such another addition as the lament. But it is not obviously so.

There remain the three passages concerning the Papacy. In the case of two of them it is impossible to decide whether they were in X or whether they are interpolations made by the compiler of d. These are the passage dealing with the decretal of Celestine III[48] and that describing the grief caused throughout Christendom by the news of Hattin, and in particular the death of Urban III, which is seen as a direct result of the shock; the succession of Gregory VIII; his reign of two months; and the election of Clement III, 'A cui Joce l'arcevesque de Sur li porta ceste novele veraiement, ensi com vos le troverés escrit ça en avant.'[49] All we can say about these two passages is that they can be removed without doing violence to the train of the narrative, but cannot be conclusively shown to have been added by the compiler of d to the material of his source X.

The third of the passages is different in kind, however, being a rapid summary of a number of events during 1191-2[50] most of which are narrated in full either before or after this point. It is fairly obviously a résumé by the compiler, who is in any case skipping about a good deal in his chronology in this part of the chronicle. Moreover it can be precisely dated by the reference to the unpopular Frederick II as *le derain*. Frederick died on 13 December 1250, just about the time when d, which includes events up to 1248, was being compiled. So this passage can be definitely attributed to the compiler.

---

[47] Cf. above, p. 105.   [48] Cf. above, p. 109-10.
[49] *RHC* ii, 66-7, *d* variant; cf. 67 main text, and n. 2.   [50] See above, p. 108.

To sum up the question of clerkly traits in the text of d, then, it is fair to say that in some cases, e.g. that mentioning Frederick II, they can be attributed with certainty to the compiler of d, and not to X. In the other cases, there must remain some doubt: none of the passages need have been in X, but we cannot assert with confidence that none of them was. This does not rule out the possibility that X was the 'chronique primitive d'Ernoul', for none of these extracts is too big to be an addition made at the suggestion of Ernoul's amanuensis as he wrote X to dictation. But it does mean that if we do finally identify X with proto-Ernoul, we shall have to revise our ideas about the nature of Ernoul's work, allowing it a much higher degree of 'literariness' than we should otherwise expect from a soldier's memoirs.

It remains to consider the other quality we expect in the work of Ernoul, namely what we may call the Ibelin factor. Here the results are most striking. The variants of d contain a very large number of supplementary references to the Ibelins, some of which are trivial, and others of general public interest, but many of which are really family history only, with no wider interest, and which have therefore been eliminated by the more rigorous cutting technique of Xi. For example, the anecdote concerning the child Thomassin d'Ibelin, already quoted elsewhere,[51] is basically a sentimental tale of interest only to historians wanting to demonstrate the quality of Salahadin's character, or those specifically concerned with the Ibelins. For the purpose of this study it has another quite fortuitous interest, in that it gives us an instance of a child of the house of Gibelet, Guillemin, being brought up in an Ibelin household, thus illustrating again the close ties between Ernoul's house and the Ibelins. But that is another story. The anecdote appears to have been conserved by the d compiler on account of his taste for *Personengeschichte*, which is observable elsewhere (cf. his treatment of Henri de Champagne). As has been shown already, it was cut out by the more strict compiler of Xi, who saw it, rightly, as of no general interest.

Sometimes, of course, the information on the Ibelins to be found in d is no more than a function of his care for detail, his interest in 'ciaus de cest païs', or his tendency to mention

[51] Cf. above, pp. 91 and 103.

people by name. Thus he describes in detail the order of Richard's march on Jaffa: 'Il ordenerent qui fereit l'avant garde et qui l'ariere garde. Balian de Ybelin et Guillaume de Thabarie firent l'ariere garde.'[52]

Again it is doubtless accuracy alone which leads him to specify that Balian d'Ibelin was the negotiator of the truce of 1192.[53] Such references cannot be taken to indicate any particular interest in Balian d'Ibelin, but only a greater precision than has been preserved in the reworking of *Xi*, an intermediary which the *d* compiler has fortunately bypassed. But in other instances there is an unmistakable tendency not only to give space to Ibelin trivia like the Thomassin story, but also to relate events and people to the Ibelins quite gratuitously, assuming them to be the *point de départ* in a way which makes them even more central than they were. Take for example this description of Joscelin III of Edessa: '. . . le conte Joscelin, qui aveit esté bailli en Acre, et esteit eschapé de la desconfiture o Balian d'Ibelin, qui faiseit l'ariere garde, vint en la cité.'[54]

Now Joscelin was a major political figure in the Kingdom, just as important as the Ibelins, and there was very good cause to remember his ill-fated guardianship of the infant Baldwin V. It is totally unnecessary to attach the name of Balian here.

Another reference which not only drags in Balian, but names him only by his first name, and assumes we know who is meant, is made in speaking of his grandson, Balian of Sidon: 'Icestui Balian, seignor de Seete, il fu fis de la fille Balian, qui avoit non Helvys, et de la reyne Marie.'[55]

Since the narrative immediately preceding has treated at length of Renaud of Sidon, it would have been quite sufficient to identify Balian of Sidon as his son, as indeed the text already has, without this superfluous information on his mother's origins.

One last example of a variant of *d* incorporating an episode in which an Ibelin is the central character, is perhaps a rather surprising omission on the part of *Xi*, dealing as it does with the kidnapping of Eschiva, daughter of Baudouin d'Ibelin, and wife of Amauri de Lusignan. Eschiva was queen of Cyprus at

---

[52] *RHC* ii, *d* variant, 194.
[53] Ibid., p. 199: 'Li messages que le roi manda, si fu Balian d'Ibelin.'
[54] Ibid., p. 69. [55] Ibid., p. 111.

the time, and therefore a person of some public importance, and the story is not without political import—Eschiva is eventually returned through the influence of Leo of Armenia, '. . . por amor dou rei Haymeri, qui estoit son ami et son acointé, et por amor Baudoyn d'Ibelin cui fille ele avoit esté,'[56] and the incident results in the establishment of good relations between Leo and Eschiva's relatives: 'Illueques conquist Lyvon de la Montaigne l'amor dou rei Heimeri et del parenté de la dame por le servise que il lor avoit fait.'[57]

But for all that, the story is primarily of interest to the 'parenté de la dame', and is eliminated by $Xi,$ along with a lot of other material on the state of Armenia—an insignificant country in European eyes—and its trivial private quarrels with the crusader states of Jerusalem and Antioch.

These are but instances of the interest in the Ibelin family displayed by the variants of d. There are others, too numerous to quote, of the same kind, and beyond that there is a bias towards the family and its interests which makes the whole thing read like an apologia for their course of action in the major events of the history of the Latin Kingdom. Indeed, an apologia is what it amounts to, in effect if not in the intention of the author, and we cannot entertain any reasonable doubt that it was written by a close associate of the Ibelins, unswervingly, sometimes uncritically, loyal to them, anxious above all to state their case. He was himself a *Polain*, opposed to Guy and his faction, but somewhat revising his opinion of Guy when he himself, apparently, profited by Guy's policy of distributing fiefs on a large scale in Cyprus. Certainly he is remarkably well informed about Cyprus, and takes a particular interest in the island. His descriptions of battles and his knowledge of military matters in general suggest that he was, or had been at some period of his life, a serving knight, but on the other hand the skill in composition, the comparatively eloquent style of his narrative, suggest at the same time a man of some learning, though not necessarily a clerk. All this tallies so closely with what we know of Ernoul that we must conclude that X, the immediate source of the d version of the *Eracles* for the period 1184-97, was indeed none other that 'la chronique primitive d'Ernoul'.

[56] Ibid., p. 206.   [57] Ibid., p. 207.

Did that chronicle end in 1197? We must assert that it did. The variants of *d* cease precisely in that year, just after the death of Henri de Champagne, with the news of the death of Henry VI (September 1197).[58] It is plain that the source which only *d* draws on stops here. After this point, what variants *d* has it has in common with at least one other text in each case, and it never gives anything materially different that is particular to itself. As we have already observed, the whole set of relationships among the texts here changes suddenly and completely, indeed a quite different stemma must be postulated to account for them after this point. One of the main differences is that *d*, hitherto a case by itself, now begins to resemble *gG* so closely that they are virtually identical from here to the end of *d*.

The original lost chronicle of Ernoul is best preserved to us in the version of *d*, though all the other continuations of William of Tyre, and the abrégé text, drew on it indirectly, and thus provide valuable points of comparison which often permit us to say whether a given trait of *d* comes from *X*, or is added by the compiler or the scribe. Where no such comparison is possible, we must accept the version of *d*, on the general principle that it is the most faithful reproduction of proto-Ernoul. From it we can deduce that proto-Ernoul was a work superior in many ways to its successors—more varied, livelier in style, and with much valuable historical information of a kind which in contemporary opinion was alas too specialized to survive the rigours of recension. To the compiler of *d* we owe a great deal, and it should be added here that the compiler would seem to have been an inhabitant, if not, like the original author, a native of Outremer, since he alone of all the compilers of the *Eracles* shared the parochialism of Ernoul.[59] What he did not preserve of his source we can only wonder, speculating regretfully on the contents of that lost source itself, for which, however, the chance preservation of the text of *d*, in a single manuscript, must somewhat console us. This one manuscript too is of Eastern origin, its miniatures being one of the few surviving examples of the work of the atelier of Acre.[60] It is known that in the second quarter of the thirteenth century there was a

---

[58] Ibid., p. 222.   [59] Cf. above, pp. 98-107.
[60] Hugo Buchthal, *Miniature Painting in the Latin Kingdom of Jerusalem* (Oxford, 1957), p. 87 ff.

short revival of the scriptorium of the Holy Sepulchre at Jerusalem; it is not too fanciful to see the *d* manuscript of the *Eracles,* compiled just about the middle of the century, as one of the products of that revival.

So we can gather from the *d* text much of what the chronicle of Ernoul contained, which would otherwise be lost to us, and by comparing the continuations with each other we can deduce that Ernoul's work ended in the year 1197. Where did it begin? The question is at once more difficult and less interesting. It is difficult because the obvious break in redaction at 1184, common to all the continuations, is determined by the end of William's chronicle, and is not therefore necessarily any indication of the beginning of the source or sources to which they then turn. It is less interesting because whereas the section 1185-97 of Ernoul's chronicle is at least largely an eye-witness account, it is to be supposed that the material covering the period before Ernoul's lifetime (as we may approximately date it) must have been unoriginal, if it was there at all. But if we are to reconstruct in its general outlines, where we cannot trace in detail, the chronicle of Ernoul, we must look at the only chronicle related to Ernoul which does not use for the early part a straight translation of William of Tyre, that is, the abrégé. Only this text can possibly afford any clues as to what the section of Ernoul's chronicle preceding 1185 contained, and by analysing its source and structure it may prove possible to determine the early as well as the late limit of Ernoul's work.

---

[61] The texts of *A* and *z* virtually identical in this early section.

VIII

THE SOURCES AND STRUCTURE OF THE ABRÉGÉ

1. The Beginning to 1197; reconstruction of Ernoul's Chronicle

F ROM THE words 'Li quens de Triple respondi',[1] to its end, the abrégé can properly be compared, as we have seen in the preceding chapters, with the corresponding sections of the continuations, to which it is closely related in that part of its text. From its beginning up to those words, however, the abrégé stands quite apart from the continuations. Whereas they all have a translation of the *Historia* of William of Tyre, it presents instead a totally unrelated text, very much shorter, but serving broadly the same purpose of filling in the history of the crusades from their beginning up to the period with which it is chiefly concerned, that is, the 1180s and 1190s. This text, covering some nine and a half chapters in the edition of Mas-Latrie, is basically a sketchy history of the Latin Kingdom of Jerusalem, but is liberally interspersed with much semi-relevant material concerned in some way with the Holy Land. What are these first nine chapters? Do they represent the beginning of Ernoul's chronicle, cut out by the compilers of the *Eracles* because the translation of William rendered them superfluous, but preserved by the abrégé compiler? Or are they the original work of that compiler himself, who found in his source a text which actually began about the year 1184, and added these introductory chapters as a run-in? If the first alternative is the case, then *X*, the original chronicle of Ernoul, began about the point at which the abrégé and the continuations begin to run parallel, that is at the words 'Li quens de Triple respondi', in the year 1185. If on the other hand the abrégé compiler found the first nine chapters along with the central section of the narrative all in *X*, and abbreviated the whole thing, then the *Eracles* continuators must have begun where it suited them, after the end of the *Historia* translation, and the chronicle of Ernoul must have begun a good deal earlier than 1185. Thus it is by examining these early chapters of the abrégé, to see precisely what they are, who could have written them, and whether there is any perceptible break between them and the

---

[1] M-L p. 116. Cf. *RHC* ii. 6, beginning of *Eracles* xxiii, 4.

central portion in which Ernoul is named, that we may hope to establish the beginning of Ernoul's original work, as the comparison of the continuations established its end.

In considering the possibility that X began at or about the year 1185, it is apposite to mention the theory propounded by A.C. Krey,[2] that Ernoul wrote as a continuator of William. We must immediately add of course that when Krey made that statement he believed the abrégé to be the work of Ernoul himself, because it mentions his name. But although we now know that such is not the case, the possibility still remains that the real work of Ernoul, X, did begin about 1185, and was thus effectively a continuation of William. An examination of Krey's arguments is therefore a useful indication of just how convincing this 'continuation' theory about Ernoul's chronicle may be.

Krey asserts that the abrégé appears to become detailed about the year 1183, just as William's *Historia* is drawing to an end, in the version without Book xxiii which Ernoul is supposed, according to Krey, to have used.[3] Krey takes this as evidence that the writer of the abrégé intended to provide a continuation to the *Historia,* indeed he goes so far as to assert that all chroniclers of the crusades after William wrote as his successors. There is an element of truth in this, in that, as we have already seen, the *Historia* and more especially its French version, the *Eracles,* were immensely popular in their time, and were much added to and kept up to date. They were in fact the standard work on the crusades, as they are still the standard contemporary authority. But in order to assert with confidence that all succeeding authors wrote in the light of William's work, it is first necessary to show that they knew that work. In the case of Ernoul, this is by no means certain.

Krey goes to some lengths to suggest that Ernoul could have read, and did read, the *Historia.* On the first point he is convincing: he suggests that one of the copies of the *Historia* made in the scriptorium of the archiepiscopal household was circulated among William's friends, including Balian d'Ibelin. He cannot be said to have proved this, but it seems highly plausible that the Ibelin household should have had a copy of the *Historia*, and that Ernoul should thus have had access to it. But this assumes that Ernoul knew Latin, a belief which

[2] Babcock and Krey, pp. 38 ff.   [3] Babcock and Krey, p. 38.

Krey subscribes to elsewhere,[4] but which is again unproved. Two other possibilities remain: either Ernoul was acquainted with the French translation of the *Historia,* or it was translated for him, perhaps orally, by some clerk in the household. The first suggestion implies two things about the translation, however, which are now known to be untrue, namely that it was made very early, say about the turn of the century, since we know that Ernoul's chronicle finished with the events of 1197, and was presumably written not very much later; and that it was done in Outremer, either in Syria itself, or Cyprus. As for the date, Mr. Goulden's work has put it in the late years of the reign of Philippe-Auguste,[5] say about 1220 to 1223, and as for the location, Ost[6] has shown conclusively that it was done in France, and that the translator was French. The second suggestion, that the *Historia* was read aloud, perhaps translated at sight, is more credible. It is well known that reading aloud was common practice at this period, and that chronicles as well as other kinds of literature were read aloud is clear from the Preface to the *Historia Hierosolymitana* of Robert the Monk: 'Universos qui hanc historiam legerint, *sive legi audierint,* et auditam intellexerint, deprecor . . . ut concedant veniam.'[7]

That the reader ever translated at sight is not attested, but the extreme popularity of William's work suggests a larger audience than the Latin-speaking minority. Doubtless the enormous demand for stories of the crusades in the vernacular outstripped the capacity of the scribes to produce written translations like the *Eracles,* and perhaps the gap was filled by the procedure we have suggested. This is of course no more than speculation, but at all events it is possible to give Krey the benefit of the doubt and suppose that Ernoul could be, and was, by some means or other, acquainted with the work of William of Tyre.

Let us suppose for the moment that he was. The *Historia* ends abruptly in the year 1184, so Ernoul aims to begin his story at that point. But like most medieval chroniclers, he has

---

[4] Ibid., p. 40.   [5] Information orally communicated.

[6] F. Ost, *Die altfranzösische Übersetzung der Geschichte der Kreuzzüge Wilhelms von Tyrus* (Halle, 1899).

[7] Robert de Saint-Rémi, *Historia Hierosolymitana* (*PL* clv) cols. 667-756. These are the opening words of the *Praefatio Apologetica.* My italics.

an aversion to a direct entry into his subject-matter. He wants
the continuity, the impression of systematized knowledge, the
intellectual respectability, that can only be achieved by beginning a good way back. So though he does not adopt what many
contemporary writers apparently regarded as the really thoroug
approach, and begin with Adam, or at least Julius Caesar, he
does, justifiably, feel it necessary to outline the history of the
Latin Kingdom. Does he draw for this on the obvious source,
that *magnum opus* which is supposed to be his prototype?
Krey thinks he does, but is forced to admit that on some
matters these early chapters of the abrégé differ considerably
from William's account, including, says Krey, the matter of
William's own death! He explains the difference by postulating an incomplete copy of the *Historia,* not containing the
twenty-third book, which he supposes Ernoul to have used.
Ernoul is, he assures us, substantially in agreement with
William in the earlier parts. In fact this assurance rests on very
little evidence indeed. Any comparison is difficult, for what
William devotes twenty-three books to, the abrégé covers in
nine and a half short chapters, and those taken up in part with
geographical descriptions, myths and legends, and historical
events not dealt with at all by William. What remains for comparison is very little, and given moreover the vast difference
in the modes of expression of the two authors, it would not
be an easy matter to detect borrowings if they did exist.
Again, between any two accounts of the same events there
will be perforce some little similarity stemming simply from
their identical subject. Between William and the opening
chapters of the abrégé there are not many glaring disparities;
but neither is there a single feature, such as a common error,
which would suggest, let alone establish, a direct relationship
such as Krey claims to perceive.

Is it in any case true that the narrative of the abrégé does
become detailed at the year 1183? It is of course difficult to
evolve any precise method of judging detail or lack of it, but
as a rough and ready guide we can take the number of pages
in Mas-Latrie's edition which each year takes up. In general
terms we may say that up to 1180 the distribution is completely random, there being no constant perceptible trend,
save that towards the late 1170s the narrative seems generally
to move less hastily. The number of pages occupied by the
1180s is as follows:

1180:	6½	1186:	12
1181:	1	1187:	59
1182:	10½	1188:	13
1183:	7½	1189:	½
1184:	3	1190:	11½
1185:	3		

Here again, no definite trend in one constant direction is at all perceptible. The only thing which does emerge is the factor to be expected in a chronicle dealing, at least ostensibly, with the loss of Jerusalem and the Holy Cross—great, indeed disproportionate, emphasis on the fateful year 1187. As for the point where William's *Historia* ends, one could certainly not even make a guess at it from the evidence of the above table. With the loss of this mainstay the 'continuation' theory propounded by Krey can hardly remain standing.

The theory is vulnerable in other respects too: no reader, even of the most casual sort, can fail to be struck by the vast differences of style and attitude to their work that separate William and his so-called successor. In William we have a man of great natural talents, developed to their full extent by the excellent education he had received, as he tells us himself, at the feet of such men as Gilbert de la Porrée, Maurice de Sully, and one Mainerus, who had been himself the pupil of Abelard.[8] This education William supplemented with wide background reading, and in addition brought to his work a scholarly conscience, a care for truth and impartiality, a sense of the responsibility of the historian to his readers, which contribute largely to the enduring quality of his chronicle. Nor was his success unintentional. He expected his work to endure, he wrote for posterity explicitly: '. . . ut regni Hierosolymorum status omnis, tam prosper quam adversus, posteritati nostra significetur opera'.[9]

He would not be surprised to know that it would still be read eight centuries after his death. As for the author of the abrégé on the other hand, it seems that literary immortality could not have been further from his mind. The work is clearly a means to an end, namely the dissemination of information, and the author has evidently no consciousness of

[8] R.B.C. Huygens, 'Guillaume de Tyr étudiant'. *Latomus,* xxi (1962), 811-29. Cf. above, p. 9 n. 2.
[9] *RHC* i, 1132.

himself as a writer at all. This is in direct contrast to William, who mentions himself, with due archiepiscopal modesty, at all the relevant points, and frequently analyses his own conscience for us in a way which tempts us to see in him a distant harbinger of Montaigne.

Now one does not necessarily expect an author whose intention it is to continue the work of another man to imitate slavishly that man's style. But one does expect the choice of material to be careful and suitable, to avoid vivid distinction between the two parts, to make some pretence at least to similarity. In short, one expects a little attempt at pastiche. The abrégé makes none. Indeed the author does not even mention the *Historia* when speaking of William, and since it was certainly a cause of pride to its author, it is particularly strange that he does not. The author of the abrégé is an admirer of William, though how far this admiration is spontaneous and how far politic it is a little difficult to judge: the context in which he mentions William is that of the scandalous circumstances of the election of Heraclius to the patriarchate of Jerusalem in 1180, and he is at pains to make clear not only William's undeniable moral supremacy over this dissolute prelate, but also that he himself is on the side of right in the matter. His description of William is unreservedly favourable, but not so exaggerated as to be evidently insincere: 'Li archevesques de Sur ot a non Guillaumes, et fu nés en Jherusalem et ne savoit on en Crestiienté mellour clerc de lui, a son tans.'[10]

This would have been the moment to add that William was the author of the *Historia,* and if it had been the abrégé author's model and inspiration it is hard to believe that he would not have added a remark to that effect here. His silence even leads one to wonder if he did in fact know the *Historia* at all, and certainly makes clear that it was not present in his mind.

All Krey's arguments for calling Ernoul a continuator of William are based of course on the assumption that the 1229 abrégé is, as it stands, the chronicle of Ernoul. As we have seen,[11] the case for believing that the abrégé itself was written as a continuation to the *Historia* is thin in the extreme. But is there perhaps a case for thinking that not the abrégé but its source, X, was written as a continuation, beginning at 1185

[10] M-L p. 82.   [11] Cf. above, pp. 118-21.

('Li quens de Triple respondi' etc.), and was used as such by
the *Eracles* compilers, but differently adapted by the compiler
of the abrégé? If this is so, then it should be possible to distinguish a clear break in the redaction of the abrégé at the
point where the compiler is supposed to have finished his own
introduction, and begun to transcribe X, abbreviating it in the
process. In other words there should be some observable differences between the first nine and a half chapters of the abrégé,
supposedly the compiler's own work, and the rest, from 'Li
quens de Triple respondi' onwards, drawn, like the corresponding part of the *Eracles*, from the original chronicle of Ernoul, X.

In fact, at first sight, the early chapters of the abrégé do give
the impression of being rather differently constituted from the
rest of it, and from the continuations proper. Whereas the continuations, and the abrégé after 1185, are more or less straight
historical narrative, the first nine chapters of the abrégé
are very mixed in content, and, at least on first reading, make
on the reader an impression of disorganization and disunity.
To discover whether they are a separate entity by themselves,
or whether they have some links with the remainder of the
abrégé and with the continuations, it is therefore necessary to
examine more closely of exactly what these early chapters are
composed, and if possible, what the sources of the material are.

The contents of these early chapters of the abrégé fall into
four broad categories: Biblical excerpts, geographical descriptions, legendary and traditional material, and history proper.

The Biblical material varies very much in extent and detail.
Some examples are no more than passing references to Biblical
stories, often incidents associated with some place in the Holy
Land which the author is describing. But others are long and
close paraphrases of Scripture, both Old and New Testaments.
The writer knows in detail parts at least of all four Gospels
(though he makes no textual reference to any epistle)[12] and
of the Old Testament books of Genesis, Exodus, Numbers,
Joshua, Judith, and the third and fourth books of Kings.[13]
The New Testament extracts are by and large accurate renderings into French of the Vulgate, with some additions, usually

---

[12] He refers elsewhere in passing to Philippi as the place of composition (sic) of the
Epistle to the Philippians. See M-L p. 95, and *RHC* ii, 23.
[13] All Biblical references are to the Vulgate, and the Psalms and the Books of Kings
are numbered accordingly.

dialogue, by way of enlivenment. The Old Testament stories, however, are in fact drawn from two sources, the Old Testament, and the works of Flavius Josephus—the compiler draws frequently on the *Antiquities* and once on the *Jewish War*. Thus for example the story of the children of Israel crossing the Red Sea is clearly based on the account in Exodus 14, and not on that given by Josephus,[14] whereas the story of Elisha healing the waters[15] is identifiable by its preamble, not found in 4 Kings 2, as an adaptation of Book iv, chapter 8, section 3 of the *Jewish War*. A particularly interesting case is that of Abraham, in a story found in Genesis 18: 'Apparuit ei Dominus in convalle Mambre sedenti in ostio tabernaculi sui in ipso fervore diei.' (Genesis 18: 1.)

This turns up in the abrégé as 'Abraham se seoit desous un arbre qui avoit a non Mambré,' and so Mas-Latrie added the words 'en une vallée' before 'qui avoit a non', as being necessary to the sense, and making the sentence a proper translation of Genesis 18: 1.[16] In fact we have here a translation, of sorts, of Josephus again (*Antiquities* i. 11. 2): 'By the oak of Mambre, at the door of his tent',[17] and Mas-Latrie's amendment is superfluous. The compiler has got things very slightly wrong, but he certainly thinks Mambre is the name of the tree.

His most blatant departure from the text also occurs in this passage and has an obvious purpose. The text of the Vulgate at this point is grammatically curious:

(Genesis 18: 1):   Apparuit ei Dominus in convalle Mambre sedenti in ostio tabernaculi sui in ipso fervore diei.
(Genesis 18: 2):   Cumque elevasset oculos, apparuerunt ei tres viri stantes prope eum; quos cum vidisset, cucurrit in occursum eorum de ostio tabernaculi, et adoravit in terram.
(Genesis 18: 3):   Et dixit: Domine, si inveni gratiam in oculis tuis, ne transeas servum tuum.

This is an opportunity not to be missed of expounding an Old Testament type of the Trinity, and the compiler makes full use of it: 'Tout si que il vint pries de lui si l'aoura. En l'aourer qu'il fist s'en vit .iii. Un en vit et .iii. en aoura; li .iii.

[14] M-L p. 69. Josephus, *Antiquities*, Bk. ii, ch. 16.
[15] M-L pp. 78-9.   [16] Ibid., p. 71 n. 9.
[17] All quotations from Josephus are from the version *The Antiquities and The Jewish War of Flavius Josephus*, translated by William Whiston (London, 1963).

estoient en un, et li uns estoit en .iii., et tout en une personne. Il li proia qu'il herbergast aveuc lui . . .'[18]

In other instances the details given by the abrégé compiler are neither in the Old Testament nor in Josephus. Nor do they always enhance the story, indeed sometimes they seem incapable of explanation except as gratuitous elaboration. The abrégé's version of the siege of Samaria in the time of Elisha, for example, is an accurate rendering of the account in 4 Kings 6, with one detail added which is not in the original text at all.

Quod cum audisset rex, scidit vestimenta sua; et transibat per murum, viditque omnis populus cilicium quo vestitus erat ad carnem intrinsecus. Et ait rex: Haec mihi faciat Deus et haec addat, si steterit caput Elisei, filii Saphat, super ipsum hodie.	Dont fu li rois si dolans qu'il descira ses dras, *et se laissa caoir de son cheval a tiere* et manda par .i. sergant Elyseu le prophete pour ocirre, pour che que c'estoit avenu a son tans.[19]

This is *per se* unlikely. It does not in the least fit in with the rest of the story as an elaboration, indeed it rather makes nonsense of it. Nor can it be seen as a mistranslation of the original, which may be the explanation of another even more bizarre statement: 'Celle cités a a non Jericop et fu fermée de pierre d'aimant.'[20]

Can the compiler possibly have misread Joshua 6: 1: 'Jericho autem clausa erat atque munita', as 'clausa erat magne', or as 'clausa erat atque magnetica'? His translating abilities do have their limitations, as is attested by another of his assertions, that Balaam, after his donkey has told him that an angel is blocking their path, actually turns back, something that happens neither in the Old Testament nor in Josephus. Alternatively, the compiler may have added this detail gratuitously from memory, having read it in some description of a city which had an *aimant* in its construction, like this one of Narbonne:

> Aymeris fet soner .xxx. olifans,
> Bondir en fet Nerbone la plus grant,
> La mestre tor et lo dur aymant.[21]

---

[18] M-L p. 72.
[19] 4 Kings 6: 30-1. M-L p. 110, my italics.
[20] M-L p. 75.
[21] *La Mort Aymeri de Narbonne,* ed. J. Couraye du Parc (Paris, 1884), v. 3361-3.

Apart from Josephus and the Bible, there are a number of statements which belong to well-attested tradition, for example the identification of Sebaste as the burial place of John the Baptist, and of Josaphat as that of Our Lady, and many other such traditional identifications of places in Palestine as the scene of this or that event. In fact most of the Biblical material is mixed in with the topographical descriptions of Palestine. Thus the mention of Jericho precipitates the story of Joshua and also an amusing digression on the habits of certain snakes which the author asserts live in that region.[22] The location seems to be his own invention, but the information on the serpents is drawn from the *Etymologiae* of Isidore of Seville.[23] The same location for these snakes is given in Jacques de Vitry's *Liber Orientalis*,[24] but this cannot be the source for the abrégé, since, leaving aside the vexed question of dating, the abrégé gives information not contained in Jacques de Vitry. For example, he says of the asp only that it is used to make antidote (*tyriaca*), whereas the abrégé has also another piece of information given by Isidore, that it avoids capture by stopping up its ears. This last is a very common story, originating in Psalm 57: 5 and 6, and is found not only in Isidore and the abrégé, but also for example in the bestiary of Philippe de Thaon, who gets it from Isidore, and who exploits to the full its symbolic possibilities.[25] As for the abrégé compiler, it looks certain, from the texts, that he could not have got it from anywhere but Isidore, and that the location of the serpents in the neighbourhood of Jericho is his own idea, possibly indeed imitated by Jacques de Vitry, as we shall see when the date of composition of this part of the abrégé becomes clearer.

The topographical descriptions themselves have been the object of much research, culminating in the edition by Michelant and Raynaud, with the preface of Riant.[26] Riant concludes that the description of Galilee is the original work of Ernoul himself, while that of Jerusalem is an expansion of

---

[22] M-L pp. 76-7.
[23] Isidore of Seville, *Etymologiae*, Bk. xii, ch. 4, sections 2, 6, 10, 11, and 12.
[24] Jacques de Vitry, *Liber Orientalis* (Douai, 1597), pp. 186-8.
[25] Philippe de Thaün, *Le Bestiaire*, ed. Walberg (Lund, 1900) vv. 1615 ff.
[26] H. Michelant et G. Raynaud, *Itinéraires à Jérusalem rédigés en français* (Geneva, 1882), pp. 23 ff. and 31 ff.; preface, pp. xiij and xv.

an older text, part of which the *Estoires* preserves in a different
redaction. It must be borne in mind of course that when Riant
wrote this, in 1882, he believed the abrégé, as edited by Mas-
Latrie eleven years earlier, to be the chronicle of Ernoul as
such. So it would be fair to revise his statement, in the light of
the preceding chapter, and to say that the description of
Galilee, as contained in the abrégé, has no extant written
source, nor can a lost one be inferred; but that a lost written
source can be inferred in the case of the description of Jerusalem,
by comparing the version found in the abrégé with that found
in the *Estoires*. In other words, we can modify Riant's attribution
of the description of Galilee to Ernoul by saying that it is the
work of whoever wrote this part of the abrégé. It is relevant to
add here that the same person also made the Biblical extracts
and the extracts from Josephus and Isidore, for they are inex-
tricably woven into the description of Galilee, often to the
extent that the event cited from the Bible, or from Josephus,
is the only information given about the place being described.
There can be no question of a previously existing topographical
text being filled out from Scripture and tradition, for such a
text could not stand by itself, indeed it would hardly exist at
all, apart from the illustrations of which in large sections it
virtually consists.

The same is not true necessarily of the strictly historical
parts of these early chapters. Though they are very much
interwoven with the other kinds of material we have just
described, it would be possible to extricate them and make
of them an independent narrative, though this would be very
thin, and though to separate it thus from its surrounding text
would involve doing considerable violence to the abrégé as it
stands. The separation one cannot make is between this part
of the historical narrative and the section centred on Hattin
and the fall of Jerusalem, which is the setpiece of the history
and fulfils the stated intention of the author, to tell his
readers how the Holy Cross and Jerusalem were lost to the
Saracens. As a historical narrative, it is remarkably homogeneous,
for all that the amount of detail it gives varies considerably. It
consists at the beginning of mere allusions, but becomes
steadily more detailed up to the early 1180s, when it can be
said, as it runs into the central events with which it deals, to
become a chronicle proper rather than a mere outline. It appears

to be original, at least, no source can be traced for it. It is not,
as Krey asserted, a résumé of William's *Historia*. Large parts of
it are of course such brief statements of fact that they might
have come from anywhere. In its more developed sections there
are some pieces which could be drawn from William (for examp
the marriage of Amalric and Maria Comnena),[27] many which
are not found at all in William (for example the history of
Gérard de Ridefort's career),[28] and some which cover the
same ground and give an account quite different from William's
Thus for example their respective accounts of the founding of
the Order of the Temple do not resemble each other in the
least.[29] It is possible, though incapable of proof, that William's
lost work, *De Gestis Orientalium Principum,* did provide the
material for the chapters on Salahadin's early life and rise to
fame. But the *Historia* is not the source for the rest of the histo
and in default of any work identifiable as its source we must
assume that it is an original work interpolated with identifiable
borrowings from elsewhere, i.e. from Isidore, Josephus, the Bib
and the anonymous description of Jerusalem which Riant established as being taken from an earlier work and partly adapted.[30]

It is not possible to detect in this part of the abrégé any
break in matter or manner such as we have discovered in the
texts at 1197. Apart from changes in scene, e.g. from Jerusalem
to Byzantium or Cairo as the subject requires, the chronology
is consecutive, unlike that of the later parts of the abrégé or of
the continuations for that matter, where it moves backwards
and forwards in a confusing and untidy fashion, often betraying
mere lack of skill in composition, rather than a deliberate cutting technique. Allowing for the changes in subject, and the
interpolations in the narrative proper of the various other
elements already analysed, the history gives the impression of
a unified narrative. It seems to be all of a piece with the section
mentioning Ernoul by name, all moving towards those events
at which he was present, looking forward to them and preparing us to appreciate the disaster fully when it occurs. That this
is in fact the case is demonstrable, curiously enough, by comparing the abrégé once again with the continuations, for though
they do not ostensibly treat of this period, before 1184, except

[27] *RHC* i. 942; Babcock and Krey ii. 344-5; M-L p. 18.   [28] M-L p. 114.
[29] *RHC* i. 520-1; Babcock and Krey i. 524-7; M-L pp. 7-9.
[30] H. Michelant et G. Raynaud, *Itinéraires à Jérusalem*, p. xvj.

in the translation of William, some of the versions do inter-
polate into the narrative of later events three sections also
found in these opening chapters of the abrégé.

These three sections are all placed chronologically in the
abrégé, but in the continuations serve as flashbacks, and in
each case the compilers of the continuations have chosen
passages dealing with events which are necessary to a clear
understanding of the later parts of the history, and which are
dealt with inadequately, or not at all, by William of Tyre. Thus
the history of the 'mariage dou Botron', the abortive attempt
made by Gérard de Ridefort to obtain the hand of the heiress
of Botron, is inserted by *a-b* and by *d* before Hattin as a direct
explanation of the ill feeling existing between Gérard de
Ridefort and Raymond of Tripoli.[31] Precisely the same reason
for telling this story—that it was a contributory factor to the
loss of the Kingdom—is given by the abrégé compiler also.[32]
Similarly the election of Heraclius as Patriarch of Jerusalem,
his scandalous life, and the description of Pasque de Riveti,
la patriarchesse, are also transposed, in *a-b* and *d*, and this
time in *gG* also,[33] to a point part way through the Hattin
manoeuvres, breaking the action off most unsuitably, but
serving the same purpose of providing a very necessary explanation of why the Christians lost: 'Dont toz li clergés en
prenoit mauvais eissample a la vie dou mauvais cheveteine;
por les pechez des quels Nostre Seignor se corroça moult
durement a ceauz qui habitoient en Jerusalem et ou roiaume
de Surie et netoia sa terre de ceauz qui le peché ovroient.'[34]

The third piece of material interpolated in this way is a
section of Byzantine history, which William had not sufficiently covered, and which is appropriately put in apropos of
Conrad of Montferrat's defence of Tyre. Again it is necessary
to give the reader this background if he is to understand
properly the current state of Byzantine politics at the time of
Conrad's enforced sojourn in Constantinople, his escape, and
the fact that he therefore arrived in Palestine too late, when
the Kingdom was almost entirely in the hands of Salahadin,
and Guy of Lusignan a prisoner of the Saracens. For part
of this section *gG* gives the same narrative as is found, at an

---

[31] *RHC* ii. 50-2.   [32] M-L p. 87.
[33] *RHC* ii. 59-61 main text, 60-1 *g* variant.
[34] *RHC* ii. 61.

earlier point, in the abrégé, while the other continuations give a fuller, but in no way contradictory version throughout.[35]

These excerpts leave us in no doubt at all about the presence in X of at least some of the pre-1184 historical narrative found in the abrégé. The continuators have not drawn these sections directly from the abrégé and interpolated them into the narrative of their common source, for they have nearly always a fuller version than the abrégé itself has. Textually, one can only explain these sections in the abrégé and the continuations as different adaptations of a common source, in which each text displays its own characteristic treatment of the source: the abrégé abbreviates, d preserves, in the account of Conrad arriving off Acre,[36] the explanation of the bell he expected to hear, and so on. In short, these three sections at least must have been in X, and it is reasonable to infer that at least some of the rest of the historical material contained in the opening chapters of the abrégé was also drawn from X by the abrégé compiler. Indeed, since as we have already observed, the narrative forms a remarkably homogeneous whole in this section, and leads straight into the section in which Ernoul is named without any discernible break or change in redaction, it is reasonable to assert that not only these three excerpts, but the whole historical narrative to which they belong comes from the chronicle of Ernoul.

What of the other material in the first nine chapters, that is the geographical descriptions, the Biblical extracts, and the adaptations from Josephus and Isidore? Since they can conceivably be separated from the historical narrative proper, it cannot necessarily be assumed that they too come from X; the abrégé compiler could well have interpolated them into the history, perhaps in the intention of producing a more varied narrative, with a wider appeal. The very fact that he has cut down on his source to an extent which often lessens the historical interest of his work considerably is evidence enough that the purely informational value of his work did not for him take primacy over its appeal to a more general public than that interested purely in the recent history of the crusades. While the history proper belongs to Ernoul, the rest might belong to the compiler of the abrégé.

---

[35] Ibid., pp. 16-25. Cf. M-L pp. 95-6 and 128-9.   [36] Cf. above, p. 101.

Were that the case, however, one would expect to find that the narrative of the continuations proper was purely historical, and this is not the case. The non-historical material in the first nine chapters of the abrégé is of course found only in that text, but all the Biblical stories which come in the abrégé after 'Li quens de Triple respondi', that is, the pool of Siloam, Elijah's fast, Solomon's building of high places, and the story of Balaam, are found in the continuations proper as well.[37] Indeed the continuations also contain one more story of the same kind, that of Gideon laying the fleece.[38] Again, as in the case of the pre-1184 historical episodes found in both the abrégé and the continuations, there is no question of the *Eracles* compilers borrowing these stories direct from the abrégé, because the Eracles has once again, in the versions of *a-b* and *d,* more accurate and usually fuller reproductions of the Old Testament, or Josephus as the case may be, than has the abrégé. Again the only possible explanation is of two independent adaptations of a common source. Again we are forced to conclude that the extracts from Josephus and the Bible which are found in both the continuations and the abrégé were contained in *X*. Again we can infer that the other material of the same kind contained in the first nine chapters of the abrégé was drawn by the abrégé compiler from that part of *X* from which the *Eracles* compilers took only the three historical extracts mentioned above.[39] And since we have already identified *X* as the original chronicle of Ernoul, we must now consider how Ernoul came to know the Bible in such detail, and also the works of Josephus and Isidore.

He may not necessarily have known Latin: vernacular translations of fragments of both Isidore and Josephus are frequently found in compilations of this period—for example the work of Jacques de Vitry and Philippe de Thaon mentioned above. But since there is no positive evidence in the form of such a text containing precisely the extracts that Ernoul uses, this possibility must remain a speculation, and we must assume, until the contrary can be proved, that the most obvious explanation is true, and that his borrowings from Josephus and Isidore come from a Latin original.

---

[37] M-L pp. 123, 126, and 127. Cf. *RHC* ii. 11, 14, and 15.
[38] *RHC* ii. 14-15.   [39] Above, pp. 128-129.

For the Bible extracts, at least the Old Testament ones, more definite clues are available. All the Old Testament books Ernoul uses are also contained in the vernacular translation known as the Acre Bible.[40] The oldest manuscript of this text, Arsenal 5211, was made for St. Louis and can be assigned to the early 1250s, but it is of course perfectly possible that older copies of the same text, or at least of parts of it, were in circulation well before that date; and Acre is geographically very much within Ernoul's orbit. Since we have a vernacular text which provides all the right parts of the Old Testament, in the right place at about the right time, it would be perverse to suppose that Ernoul necessarily used the Vulgate. But this still leaves the New Testament extracts to be accounted for, and here we are again reduced to speculation. They could all come from a Life of Christ, and these are commonly found in early vernacular translations of the Bible; but in this case there is no positive evidence, as there is in the case of the Acre Bible, of the availability of such a text. We can consider it quite possible, even probable, that there was one available, but we cannot rule out the contrary possibility, that Ernoul drew directly on the Vulgate. Since it appears thus that there is at least a good chance that Ernoul did know Latin, we must add this trait to our mental image of him. He could of course have had an amanuensis who translated for him the appropriate texts, but it is equally possible that he did it himself.

Each element of the opening nine chapters of the abrégé, then, is clearly seen not to be particular to those chapters, but is found also in the rest of the text, and in the *Eracles* compilations as well. There is no perceptible break in the text of the abrégé between the early and later parts. In the sections of the early part which we can compare with the *Eracles,* because the *Eracles* compilers have transposed sections belonging to the early part of their common source *X,* we can observe that the abrégé compiler has consistently cut down on his source, and has sometimes cut out pieces (e.g. the story of Gideon), but has never added anything material, as far as we can see. We must conclude that the pre-1184 section of *X* is represented

---

[40] I am grateful to Mr. C.R. Sneddon of St. Edmund Hall, Oxford, for suggesting the Acre Bible as a possibility.

in little, and with omissions but no additions, by the first nine and a half chapters of the abrégé as edited by Mas-Latrie; that it began, like the abrégé, with a rapid résumé of the history of the Latin Kingdom from its foundation to the late twelfth century; and that it contained, as well as history proper, the same mélange of relevant and semi-relevant material as the beginning of the abrégé. In other words, we find in the first nine chapters of the abrégé a reduced-scale reproduction of the early part of the chronicle of Ernoul. The contents of these chapters are the work, if not of a scholar, at least of a well-read man. This is the Ernoul whom Philippe de Novare describes: '. . . messire Harneis et messire Guillaume de Rivet le joune, qui moult estoient grans plaideors',[41] and whom Mas-Latrie envisaged as '. . . aussi apte, comme la plupart des chevaliers des Assises, à dicter un livre qu'à soutenir une discussion féodale'.[42]

The identification of the sources Ernoul used has proved Mas-Latrie a true prophet once again, for it has shown the book Ernoul composed to be a work more learned, more elegant, more a coherent whole, than Mas-Latrie, on the evidence available to him at the time, could possibly have known. Thinking of that disastrous occasion in 1232 when Ernoul, left in charge of Cyprus, demonstrated his military ineptitude by failing to provision the castle of Dieu d'Amour, and nearly causing his own death and that of the king's sisters who were in his care, we may well conclude that he was in fact much more talented with the pen than with the sword.[43] Certainly among the authors of his day he stands out as particularly skilful.

So the chronicle of Ernoul, one element among many, emerges from among the assorted raw materials of the various French chronicles of the William of Tyre corpus. By putting together the pieces culled from each we can finally reconstitute Ernoul's work, a work unexpectedly scholarly in its sources, but in its composition pleasantly free from the trammels of scholarly convention. We can summarize its structure briefly thus:

---

[41] *Le Livre de Philippe de Navarre,* ch. 49. *RHC Lois* i, 525.
[42] M-L p. 500.   [43] *Eracles* xxxiii, 33. *RHC* ii. 399.

The beginning to 1185: The first eight chapters, and the first part of chapter nine, of the abrégé as it stands in the edition of Mas-Latrie, as far as the words 'li enfes fust d'eage' (M-L p. 116). But MS Saint-Omer 722 (ff. 4b-26b), unknown to Mas-Latrie, should be used in preference to his base MS, Brussels 11142. Also the three extracts made from *X* by the *Eracles* compilers, which are fuller versions than the corresponding sections of the abrégé, should be taken from MS Lyon 828 (*d*). These sections form in the Académie edition chapters 11-16, 34, 38, and 39 of Book xxiii.

1185-1197: From the words 'Li quens de Triple respondi', to the end of Book xxvii chapter 5 of the Académie edition, from MS Lyon 828, ff. 287b-343. The description of Jerusalem found in Saint-Omer 722 immediately before the account of the siege of Jerusalem (ff. 39b ff.) should be added at the same point. The sections already taken from MS *d* and replaced in their proper chronological order, sc. xxiii. 11-16, 34, 38, and 39, should of course be omitted.

Probably one ought also to include in this reconstruction at the appropriate places those sections in the *Estoires d'Oultremer* concerning Salahadin's wars against the King of Nubia.[44] What evidence there is about the text which alone includes them does suggest that they probably were contained in *X*. But there is much less evidence about them than about the rest of the text of the reconstruction, and so they should certainly not be included without reservations, at least until more is known about the *Estoires d'Oultremer* in the two extant manuscripts.

What we have thus arrived at does not pretend to be verbatim the chronicle which Ernoul 'fist metre en escrit'. Even *d*, the nearest text to the original chronicle of Ernoul, is still a compilation, a reproduction of Ernoul and not Ernoul himself. Where its faithfulness to the original is greater and where less we cannot say; what we can say is that it is the best reproduction available. Similarly, the abrégé, in the sections which can be compared to the continuations, has obviously abridged its source, *X*, considerably, and we may safely infer that the early chapters, peculiar to the abrégé, are equally a précis, rather than a copy, of the corresponding chapters of *X*, so that they provide us with a shadow, and not a picture, of that section of *X*. But once again, they are the best reproduction, indeed the only one, that we have at present, and we can at least know that though they are not an exact likeness, neither are they a gro distortion. This reconstruction of Ernoul has its limitations in

---

[44] Cf. account of extant texts, especially pp. 14-16.

short, but it is the best we shall ever have, unless and until new
manuscripts are discovered, offering not merely variant readings
of the texts now extant, but radical differences in composition.
Even with these few reservations, the text thus reconstituted
does at last make sense of the great variety of the continuations
of William of Tyre in this first period, which before were seen
as related in a confused and undefined manner, and which now
can be seen as deriving directly or indirectly from this prototype Ernoul.

What is more, we have at last in this reconstruction a text
which fulfils the task the author sets himself in the opening
sentence of the abrégé. It has become something of a common-
place in Ernoul studies to observe that the opening words of
the abrégé are anything but an accurate statement of what the
book contains:[45] 'Or entendés conment le terre de Iherusalem
et le sainte crois fu conquise des Sarrasins sor Chrestiiens.' (MS
z, f. 4b.)

Admittedly the year 1187 does occupy very much more
space than any other single year,[46] but it is still very misleading to announce these events as the subject of the abrégé, for
even in the shortest version of the work, that ending in 1227,
the account of them still forms only one section among many.
In fact the abrégé compiler, far from having any good reason
to fabricate this inappropriate opening specially for his own
composition, has slipped up in including it. It is without doubt
lifted ready-made from his source, a work to which it really
was appropriate, which did deal only with the period immediately relevant to the loss of Jerusalem and the Holy Cross,
which began with the Latin Kingdom apparently securely
established, and ended with it in ruins. From this work comes
the orientation of the opening chapters of the abrégé towards
the loss of the Holy Land, the description of Gérard de
Ridefort included, 'por che . . . que ce fu .i. de ciaus par coi
la tiere fu perdue', the mention, by d, of the political song
against the Polains as an illustration of the division of the
Kingdom against itself—'Cest haine et cest despit firent perdre
le roiaume de Jerusalem.' If we postulate the above reconstruction

---

[45] M-L p. 495: 'Contrairement aux termes de son début . . .'
[46] Cf. above, p. 121.

of *X*, the chronicle of Ernoul, all these features of the abrégé and the *Eracles* make sense, and the description of the contents has a text to refer to.

Reading through the text we have now attributed to Ernoul, the emphasis on the Ibelin family comes out even more clearly than before, indeed the chronicle begins to look like an apologia for their conduct in the period in question. It may even have been written as such, at the request of the Ibelins, to defend them against the general ill feeling and the specific accusations frequently directed against them, which related more often than not to the time, precisely, when Jerusalem and the Holy Cross were lost. There was first their opposition to Guy—some who agreed with Ernoul that the Kingdom fell because it was divided against itself disagreed, however, in laying the blame on one faction rather than the other. There was too the fact that at Hattin, while Guy and many of the barons were taken prisoner, Balian d'Ibelin and Raymond of Tripoli had escaped— by chance or by design? Then Balian himself had conducted the negotiations with Salahadin for the surrender of Jerusalem: why had he not rather held out against the Saracens to the bitter end? It was Balian too who drew up the terms of the 1192 treaty between Salahadin and Richard Lionheart, a treaty which no one could call favourable to the Christians, but which included among its terms the personal gift from Salahadin to Balian of the castle of Caymon. In short, while the Latin Kingdom was falling about their ears, the Ibelins had main- tained for themselves a relatively secure position, and those who had come out less well were more than ready to point out the most obvious reasons for the difference. There might be other more laudable reasons, but they were far less self-evident, and needed to be pointed out clearly. What had really happened in 1187? That is precisely what Ernoul sets out to tell us: 'conment le terre de Jherusalem et le sainte crois fu conquise des Sarrasins sor Crestiiens'. This is the story from the Ibelin point of view, answering by implication all the criticisms of those who saw the Ibelins as the villains and not the heroes. It does for the Ibelins what Villehardouin did for the leaders of the Fourth Crusade.

Lastly, this chronicle of Ernoul must be recognized as one of the few, very few, literary works produced in Frankish Outremer. As Runciman points out, Outremer did not on the whole make a very large contribution to the culture of the West. Among the exceptions are the chronicles of William of Tyre and Ernoul.[47] Now that Ernoul's work can be recognized as something much superior to the abrégé with which he has until now been credited, we may perhaps take a very slightly more optimistic view of the size of his contribution. It is a sort of by-product of that abiding and universal interest in legal affairs which characterized the knight in the crusader states, and led to the accumulation of the enormous body of writings on the *loi coutumière* collectively known as the *Assises de Jerusalem*. If Ernoul's career as a soldier gave him the material for his chronicle, it was his experience in the law courts which doubtless gave him the means of expressing it. So the particular culture of Outremer, with its insistence on the linking of these two, gave him a unique background which he could not have found elsewhere. His chronicle is the product of that culture, giving us at once greater insight into its nature, and a greater appreciation of its own peculiar merits, of which indeed little trace otherwise remains.

2. *The Abrégé and the Continuations, 1197-1231*

The early chapters of the abrégé do, then, give us a version of sorts of the beginning of Ernoul's chronicle. It now remains, in analysing the abrégé, to clarify the structure, and if possible the sources, of the remainder of the abrégé, from 1198 to its end, and here we can once again profitably take the abrégé and continuations together. Indeed, as we shall see, some versions of the continuations correspond so closely to the abrégé in this section 1198-1231 that they and it must be regarded as a single text.

But the abrégé, and the continuations, are by no means a unified whole over all this period. In fact there is another break in redaction, another shift in the relationships of the texts to each other, just as discernible as that which we have established at 1197, and it divides the 1198-1231 period sharply in two. Unlike the 1197 break, however, it does not simply occur in the course of an apparently unified and chronological narrative; rather in this case the two sections of text overlap chronologically. In other words, the break in

---

[47] See Runciman, Vol. iii, Appendix 2: 'Intellectual Life in Outremer'.

redaction at 1197 can only be observed by comparing the structure of the various texts one with another, but the second break is evident in any single text because the chronology, from being consecutive, suddenly takes a leap backwards and starts again. Thus we have, immediately after the section based on Ernoul and ending in 1197 which we have just analysed, a narrative which, though it mentions events in Constantinople as late as 1228, basically covers the period 1198-1216, ending with the death of Otto IV and the election of Frederick II as Emperor. Then the narrative starts again at 1205, and continues once more chronologically to 1231. The relationships between the texts in these two sections differ totally. We shall consider each separately in turn.

The first section of narrative, that following immediately after the end of Ernoul and extending in the *Recueil* from xxvii. 6 to xxx. 10,[48] is relatively simple in structure. All the texts cover the same events: the Kingdom of Jerusalem under Amalric, contemporary events in the Byzantine and Roman Empires up to 1228 and 1216 respectively, the last battles of Richard Lionheart, and the Fourth Crusade. The only exception to this general agreement between the texts occurs at the beginning of the section, when *cJ*, *gG*, and *d* insert a certain amount of material on Armenia[49] which has already been given by *a-b*, in a slightly different and shorter form, at xxvi. 25-7 inclusive. Nearly all the events narrated in these passages have already been related by d[50] in a much fuller form, of which this second version is fairly evidently a précis. In other words, this material was indeed contained in X, and is preserved by d in what we may assume to have been its original place in the pre-1197 section of his chronicle, but it was apparently abbreviated by Xi from where it passes with the rest into *a-b*, and also, though at a different point, into y, and thence into *cJ* and *gG*[51] The interesting thing is of course that it also somehow finds its way into d, a text which for the period ending 1197 is not dependent on Xi. The reason for this is obvious: after 1197, when X ceases, d takes up a new source, and that source is y, which *cJ* and *gG* have been drawing on all along. Following this source with his usual lack of ability to compile a really

---

[48] *RHC* ii. 224-304.   [49] Ibid., pp. 228-31, *c, g,* and *d* variants.
[50] Ibid., pp. 207 ff., *d* variant.   [51] See stemma, p. 96.

consistent text, *d* blindly copies these sections on Armenia, oblivious of the fact that they are nothing more than an inferior version of an earlier part of his text.

Apart from this variant, there are only two other short passages where any divergence occurs between the various texts. The first covers the taking of Gibelet and Beyrouth and the assassination attempt on Amalric.[52] Here *cJ, gG, d,* and the abrégé give basically the same account as *a-b*, but much abbreviated, and with the order of events reversed. The second passage, the account of an attempt by Tancred's son-in-law Gautier de Brienne to reconquer Apulia,[53] is a straightforward case of drastic abbreviation, by *cJ, gG, d,* and the abrégé, of the text given by *a-b*. For the remainder of the 1198-1216 section all the texts give the same account, covering the Fourth Crusade, events in the Byzantine Empire up to 1228, rather sketchily described, and a more thorough account of the Holy Roman Empire from 1208 to 1216. Here, after the death of Otto IV and the election of Frederick II, a natural break presents itself: 'Ci endreit dist li contes que il vos laira a parler dou roi Fedric d'Alemaigne . . . si dirons de la terre de Jerusalem.'[54]

The chronology of all the narratives, which up to here has been reasonably consecutive, breaking off only for breaks in the subject-matter, now jumps from 1216 right back to 1205, where the narrative starts afresh with the death of Amalric.

Of the first section, which ends at this abrupt shift in chronology, subject-matter, and relationship of the texts to each other, there is not much more to be said. As has become clear in the description of the contents of this section, the texts all have one common source, with two intermediaries, *a-b* deriving from one, and all the other texts, *cJ, gG, d,* and the abrégé, from the other. Nor indeed are the two intermediaries very widely different one from the other; no material is found in either that is not also found somewhere in the texts dependent on the other. Rather they differ only in that the intermediary source of *cJ, gG, d,* and the abrégé includes material dealt with earlier in *a-b* and abbreviates two passages of which *a-b* has a

[52] Ibid., pp. 224-7 main text and variants.
[53] Ibid., pp. 234-8, main text and variants.
[54] Ibid., p. 304. Beginning of *Eracles* xxx. 11.

fuller form.[55] Thus the stemma for this section of the continuations does not greatly differ from that already given[56] for the
section ending 1197. The two differences are that X, the original
chronicle of Ernoul ending in 1197, no longer appears at all,
and d, which up to 1197 had been directly dependent on X,
is now seen to be dependent on y, and thus closely related to
cJ, gG, and the abrégé. The relationships of the texts to each
other for the section 1198-1216/1228, covering the *Eracles*
xxvii. 6 to xxx. 10 inclusive, may therefore be represented thus:

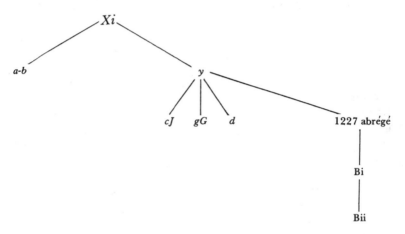

For the remaining portion of the continuations which comes
within the subject of this study, that is the narrative beginning
in 1205 (*Eracles* xxx. 11) and ending in 1231, no such simple
explanation can be found. The text presents interesting features
both from a historical and a textual point of view, and demands
a much closer examination than does the 1198-1216 section.
Only one thing can be said of the 1205-1229/31 narrative at
the outset, and that is that there are basically two versions in
this section, one in *a-b*, the other in all the other texts (*cJ*, *gG*,
d, and the abrégé) which all agree very closely throughout,
and which indeed can properly be regarded as containing a
single text from 1205 to 1227, where the shortest version of
the abrégé ends. The most convenient way to analyse this part

of the continuations therefore is to look at the relationship of
the *a-b* version to that of the other texts.

Four main topics are treated in *a-b*: Jean de Brienne and
Frederick II, both separately and in their dealings with each
other; Frederick's war against Cyprus; relations between
Armenia and the principality of Antioch; and the siege of
Damietta. For each of these the relationship of *a-b* to the
other version is different. The Imperialist-Cypriot war is completely omitted by *cJ, gG, d*, etc., as is the short section on
Armenia, which in any case gives every appearance in *a-b* of
being an interpolation into the main body of the text. The
two versions differ totally in their accounts of the siege of
Damietta—the only resemblance between them is in the basic
facts, and even that is often far from obvious. For the narrative
concerning Jean de Brienne and Frederick, however, the situation is much more complex. The two narratives are not at
first sight similar, but closer inspection shows that their material, though not their manner of expounding it, is very similar indeed. The following passage is a typical example:

Abrégé (*cJ, gG*, and *d* similarly)

Ne demoura gaires puisque li rois
Jehans fu en France que li rois
Phelipes morut. Si laissa grant avoir al
roi Jehan, et grant avoir a envoier en
le tiere d'Outremer. Li rois Jehans fu
a Sainte Denise a l'enfouir le roi
Phelipe. Apries si fu au coroner le roi
Loey sen fil a Rains. Puis prist congié
en France, si s'en ala a Saint Jakme.
Al revenir k'il faisoit de Saint Jakme
fu li rois d'Espagne a l'encontre a
Burs, qui grant honor li avoit faite en
se tiere et fist encore. La li dona li
rois a feme une sereur qu'il avoit, si
l'espousa et grant avoir li donna.

Quant li rois Jehans ot epousee se
feme si prist congié si s'en ala en
France. Quant il ot esté une piece en
France si prist congié al roi Loey et
as barons si dist qu'il l'en estovoit
raler, que li emperere l'atendoit en
Puille por passer mer et por se fille
espouser. Il s'en ala, et erra tant qu'il
vint en Puille a l'empereur.[57]

a-b

Li rois Johans se parti de France et s'en
ala en Espaigne en pelerinage a mon
seignor Saint Jaque. Et quant il ot fait
son pelerinage, si ala voir le roi de Castele,
qui moult li fist grant onor, et li dona de
beauz dons, et en la fin se acorderent a
ce que li rois Johans esposa une suer dou
roi de Castele et s'en revint o tout lui en
France. Quant il fu venus ne tarsa gaires
que li rois Phelipes acocha au lit de mort,
si que il fist sa devise et laissa a la Sainte
Terre C.L. mile mars d'argent, les L mile
en la main dou roi Johan, et les L mile
en la main dou Temple, et les L mile en
la main de l'Ospital; et moult de autres
aumosnes fist en sa devise beles et granz.
Ensi trespassa li bons rois Phelipes qui
longuement et honoreement avoit vescu.
Ne tarsa guerres apres que ses fiz Loys
fu coronez a Rains hautement et a grant
honor.

Et quant li rois Johans sot que li
termes aprochoit dou mariage de sa fille
et del empereor, si s'en vint en Puille.[58]

[57] M-L pp. 450-1. Cf. also *RHC* ii. 366-7, *c* variant, and 367, *g* and *d* variant.
[58] *RHC* ii. 356-7.

Here we have basically the same events related in each case: the death of Philip Augustus and the coronation of his son Louis VIII, Jean de Brienne's travels in France and Spain around the time of these events, and his marriage to Berengaria of Castille. The order of events, however, is completely different, and the selection also differs slightly. For example, the abrégé, and the continuations agreeing with it at this point, do not mention the terms of Philip Augustus's will, but do on the other hand describe briefly (just before the extract quoted) Jean's visit to the English court, which is omitted by *a-b*. But there is no great disagreement on matters of fact between the two versions. In this too the passage quoted is typical in that the two versions disagree only on whether Jean de Brienne visited Spain before or after the death of Philip Augustus, and whether he went to Burgos to see the King of Castille, or whether the King came specially to meet him. Neither point is vital to the thread of the narrative or to the chronicler's interpretation of events. Indeed the biggest contradiction between the versions in their entire treatment of the topic of Jean de Brienne and Frederick is the motive they attribute to Frederick for not sailing from Brindisi with his fleet: the one asserts that he was ill, the other sees it as a piece of trickery. This kind of difference has a familiar ring. It is another instance of idle uninformed speculation after the events, and belongs with the motives attributed to Henri de Champagne's dwarf for falling, or as the case may be throwing himself, out of the barred, or unbarred, window.[59] Such minor differences in no way argue against an ultimate common source for the two accounts, but only indicate a common intermediary for those texts which agree precisely with each other, i.e. *cJ, gG, d,* and the abrégé. In fact the combination of agreement and difference found between their version and that of *a-b* is exactly the same as that already observed in the variants of the 1198-1216 section, concerning the taking of Beyrouth and Gibelet and the attempted assassination of Amalric.[60] The stemma[61] which explains the relationship of the two versions in that section also holds good for their accounts of Jean de Brienne and Frederick in this last section of the first period of the

---

[59] Cf. above, pp. 86-88.   [60] p. 139 above.   [61] p. 140.

continuations, though it does not apply (and this must be emphasized) to the treatment of the other three topics dealt with in this last section, namely the Imperialist war with Cyprus, Armenia's dealings with Antioch, and the siege of Damietta. For these parts of the 1205-27 section, as we have already observed,[62] the two versions give no evidence of being related to each other at all.

There remains one last problem concerning the 1205-27 section of the continuations, and that a difficult one. It concerns the very end of this section of the texts, which, as may be gathered simply from the difficulty in deciding on an end date for the section (1227? 1229? 1231?), differs in the various texts. A fairly detailed description of the contents of the various texts in this section and the breaks in redaction which are discernible in them is necessary if their significance is to become evident.[63]

To resume briefly the situation: the texts of *cJ, gG,* and *d* have been in exact agreement, have indeed virtually presented a single text, ever since the death of Amalric, A.D. 1205, beginning at xxx. 11 in the *Recueil*.[64] This same text is also given by the abrégé, beginning at chapter 35 of Mas-Latrie's edition.[65] The agreement between *cJ, gG, d,* and the abrégé continues right up to the end of the longest version of the abrégé, that is Bii, the full text as published by Mas-Latrie, the last events dealt with being the pact of San Germano and the absolution of Frederick II (9 July and 28 August 1230), and in the last chapter of Bernard, and the corresponding passages in the continuations, the proposals made to Jean de Brienne by the distressed citizens of Constantinople, his hesitation in accepting their invitation, and finally his journey there, the marriage of his daughter to the infant Emperor Baldwin II (September 1231), and the promise of personal supremacy for Jean himself for his lifetime. In the *Recueil*[66] this ends the long variant of *cJ, gG,* and *d.* In fact the version of *cJ,* like the abrégé, stops here. But *gG* and *d* go on to take up the same text as

---

[62] p. 141.
[63] The section in question covers the end of ch. 40 and the whole of ch. 41 of the abrégé (M-L pp. 467-72), the corresponding parts of *cJ, gG,* and *d (RHC* ii. 376-9 variants) and in the *a-b* text the end of xxxiii, 12 and all the following three chapters 13, 14, and 15 (*RHC* ii, 379-82, main text.)
[64] *RHC* ii, 304.   [65] M-L p. 406.   [66] Ibid., p. 379, variants.

a-b, at xxxiii. 13, although this involves them in repeating, in xxxiii. 14 and 15, much of the information they have just given about Jean de Brienne's new political career in the Byzantine Empire. In other words, there is clear duplication of a sort which indicates beyond doubt a change in source by the compilers of *gG* and *d*.

Further evidence of a clear break in the texts between xxxiii. 12 and xxxiii. 13 is provided by a family of manuscripts which in general lie outside our consideration, but can clarify at this point the structure of the texts with which we are concerned. It is the family containing the continuation known as the Rothel a text which we have already described briefly,[67] which is totally different from all the other continuations, and, except for the geographical descriptions it contains, quite unrelated to them. The point is that it begins, in the manuscripts which contain it, at precisely this point, after the end of xxxiii. 12. So there is one continuation, shared by the Rothelin family and *a-b,* which ends at xxxiii. 12, after which the Rothelin text begins the continuation peculiar to itself which distinguishes it from all the other texts, while *b* and *gG* and *d* all take up, at xxxiii. 13, a new continuation. In *b* this follows on well enough from the preceding text, indeed it might have been written for the purpose or at least very thoroughly adapted by the compiler; but in *gG* and *d* it follows very badly.

Now when we come to look at the section of *a-b* ending at xxxiii. 12,[68] we see immediately that the very end of it resembles the treatment of the same events by *cJ, gG, d,* and the abrégé in the same vague yet undeniable way as the rest of their accounts of Frederick and Jean de Brienne, that it is in fact one of the parts of *a-b* which has been drawn from the common source with the other continuations and the abrégé, and not one of the totally unrelated sections. The relationship between the texts for their accounts of Jean and Frederick is, as we have already seen,[69] the same as that between the texts for the period 1198-1216/28, and can be represented by the same stemma, though it is necessary to use different letters for the unidentified common source and for the postulated intermediary text in order to avoid the impression that the

---

[67] Cf. above, p. 20.   [68] *RHC* ii. 378.
[69] See above, p. 142, and stemma p. 140.

same documents were necessarily involved in each case. So, for the topic in question, and for no other, in the section 1205-1227/ 29/31 of the continuations, we may represent the derivation of the material they have in common thus

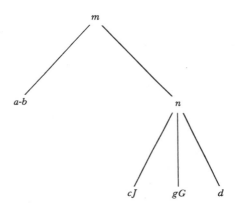

We must now consider another fact about the content of xxxiii. 12, in the *a-b* text, namely the point at which it ends, since we have already established that this was the end of a source text, the source which *a-b* has in common with the Rothelin family. The chapter ends thus: 'Dont il avint puis que des princes d'Alemaigne, li patriarches d'Aquilée, et li arcevesques de Sauseborc, et le duc d'Osteriche, et le duc de Merain, et moult d'autres hauz homes vindrent a Rome et firent la pais, par quoi li empereres fu asot. Et y ot plusors covenances en cele pais.'[70]

Strikingly enough, it is precisely at this point that Pipino tells us his manuscript of Bernard ended, indeed his last words before the note on Bernard express, though as is his habit, more concisely, exactly the same information: 'Interim Dux Austriae inter Papam et Imperatorem pacem composuit, et sic tunc imminens cessavit quassatio. Haec de gestis Regis Johannis sumta sunt ex Historia Bernardi Thesaurarii. Qualis autem fuerit exitus non inveni, vel quod Historiam non compleverit, vel quod codex, unde sumsi, fuit imperfectus.'[71]

---

[70] *RHC* ii. 379.   [71] *RIS* vii, col. 846.

As we have already established, Pipino's manuscript was not *imperfectus,* rather it was a copy of the first recension Bernard made of his chronicle, the lost text we have called Bi. So the picture that begins to emerge is this. The text given by *cJ, gG,* and *d* for the period 1205-31 is exactly that of the longest version of the abrégé, Bii, the text published by Mas-Latrie. To this text, in so far as it concerns Jean de Brienne and Frederick II, the text of *a-b* bears a resemblance which, though its existence cannot be denied, is an elusive and variable one, now close, now faint, and suggesting a distant relationship between the two texts, such as is represented by the stemma on p. 145. When the two continuations treat of any other subject—for example the Imperialist war against Cyprus, or the siege of Damietta—they appear to be completely independent and unrelated, and this remains true even when there are rapid switches from one subject to another. So we must conclude that their common source, *m* in the stemma, was a document concerned exclusively with the dealings between Jean and Frederick, and that it ended, as we can infer from the change of redaction in *a-b* and the Rothelin texts, and from the overlap in *gG* and *d*, at August 1230, the point at which Pipino tells us Bi also ended. But *n*, the intermediary text on which *cJ, gG,* and *d* drew for the same topic, continues without visible break through to September 1231.

The answer to the riddle is now obvious. In describing *m* and *n* we have in fact described accurately the accounts of Jean de Brienne and Frederick to be found in Bi, as we know it from Pipino, and in Bii as at present extant. Is it then true that *m* is Bi, and *n* is Bii? That is to oversimplify, for while there is no objection to identifying Bii as such with *n*, indeed all the evidence is in favour of doing so, Bi only resembles *m* for the material on this one topic, and for nothing else. So it appears that *m* was rather the source on which Bernard drew, in compiling Bi, for the information on Jean and Frederick, and which was also drawn on, for the same purpose, by the compilers of *a-b* and of the texts which after xxxiii. 13 diverge into the Rothelin continuation. This answer explains all the observable facts: the vague nature of the resemblance between the two versions; the manner in which agreement on this topic is mingled with total independence on all other topics; the change of redaction at xxxiii. 13 in *a-b* and the

Rothelin continuation, and the absence of such change at this point, together with the subsequent repetition of information, in gG and d. The intermediary n was Bii. The common source of all the continuations, m, was a document dealing with a single topic only, and ending in August 1230, which the various compilers, including Bernard, mixed with material on other topics, perhaps from other sources, or perhaps written by themselves, to produce in the one case the continuation we now have for the period 1205-27 in the version of a-b and the Rothelin manuscripts, and in the other the lost text Bi, known to Pipino. This latter was subsequently extended by Bernard to 1231, forming the text we know as his chronicle, Bii, and it was on this that the compilers of the *Eracles* versions found in cJ, gG, and d drew for the entire period 1205-31.

So for the history of Jean de Brienne and Frederick II, up to Frederick's absolution in August 1230, we can represent the derivation of information from one text to the other thus:

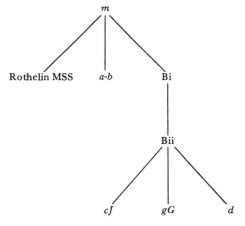

This knowledge clarifies still further for us both the structure of this period of the continuations, and also the sources and structure of Bernard's chronicle, and the methods he used in compiling the two versions of it. We are now sure that for the history of Jean de Brienne and Frederick up to August 1230 he had a written source, m; equally, it seems clear that after that point his material is original. We still do not know of course where he, or rather the compiler of the 1227 abrégé, got the rest of the material for the period 1205-27, or whether there was a written source at all. Again, it is now evident that Bernard's chronicle, in its second recension, served as a source for the *Eracles* text contained in the versions of *cJ, gG,* and *d,* at least for the period immediately preceding 1231, and most probably, to judge from the continuity of their texts from 1205 to 1231, for the whole of that section. In other words, Pipino is not in fact the first chronicler to use Bernard's work as a source. Long before he wrote, three *Eracles* compilers had already used a substantial part of Bernard's chronicle as part of a larger work, and with far less adaptation than Pipino was later to find desirable. The earliest of the *Eracles* compilers the man who produced the *cJ* version, ending in 1231, may have worked relatively soon after Bernard. All in all, it seems that, unoriginal though we must admit Bernard to have been on the whole, his ability to compile from other men's work a coherent, interesting, and useful chronicle was considerable. His talent, and the value of his work, was apparently recognized fairly quickly by other compilers, who judged it worthy to form part of a compilation which also drew on the invaluable eye-witness chronicle of Ernoul, and whose beginnings reached back to no less an author than William of Tyre himself.

IX

THE PLACE OF THE CONTINUATIONS
IN OLD FRENCH LITERATURE

IN CONSIDERING the first branch of the continuations, and the chronicles related to it, as literature, and in trying to make on them any kind of literary judgement, we are immediately presented with a number of difficulties. The main one is that we are not here dealing with a single author who, having a more or less clear purpose in writing, may be judged by the extent to which he has fulfilled that purpose. Nor are we evaluating a conscious exposition of a particular literary genre that has its own criteria, rigid or flexible, as would be the case say for a classical tragedy. Nor even are we dealing with a work of fiction, which is more easily seen by modern critics to be an art than is the setting down of material provided by real events, or at least by events purporting to be real. What we have in these chronicles is a corpus of writings of varied content, which has passed through the hands of many writers with differing aims, differing views of their task, and differing methods of accomplishing it. Clearly any literary merits there may be in this patchwork can only possibly belong to the individual pieces, since the whole is more the product of chance than of design.

Even having determined to take each element in the chronicles separately, as far as is possible, our task is still not straightforward. To consider as literature at all a genre which is primarily informative rather than decorative is a procedure whose validity is sometimes disputed. Rudolf Brummer, for example, in his survey of early narrative prose, deliberately excludes all chronicles from his consideration at the outset, 'da es sich bei ihr nicht um erzählende Prosa*dichtung* handelt, sondern um eine Gattung, die der wissenschaftlichen Darstellung nahekommt. Aber es gibt auch Grenzfälle . . .'[1] Despite this last qualification, however, Brummer does not admit as borderline cases any of the texts which are our subject, though two of them at least, the abrégé and the *Estoires d'Oultremer,* have irrefutable

---

[1] Rudolf Brummer, *Die erzählende Prosadichtung in den romanischen Literaturen des dreizehnten Jahrhunderts* (Berlin, 1948), i. 26. Author's italics.

claims to that description, containing as they do a very high proportion of *Dichtung* to *Wahrheit*. They are not really historiography proper, in the same way that the continuations are, and *wissenschaftlich* is the last word one would use to describe them.

On more general grounds, too, one would dispute the exclusion of even completely non-fictitious works from a survey of the rise of vernacular prose. Unoriginality of matter does not necessarily imply unoriginality of manner, especially in this period. Reading the chronicles, one may often be struck by the authors' failure to achieve an effective, striking style which holds the reader's interest, and helps in conveying to him what the author means him to think and feel about the subject in hand. But that is not the same thing as saying that the author had no consciousness of style, that his stylistic weakness springs from negligence rather than incompetence; nor does it at all support the claim made by Brummer, that such works are not a proper subject for aesthetic judgements. What is more, the omission of historiography from any consideration of the rise of vernacular prose seems all the more unjustifiable since it was one of the first fields in which the new medium was extensively used. Lastly, the very fact that the distinction between fact and fiction is in some chronicles so very unclear is in itself indicative of the author's mentality, and worth considering for its own sake. All in all, it appears that the chronicles are not only a proper subject for critical examination as examples of Old French literature, but are likely to be reasonably rewarding in this respect.

Taking first the relationship of fiction and fact, a work which announces itself as a record of real events provides a unique opportunity for us to see in operation the author's criteria of fact, as opposed to his notion of reality or of truth. Of course fiction can be used to convey all these three, that is, fact in the sense of exterior events which really did take place, and can be proved to have taken place, or reality in the sense in which Auerbach uses the word, that is, internal psychological reality, or truth, as the poet sees it, either philosophical or poetic. Dante did not, historically speaking, really go for a walk in a wood, and there meet a leopard, a lion, a she-wolf, and finally the ghost of Virgil, and indeed he makes no attempt to conceal his fiction, for his very first line tells us that his path was the 'cammin di nostra vita'. But once he has embarked on the fiction he continues it without any reminder that it is a fiction, and uses it to convey the truth as it appears to him. Similarly, Jean de Meun, to name but one, uses a fiction, and within that another fiction, to convey not this time truth, but at all events something which had for him a reality, in Auerbach's sense, and also a certain amount of factual information. Descending to a more factual level still, to the conveying of fact by fiction, those chroniclers who relate that Godrey of Bouillon refused to wear the crown of Jerusalem out of humility presumably thought that the refusal was a historical event.[2] But that is not their main interest in relating it. Rather they are interested in what it says about Godfrey's character, and if the incident had not happened (or indeed did not happen) they would have been obliged to invent it; nor would the invention have diminished their own honesty, or the parabolic value of the story. In examining a story like this, the historian asks himself, did it happen or not? But the literary critic asks, did the author think it happened, did he care whether or not it had happened? The historian is interested primarily in what the author can tell him about contemporary events, and the contemporary mentality. But the critic asks, what were the author's criteria of reality, and what did he regard as subject-matter worthy of his literary attention? It is in this way that a self-styled historical narrative provides material for his inquiry which cannot be provided by an openly fictitious work, for he has, in other accounts of the same events, and in archaeological evidence, a measure of what is or is not factual in the author's material, and though he cannot always be absolutely certain, he can go some way towards separating fact from fiction, and fiction intending to convey fact, or reality, or truth, from fiction for its own sake.

In other words, imagination has a function of conveying what is not imaginary in itself, and is used for this purpose by the chroniclers. If direct speech makes a scene more convincing, the chronicler will not hesitate to make up the necessary dialogue, and to assert that the characters said those words,

---

[2] e.g. *Historia* ix. 9 (*RHC* i. 376-7); Babcock and Krey i. 392-3. Cf. also *Li livres de Jean d'Ibelin, RCH Lois* i. 22, and Pierre de Beauvais, 'Les Olimpiades', MS *z* f. 4b and Bodleian MS Hatton 77 f. 393.

with the same degree of conviction with which he asserts that
the scene took place, even though he himself knows that he
has invented the one and not the other. This may not square
with the modern historian's notion of exactitude, but as an
artistic procedure it is obviously valid, and usually successful.
But it must be admitted that the boundary of imagination's
proper use is far from clearly delineated in this period, or
rather should we say that it was not envisaged that there might
be a boundary beyond which its use becomes improper. It is
probably no exaggeration to say that where we have a relatively
sober and unvarnished narrative, such as that of Villehardouin,
it is more the automatic product of the author's temperament
than of a deliberate attempt to reject the vagueness of contemporary notions about fact. In general anything would pass for
credible in an age when Geoffrey of Monmouth was taken
seriously.

To separate a chronicler who works in this way then from a
writer like Chrétien de Troyes, who might also take a ready-
made story, and rework it at will, seems quite arbitrary. The
chronicler is more restricted by his *matière* than is the writer
of romances, but not to such an extent that nothing is left to
his inventive powers: if fact provides almost all his *matière*,
and politics to a large extent determine the *sen*, the *conjointure*
is all his own. The difference between the two writers is of
degree, not kind. They are both in different ways artistically
inventive, and their works are therefore susceptible of the same
kind of criticism. The difference is that in the one case such
criticism will apply to the whole work, in the other to only one
aspect of it: a chronicle may be stylistically abominable, yet
still provide valuable information. Conversely, the aesthetic
pleasure we take in a work may endure long after its practical
value has faded away: what modern reader of the *Livre du
trésor*[3] is looking for practical advice on the art of good
government?

In other words, there are two separate kinds of excellence
we may demand of a non-fictional work, informative and
aesthetic, and the two need not exist in inverse proportion to
one another. It is a very modern notion to perceive ornament
as detracting from the reliability of a work, and to expect the

---

[3] Brunetto Latini, *Li Livres dou Tresor*, ed. P. Chabaille (Paris, 1863).

nature of the content to predetermine the style. So we do not
find that the *Estoires d'Oultremer* is more elaborately written
than, say, the translation of William, or the continuation of
a-b, though it is far less factual than either of these. Indeed
the text we have picked out as the most informative, the
continuation of *d,* is as we shall see, also one of the most
charmingly written. The writer is not limited in his choice of
style by his desire to be exact.

He is limited, however, and seriously, by the language he
is using, a newly emerging literary medium as yet not quite
adequate to its task. As the scribe of the Strasbourg Oaths, the
first to attempt to write down something we can call French,
had had to invent new graphies for new sounds, so these early
French chroniclers had to invent new vernacular expressions
for the new material they were expressing for the first time
in vernacular prose. Where they got many of their devices
from has been satisfactorily examined by P.M. Schon—they
took much from their predecessors, the Latin chroniclers, and
much also from the stock-in-trade of the *jongleur,* who like
them had often dealt with heroic characters and military themes,
and had acquired a fairly extensive vocabulary suitable for the
purpose.[4] For the rest the chroniclers had to improvise, and
the chief deficiency of the vernacular was its limited syntactic
possibilities. This is very much evident in the French translation of William's *Historia,* where the restriction of French
syntax show up particularly clearly by comparison with the
great stylistic possibilities of Latin, of which William is a
competent exponent. For example: 'Porro Aegyptius calypha,
inter caeteros infidelium principes divitiis et militia
potentissimus, nuntios suos ad nostros direxerat principes:
cujus legationis causa haec erat.'[5]

This looks like, and is, a quite simple Latin sentence. There
is one main clause, one adjectival phrase describing the subject,
and one subordinate relative clause describing the object. But
when we look at the French translation, the subtleties of the
very simple Latin, the art that conceals art, immediately becomes apparent: 'Entre les autres mescreanz princes, li califes

---

[4] P.M. Schon, *Studien zum Stil der frühen französischen Prosa* (Frankfurt, 1960)
(Analecta Romanica 8).
[5] *Historia* iv. 24. *RHC* i, pt. 1 p. 191. Cf. translation Babcock and Krey i. 223.

d'Egypte estoient [sic] li plus puissanz de genz et li plus riches d'avoir. Icist envoia ses messages as barons qui estoient en l'ost. Si vos dirai par quele achoison.'[6]

This includes accurately all the information of the original, but conveys nothing at all of the style. To be sure, there are ways in which the translator might have made a better job of it with the same materials, for example one sees no reason for not rendering 'nostros principes' as it stands, instead of the longer 'barons qui estoient en l'ost'. But there are basic inadequacies. The phrase 'divitiis et militia potentissimus' is of such a common construction that in reading it we do not notice it as a cunning stylistic device; but on seeing what expansion is needed to convey the same information in Old French, we begin to realize just how expressive and economical it is, and how much is lost when no similar construction can be found to replace it. The main difference between the original and the translation, however, and the one which has the most radical effect, is the main verbs—one in Latin, three in French, the last one preceded by the ubiquitous *si*. Parataxis may come into its own in the *chanson de geste,* where short striking phrases suitable for declaiming are precisely what is needed, and where the audience would have forgotten what the beginning of the sentence had been if too many subordinate clauses intervened before the end. But for a reader faced with a lengthy prose narrative it is hardly ideal. Nevertheless Old French, at least at the period we are dealing with, still tended to be primarily paratactic, and the author who attempted long sentences did so at his reader's peril, as this example from the *Eracles* will show.

> Il avint quant Androines ot copée la teste a Alexe, qui avoit l'empire de Costantinople en se garde et l'enfant, qui fu fiz de l'empereor Manuel; vint lors Androines, si se pensa d'une grant traison, et par le conseil d'un suen escrivain, qui avoit nom Langosse. Adonques fist il prendre le juene enfant, qui baron estoit de la fille dou roi de France Loys, que il deveit garder en bone foi, et le fist metre en un sac, et porter en un batel par mer et le fist geter ens, et fu noiés.[7]

The trouble here is that these two sentences are really nothing but a long series of juxtaposed clauses, all linked by

---

[6] *RHC* i. 191.   [7] *RHC* ii. 17. MS *a*, f. 313a, MS *b*, f. 248b.

'et' or by relative pronouns, all carrying about the same weight as each other, and none standing out above the rest. The total impression is of amorphousness. What is more, in *gG* and *d* at this point we find the same two sentences are one:

> La nuit quant Androines ot la teste copée a Alex qui avoit l'empire de Costantinople en sa garde et l'enfant qui fu fis l'empereor Manuel, vint lors Androines, si se pensa d'une grant traison, et par le conseill d'un sien escrivain qui avoit a non Langosse, et fist une nuit prendre le juene enfant qui baron estoit a la fille dou roi de France Loys, que il devoit garder en bone foi, et le fist metre en un sac et porter en un batel par mer et le fist geter ens et si fu noiiés.[8]

This is even more rambling, but makes much better sense, and we must accept it as the better reading, the *lectio difficilior* which the compiler of *a-b* has tried to improve and clarify, unfortunately losing the sense in the process.[9] In both there is obscurity of meaning at the end: Androines has been the subject of every verb up to the last one, and it is only common sense, not grammar, that tells the reader there is a change of subject at 'et si fu noiiés'.

These two examples illustrate at once the influence of Latin on the emerging vernacular—the attempt to imitate the parallelism of 'divitiis et militia' is typical—and also its limitations, which are those inherent in the language itself. In the selection and presentation of material the influence is much more apparent, and here the divergence between the 'pure' histories, the continuations proper, and the 'mixed' compilations, the abrégé and the *Estoires d'Oultremer,* shows up most clearly. They are related by the identity of much of their material, but belong in fact to quite different literary species. There are no radical differences in the language used or in the use made of it—all the characteristics described by Schon are found in these chronicles as in the ones he analysed; the difference lies entirely in the application of the same resources to different ends. Can we really call the abrégé, and *a fortiori* the *Estoires,* chronicles at all, or should they rather be described as romances which happen to have a high historical content, as ancestors of

---

[8] MS *d*, f. 290a. MS *gG* similarly.

[9] Another of many readings not noted by Streit (see above, pp. 34 ff.) but supporting his preference for *gG* over *a* and *b*. This reading is also one of many which indicate the superiority of *d* over *a* and *b* in the sections which they have in common.

the modern historical novel? To answer the question it is necessary to ask, not only what are their contents, but what did the
author intend to produce from those contents, as far as we can
judge his intention by his composition?

The abrégé seems at first sight to contain a quite astonishing
variety of materials, and makes on the reader an impression of
disorganization and disunity. It jumps from subject to subject,
puts in a long description of Jerusalem at a place where it breaks
the mounting tension of the narrative most irritatingly,[10] and
in general seems to be constructed as a long string of associated
ideas, with shorter strings branching off as and when the author
sees fit, rather than according to any predetermined plan. But
here precisely is its unity. The author, or more strictly speaking
the compiler, has an idea in his mind, and chooses his material,
and arranges it around that idea. He has set out, as he told us
in his first sentence, to tell us how Jerusalem fell to the Saracens
and how the Holy Cross was lost, and everything which that
theme suggests to him is considered relevant. Thus the chronological line of the story, the series of events in the order in
which they happened, is of secondary importance and can
properly be sacrificed, when a choice arises, to the compiler's
train of thought, which is the real unifying principle of the
work. In this respect it is quite true to say that he is writing
not so much history as *histoire romancée*, history being made
to serve the end of good narrative, and the end result is very
like the prose romances of chivalry as far as the shape of the
story is concerned—diffuse, meandering, with sub-plots and
minor characters in profusion, but still with one theme in
mind. This is true of course of the abrégé only up to 1197, as
far that is as it draws on the original chronicle of Ernoul, from
which the theme comes. After 1197 it is much more like the
other chronicles, a straightforward account of events, told
usually in chronological order, with varying degrees of accuracy,
and without the story-telling element. To sum up the abrégé
as a piece of literature then, we may say that up to 1197 anyway it is really a story, of which the theme and most of the
material have been taken by the compiler from his source,
proto-Ernoul, and which he has made, by selection, abbreviation, and some additions of his own, into a narrative of which
the main aim is to interest the reader, but in whose high factual

[10] M-L pp. 190-210.

content we may also discern a strong, though secondary, desire to inform. After 1197 only the second of these aims remains, and the rest of the abrégé is consequently far less readable. It is not, taken all in all, a work of any particular literary merit, though it is agreeable enough.

In the case of the *Estoires d'Oultremer*, unpublished and almost unknown, the technique of mixing fact and fiction all relating to and illustrating one subject is even more evident, because the fictional interpolations are quite obvious and have an obvious purpose. The compiler does not really care at all whether Salahadin was really dubbed a knight in secret, or whether he was descended from the Counts of Ponthieu. But he does want to draw attention to those facets of Salahadin's character which these stories purport to explain, and, conversely, he wants to paint a more convincing psychological portrait of his hero by offering explanations of what would otherwise be seen as dissonant elements in the character of a man who was after all the arch-enemy of the French, that is, of the author's audience. Salahadin is clearly seen from his behaviour in the course of the history proper which the book contains, to be a complex character, and must be provided with a past to account for this. The criterion by which the events of this past are chosen is not that they really happended, or even that they fit in smoothly with the rest of the story, which they do not, but Lessing's requirement for any convincing fiction: 'es hätte geschehen können.' To be sure, the thirteenth-century idea of what might have happened differed vastly from that of Lessing's day, but *mutatis mutandis* the principle still applies.

So the unifying theme of the *Estoires* is the same as that of the abrégé, a theme in the mind of the author. But though both have ostensibly the same subject, the loss of Jerusalem and the Holy Cross, the *Estoires* is in reality much more consistently preoccupied with the subject of Salahadin, a preoccupation chiefly visible in the two fictional interpolations, and also in the fairly extensive passages dealing with his wars against the king of Nubia, which are not mentioned in any of the other texts at all. Here the secondary unifying element in these works also becomes evident, that is, the author's view of his theme. It is this which is more important in the *Estoires* than in any of the other texts, more important even than the Ibelins in *d* for while the author's loyalty to them does undoubtedly bias the history it contains, indeed to the extent of helping us to identify the change in source, it is still only one factor in the much larger narrative. In the *Estoires* the theme of Salahadin does not merely colour the narrative, as does the theme of the Ibelins in *d*, it dominates the whole work. This strong sense of the author's intention, the impression that though he may digress at times, he will not bore us with a pointlessly meandering narrative, helps to make the *Estoires* much lighter and more entertaining than the abrégé, which seems at times to have lost all sense of direction. Another factor in the composition of the *Estoires* that makes one regret it is so inaccessible and so little known is the diverting habit of the compiler of one of the manu scripts (B.N. f.fr. 770) of putting right details in the text which offend his sense of exactitude. For example: 'Sor cele mer fu çou que Nostre Sire fist de l'aighe vin quant il fu as noces de Sainte Eglyse, mais non pas d'Archedeclin com on dist en ces roumans rimés. Archedeclin fu uns asaieres de vins. Nan pour quant il estoit princes entre les mengans, et ce fu fait en la cité de Tabarie.'[11]

This is not only true but amusing, and so we forgive the author the distinct tone of self-congratulation with which he puts right his erring source. These observations contribute to the fairly wide variety of style and subject that is to be found in the *Estoires*, and which means that, for all that it is an un-reliable text whose mixture of fact and blatant fiction leaves us at liberty to disbelieve what it contains, it is certainly pleasant to read in.

When we turn from these two compilations to the continu-ations proper, we find that the dominating purpose is different, and imparts a different shape to the work. Here, to a very large degree, the author is giving first priority to the recording of facts and events as they are, and so the continuations tend to exclude the more highly coloured of the legends, and to mani-fest an idea of relevance which comes much closer to the modern one. The order of the narrative is by and large more strictly chronological than is the case with the abrégé or the *Estoires*, and the exceptions to this rule, apart from those caused by a change in redaction, are of a sort we easily accept, that is references back to past events which elucidate the present situation, or forwards to the result of the action being

[11] MS B.N. f.fr. 770, f. 330a, col. 3. Cf. M-L p. 65.

described, which permit us to view it with hindsight. The kind of stream of consciousness technique which led the abrégé compiler into strange and devious paths is here absent; at most the digressions consist of a paragraph or two. The only exception is the text called the Rothelin continuation[12] which does not strictly belong to the first branch anyway, but which is a hotch-potch of legend, geographical description, and extracts from Jacques de Vitry, the whole as variegated and the elements as far-fetched as anything the *Estoires* can offer. Apart from this the continuations are, in a word, sober.

That is not to say that they are in the least dull. The new vernacular prose had to prove its respectability, its suitability for serious works in fields which until now had been the exclusive province of Latin. But there was good precedent for being serious without being dull: even William himself, for all his gravity, had not scorned to illuminate his history with such diverting episodes as the beheading of a camel with a single stroke of the sword by Godfrey of Bouillon.[13] Fact, if properly exploited, can provide amusement as well as fiction can, and though the continuations lack the ever-surprising variety of the abrégé and the *Estoires*, they draw enough interest from the material itself to compensate for this. After all, the material they are using is inherently capable of arousing a wide range of emotions in the reader—Jocelin of Brakelond tells us of the reaction of Abbot Samson, '. . . qui, audito rumore de capta cruce et perdicione Jerusalem, femoralibus cilicinis cepit uti, et cilicio loco staminis, et carnibus et carneis abstinere.'[14] Certainly the rise and fall of Frankish prosperity in the East was a vital topic that could always command attention with the greatest of ease. By virtue of their subject-matter, the continuations were almost guaranteed success; the very large number of manuscripts still extant, together with the fact that they were copied and recopied right up to the advent of printing, and then printed,[15] bears witness to that success. The *Eracles* clearly enjoyed widespread and lasting popularity.

But though the topicality of their material accounts for this popularity for the first hundred years or so of the chronicles'

---

[12] *RHC* ii. 489 ff. Cf. above p. 20.
[13] *RHC* i. 398-9. *Historia* ix. 22. Babcock and Krey i. 413.
[14] *Chronicle of Jocelin of Brakelond*, ed. H.E. Butler (London, 1949), pp. 39-40.
[15] Cf. above, pp. 24-5.

existence, we must look after that for another explanation.
It would appear to lie in the skill with which the material is
presented, the way in which the cathartic possibilities of the
stories are drawn out, and given universality and permanence,
and it is therefore this quality which must be the subject of an
aesthetic judgement after seven hundred years have removed all
the immediate impact of the events recounted. They have of
course replaced it with something that could not exist at the
time, that is, an antiquarian interest, but that cannot reasonably
be supposed to have come within the intention of the author,
and so is quite another question. For the moment, some examples
of the way in which the compilers of the continuations present
their material will illustrate how they gave lasting interest to
events whose primary interest was bound to fade with the passage of time.

The first example forms in the *Eracles* the twentieth chapter
of Book xxv,[16] and tells the story of a Norman knight who saved
a large number of pilgrims from death at the hand of Isaac
Comnenus, knowing that to do so would mean his own certain
death, since he was a mercenary in Isaac's service. A dramatic
enough story *per se*, but the style in which it is recounted is
extremely flat. A number of emotive words and phrases are
inevitably used, e.g. *cruel* (twice), *martire* (twice), 'esmeu de
grant pitié et de grant tristece', and so forth, but they are all
used without further emphasis. Nor is the word-order of the
sentences particularly designed to dramatize their effect.
Statement follows statement in a very matter-of-fact way, and
the hero is not even named, but merely referred to as 'un
chevalier qui estoit nez de Normendie'. Probably the author
did not even know his name. In short, the whole keynote of
the episode is understatement, even, we might say, a throw-away
technique which by its very nonchalance heightens the essential drama of the content and allows it to stand out without
any of the rhetorical ornament or exaggeration which in de
Clari's writing for example so often has the opposite effect to
that he evidently intends, and by piling superlative on superlative
dulls the reader's perception and detracts from the impact of
the subject itself. The *Eracles* compiler is helped in this instance
by the fact that the qualities he is holding up for our admiration are universally accepted as admirable anyway; indeed

[16] *RHC* ii. 162.

from that point of view the story is a rather obvious one. But
by his undramatic technique he makes it tell all the same.

Another instance of brevity and simplicity giving effective-
ness to a fairly unremarkable episode is the arrival of
Berengaria of Navarre at Acre, narrated thus in all the versions
of the *Eracles* except *d*, and in the abrégé:

> Quant li rois de France sot que li rois d'Engleterre venoit, et que il
> avoit feme espousee, si en fu moult dolenz. Et por ce ne laissa il mie
> que il n'alast encontre lui. La fu li rois de France de si grant humilité
> que il descendi de son cheval a terre et prist la feme dou roi Richart
> entre ses braz et mist a terre hors dou batel, si come l'en dit.[17]

An interesting contrast is provided by the treatment in the
d version of exactly the same event, which is narrated in almost
exactly the same terms, but with a sting in the tail:

> Au descendre la feme dou roi Richart, le rei de France fu de si grant
> humilité que il ala encontre yaus au rivage. Il meismes enbraça l'espouse
> et la descendi en terre, et n'i vost descovrir son corage, ne semblant n'en
> fist de l'outrage que le rei Richart li avoit fait. Ce est assaveir de ce qu'il
> avoit laissié le mariage de sa seror por le mariage de Berengiere la suer
> dou rei de Navarre. Il li mostra bien quant il torna en France.[18]

This is an excellent example of a habit which distinguishes
the compiler of *d* from all the other chroniclers, that of adding
a sudden brief and apposite comment which casts a quite different light on the whole episode, and shows up by contrast
the mild tone of the version given by the other continuations,
which again relies on understatement to produce an effect of
poignancy.

These two are both minor incidents in the history of the
crusades, but a major event which forms one of the strongest
points of the continuations' value historically also provides
one of the best illustrations of purely literary devices used,
successfully, to make the story live apart from the information
it contains. It is the account of Balian d'Ibelin's negotiations
with Salahadin for the ransom of the Franks of Jerusalem
before the surrender of the city in 1187. This was of great
political importance, and the continuations give us a particularly full account of it. But curiously, the political aspect of
the negotiations is very much played down, almost one might
say neglected, while the author concentrates all his efforts on
personalizing the story, so that it becomes as it were part of

[17] Ibid., p. 170. M-L p. 273.   [18] *RHC* ii, *d* variant, 169.

the body of stories about Salahadin as an individual, rather
than as a public figure. The story covers two long chapters,[19]
and the major part of it is in direct speech, in the form of
dialogues between Salahadin and Balian d'Ibelin. This alone
makes it immediate and dramatic. We have very easily the
impression that the scenes are being played out before us, and
see the characters as real figures, acting on their own impulse,
rather than as puppets of the author. It is a very convincing
fashion in which to present a conversation. It also has the
virtue of allowing a great deal of detail to be expressed without
undue tedium: the passages which are in indirect speech tend, by
contrast perhaps, to a severe degree of monotony, with much
repetition of *dist que* and *distrent que*. The wealth of detail
which the author includes in his account adds nothing to the
information he gives us; he could have expressed it all very
much more succinctly. But it does serve to involve the reader
in the development of the negotiations—we see it happening
step by step, instead of being told everything at once in a
straight report—and it adds to the quasi-theatrical atmosphere
the author has built up. This in turn does add something to
our view of the surrender as a historical event, not to our
factual information about it, but to our evaluation of its importance, and of the importance it had for the Franks at the
time.

This episode is perhaps the best example in all the continuations of a piece of material which was bound to have some
value—as pure information—to any reader, and therefore to
enjoy some success even if treated by a mediocre author. But
this author, by the techniques he has used, and by the view
of his subject which those techniques helped to convey, has
given it not one value but two: without sacrificing any of the
information it contains he has made of it almost a piece of
armchair theatre. He has seen what dramatic possibilities the
story has, and has exploited them efficiently, so that what
might have been simply an episode in the war, with an im-
personal political interest only, has become also a skilful
psychological portrait of two men and the relationship between
them, a striking miniature account of a battle of diplomatic
skill, with the tension kept high by the knowledge that the

---

[19] *Eracles* xxiii, 59 and 60. *RHC* ii. 88-93. Cf. M-L pp. 222-4.

lives and freedom of thousands of Franks are at stake. It is thanks to the author's skill as a chronicler, that is, to his ability to marshal facts and present them clearly, that we are left at the end of the account well informed about the surrender of Jerusalem; that we also feel involved in the outcome, that we are interested in the fate of the Franks, is a measure of his skill as a narrator.

So far, all these examples have been common to all the continuations, and by implication attributable to their common source, proto-Ernoul. But it would be of course quite mistaken to treat all the versions of the *Eracles* together, as though they had one common style, and one appeal to the reader. This is true of the passages they do have in common, like the ones quoted, but there are also the long sections found in only one or two of the versions, and not in the others. The most strikingly individual version, from the stylistic point of view as well as in its content, is *d*. Here all the vivacity, the immediacy, the variety of technique which go to make all the versions readable, are doubled. Accepting that this is the version closest in content to the original chronicle of Ernoul, we must also accept that it gives us the most accurate impression of what his style must have been, and in doing so makes us regret more than ever that the original is lost to us. This closeness to Ernoul offers the clue to the lively style of the work: it springs from the author's involvement in the story he is telling, which is less diluted in this version than in the others. Ernoul's own involvement comes over to us clearly here, so that we ourselves identify more easily with him than in those versions which have become more dispassionate, calmer, and so less telling. We have already seen an example of *d* adding a personal comment to a narrative similar to that of the other versions, and thereby transforming the whole story at a single stroke, in the account of Berengaria's arrival at Acre.[20] An even more personalized account, in which indeed the evident personal interest of the author forms the main feature of the presentation, deals with Guy's division of Cyprus into fiefs after he had bought the island from Richard in 1192.[21] All the versions of the continuations make some comment on his handling of the situation, but in *d* this is carried much further than in the rest.

---

[20] See above, p. 161.   [21] *RHC* ii. 188-90, *d* variant.

It is *d* alone who tells us that when he acquired the island, Guy sent to Salahadin for advice on how to administer it, having apparently learnt by his mistakes. We have already seen that the author's attitude to Salahadin as displayed here is typical: Salahadin acknowledges that Guy is his enemy, but nevertheless behaves honourably towards him—*leiaument* is the key word. The rest of the story is a demonstration of how Guy put into practice the advice Salahadin gave him,[22] by offering fiefs to the knights who had lost their lands in Syria as a result of Salahadin's conquests.

> Les chevaliers et les serjans et les borjeis, cui Sarasins avoient deserités, oirent le comandement dou rei Guy. Il murent et vindrent a lui, et des dames juenes et des orfenins et orfenines a grant planté, iceles cui les barons et les peres estoient mors et perdus en Surie. Il lor dona riches fiés, et as Griffons et as chevaliers que il avoit menés o lui, et as corversiers et as massons et as escrivains en Sarraisneis, ensi que la Deu merci, sont devenus chevaliers et grant vavassors de l'isle de Chypre.[23]

There is an unmistakable personal note in this interjection of 'la Deu merci', which, like the dialogue form of the negotiations between Balian and Salahadin, gives us an insight into the significance of the event for the people involved. It is also, incidentally, corroborative evidence for identifying Ernoul the author with Ernoul de Gibelet, who was deprived of his family lands by Saracen conquest, and did become a 'grant vavassor de l'isle de Chypre'.[24] Personal gain from Guy's policy would explain too how the author who before had seen Guy as the weak ruler who lost Palestine suddenly finds that he has after all some qualities.

After this enumeration of the people who came to colonize Cyprus under Guy's rule, *d* makes, like all the versions, a comparison between Guy's success in Cyprus and the failure of the contrary policy operated by Baldwin in the Empire of Constantinople. But again *d* adds a remark of his own, this time a proverb, 'et l'en dit en reprovier, qui tout coveite, tout pert'.[25] This is a little sententious perhaps, a little heavy-handed,

---

[22] For 'qu'il la teigne toute' (*RHC* ii, 188) read 'qu'il la doigne toute' (MS *d*, f. 330a). Also in this passage, for 'perdue . . . il fu mort' (*RHC* ii, 190) read 'perdue. Car il fu mort' etc. (MS *d*, loc. cit.).

[23] *RHC* ii. 188-9, *d* variant.   [24] Cf. above pp. 44-5 and 114.

[25] *RHC* ii. 190, *d* variant.

but nevertheless it relates the author immediately to his subject, and by indicating his interest in the implication of Baldwin's error, gives it a particular twist for us which sharpens the impact considerably. It also displays another feature of *d*'s style, that is his love of cleverly turned phrases, of aphorisms, of a few words, or even single words used evocatively. Salahadin sending advice to Guy provides us with a good example of this use of words.

> Salahadin repondi as messages que il n'ameit gaires le rei Guy, mais depuis que il li requereit de conseill, il le conseillereit au miaus que il savreit. Car puis que l'on demande conseill a autrui, soit ami ou henemi, leiaument li doit conseillier, et sur ce dist as messages: 'Je conseille au rei Guy que, se il viaut que l'isle soit tote soue, que il la doigne toute.'[26]

There is in this passage first the use of *leiaument* already noted, which here evokes instantly Salahadin's whole attitude and behaviour towards Guy in the matter, and the moral standard to which he is conforming, which was after all that of the Franks themselves. We are reminded of Ganelon, an essentially admirable knight with many virtues, which, however, availed him nothing because he lacked the one indispensable virtue:

> Devant le rei la s'estut Guenelun.
> Cors ad gaillard, e.l vis gente color;
> S'il fust leials, ben resemblast barun.[27]

The *d* author, by using of Salahadin a word with so many overtones, implying by itself a whole moral code, has made us see Salahadin as he wants us to see him more effectively than a lengthy description ever could, and more subtly. We have accepted his evaluation without even noticing that we have not made it for ourselves.

Secondly, Salahadin's words offer us another example of the kind of parallelism *d* loves—'soit ami ou henemi'—two opposites in meaning but similar in sound, and having the same effect therefore as 'qui tout coveite tout pert', a rhythmic sound, with the same vowel in the first example, and in the second the same word, repeated in the two halves of the phrase. This kind of sentence structure, almost universal in

---

[26] Ibid., p. 188.   [27] *La Chanson de Roland*, ed. Whitehead, vv. 3762-4.

folk-sayings and proverbs, evidently appeals to *d* a great deal, and to his fondness for rhymes and jingles we owe the preservation of the popular political song,

> Maugré li Polein
> Avrons nous roi Poitevin.

Here again the two similar sounding words, *Polein* and *Poitevin*, express the antithesis which is the root of the sentence' meaning.[28]

The last point in Salahadin's words which illustrates the particularities of *d*'s style is the way in which the advice itself is formulated, 'se il viaut que l'isle soit tote soue, que il la doigne toute'. Here there is no play on words, but the thought is formulated in a paradox, and since we can confidently assume that the author did not know verbatim what Salahadin had said, we can also assume that, knowing what had been said in essence, he himself chose this way to express it.

It is this love of cleverly turned phrases, of metaphor and proverb, that leads *d* in a particularly tense passage to a very amusing mixture of figures. He is describing the siege of Acre by the Christians in 1189, an apparently hopeless enterprise when it began, since the besieging army was pitifully small, and the town well defended. In an effort to convey to us the inequality of the two forces, *d* is carried away by his own eloquence:

> Grant fu la fei des feaus de Deu, quant ensi poi de gent oserent enprendre si grant fait com de metre siege devant Accre. Car tant i avoit des Sarazins dedens la cité d'Acre que a peine i avoit un Crestien a dix Sarazins. Il se mistrent entre le maill et l'enclume, et se cil de la cité vosissent, il eussent devoré les Crestiens et pris si come fait l'espervier le petit oiselet.[29]

Here alas the author goes too far, and where in most cases he has achieved a dramatic or pointed effect, we have in this instance only unintentional and incongruous amusement. But this is the exception to the general rule that the *d* author stands head and shoulders above the other *Eracles* writers not

---

[28] Another more minor example is the phrase used by Renaud de Saete: 'Le cors est entre vos mains et le cors est en la main de Dieu' (*RHC* ii. 111, *d* variant), probably the commonest of all puns in Old French.

[29] MS *d*, f. 316a, col. 1. Cf. *RHC* ii, 126, *d* variant.

only by the intrinsic interest of his material but also by his
artistic skill in expressing it, and that his is the most admirable
of all the continuations in both these respects.

The virtues of the *d* continuation, and as we have seen they
are considerable, are the closest imitation we have of the virtues
of Ernoul's original work. Judging by what *d* has preserved for
us, we can say that as a writer Ernoul was skilful to a considerable degree. His writing has the vivacity of Robert de Clari, but
without the singular lack of descriptive vocabulary that is de
Clari's undoing. Whereas de Clari's most forceful description
is the assurance that he really cannot describe his subject at all,
Ernoul is rarely at a loss for words. In fact as a chronicler he
combines the individualism of de Clari with the intelligence of
Villehardouin, and as a writer he is more skilful than either.
Neither of them expresses himself in anything like the wide
range of modes employed by Ernoul. When Salahadin orders
the Templars to be killed Ernoul gives us his own opinion, that
it was an error of judgement, but he also adds an impartial
analysis of Salahadin's motives.[30] On the subject of the German
crusaders on the other hand he is unashamedly partisan.[31] He
is capable of a minutely detailed exposition of a complicated
subject—for example he traces with admirable clarity the evolution of the procedure for electing the Patriarch of Jerusalem[32] —
but he can also convey his meaning in few words, as in his
evocative thumb-nail sketch of Henri de Champagne.[33] He is
sarcastic or sentimental, lucid or impressionistic as the subject
and occasion require, petty and generous by turns. Indeed
versatility is perhaps his main virtue, both in the means of
expression he uses, and in the range of topics he deals with.

He differs from his contemporaries too in his conception
of his subject; *conte* is precisely the word for his work, for he
is a born teller of tales as well as a historian. Schon has demonstrated convincingly that the early vernacular chroniclers
took from the tradition of the *chanson de geste* much vocabulary and many stylistic tricks.[34] Ernoul at any rate also shares
with them his approach to his subject. To be sure he is infinitely
more faithful to fact than are the *jongleurs*, but like them he

---

[30] *RHC* ii. 122-4, *d* variant.   [31] Ibid., pp. 220-2.   [32] Ibid., pp. 203-5.
[33] Ibid., p. 220.   [34] P.M. Schon, op. cit., pp. 134 ff.

sees his heroes as heroes in both an artistic and a historical sense, and he transmits this dual concept to his audience. This in turn allows him much more subtlety in his treatment of character than is possible in the framework of most chronicles, for the two parts of his vision—the historical and the artistic—can be separated if necessary. Thus Richard Coeur-de-Lion is a hero in both senses, while Salahadin is a political villain, but an artistic hero all the same. It is in this way that the rigid division of characters into Franks and therefore good, and Saracens and therefore bad, is avoided, and we have a picture at once more informative of the true state of affairs, and more convincing psychologically. Here the artistic and the historical, far from conflicting with each other, go hand in hand, and a single technique benefits the work in both ways.

In fact these two aims, the informative and the literary, are the two mainsprings of Ernoul's work, and on the whole he balances the two fairly well. He does not allow the necessity to inform to obscure the desire to amuse, nor is he carried by fantasy too far from reality. By contrast with those parts of the *Eracles* which are not dependent on his work Ernoul's writing seems full of entertainment, if perhaps a little lacking in sobriety. By contrast on the other hand with the barely disciplined farrago that is the *Estoires d'Oultremer*, it appears ordered, informative, polished. Mas-Latrie, following Philippe de Novare's description of *messire Harneis*, envisaged him as 'aussi apte à dicter un livre qu'à soutenir une discussion féodale',[35] and once again Mas-Latrie has proved a true prophet. The informative value of Ernoul's work, even though its form was uncertain, has been long recognized by the historian: it remains to recognize also his considerable skill as a writer who among his contemporaries deserves no mean place.

Such then is the aesthetic value of the chronicles that endures even after the lapse of some seven hundred years. No doubt in their day they were appreciated for other reasons too which now escape our modern sensibilities. But with the passing of time they have acquired an interest for us which they could not have had originally, that is, the interest of museum pieces, and though this is hardly a form of literary merit, it has a literary interest in the sense that it provides us with a great deal of

[35] M-L p. 500.

information about the anatomy of one kind of medieval literature. To a certain degree of course any single work tells us
something about the genre, the age, or the school to which it
belongs, but in the *Eracles*, the *Historia*, and the chronicles
related to them we have something infinitely more valuable
than a random collection of specimens: we have a series of
works which by their very relatedness and variety illustrate
quite fully the evolution of their species. They include most
of the basic work methods of medieval chroniclers, and cover
between them almost all the thirteenth century, give or take
ten years at either end, a vital period in the development of
the vernacular chronicle. Among them we find the most diverse
works, whose inclusion in the same family tree demonstrates
for us what different ends could be achieved by writers who
all used largely the same basic materials. What can the chronicles teach us in these respects?

The original element of the corpus was all that the rest are
not: coherent, unified, painstaking, learned, deliberately and
successfully intended to endure. William of Tyre was in the
ideal situation to write a history of the crusades. He was a
native-born Syrian, but had been educated, as he tells us, in
his parents' homeland, France, where he had been taught by
such men as Maurice de Sully, Peter Lombard, and Gilbert de
la Porrée.[36] His education finished, he returned home to
Palestine, and became successively tutor to the young Baldwin
IV, Chancellor of the Kingdom of Jerusalem, and Archbishop
of Tyre. Thus he had access to the state papers of the Kingdom,
influential friends to encourage him in his task, and all the
resources of an archiepiscopal household, scribes, translators,
and so forth at his disposal. He produced two major works of
history, the *Historia Rerum in Partibus Transmarinis Gestarum*,
and another piece which he mentions in the *Historia*,[37] a
history of Egypt, usually referred to in William's words as the
De Gestis Orientalium Principum, and now alas lost.

Despite all these advantages of natural talent and fortunate
circumstances, however, William was a reluctant author, who
wrote his masterpiece only from a pressing sense of the responsibility of the historian. He is acutely aware of his position

---

[36] See *Latomus,* xxi (1962), 822-4.   [37] *RHC* i, 15. Babcock and Krey i. 56.

and its dangers: one may fall prey to bias and prejudice; one
may be tempted to modify the truth in order not to alienate
one's friends. This point seems to weigh with him particularly,
and he invokes one of his favourite authors, Cicero: 'Nam, juxta
Ciceronis nostri sententiam, Molesta est veritas, siquidem ex
ea nascitur odium quod est amicitiae venenum; molestium
tamen obsequium, quod vitiis indulgens, amicum sinit ire
praecipitem.'[38]

In the end it was almost under duress that he accepted the
task proposed to him by Amalric, and for a reason which
would appear to militate against the impartiality he has just
extolled—patriotic loyalty. 'Inter tot igitur periculorum
insidias et anceps discrimen, tutius fuerat quievisse; silendumque
erat, et otium calamis indicendum: sed urgentissimus instat
amor patriae; pro qua vir bene dispositus, etiam si id necessitatis
articulus exigat, vitam tenetur impendere.[39]

This motive was, however, balanced by another more prom-
ising one, which comes particularly into evidence towards the
end of the work. The fortunes of the colonials were declining
sharply, and it became painful to William to have to relate
things detrimental to his countrymen and his country. He was
only able to continue, he tells us, because of a desire, not to
extol his native land, but to make an accurate record for
posterity. It is interesting, and indicative of his mentality and
background, that he takes once again classical authors as his
example, this time Livy and Josephus, who had both recorded
the fortunes of their peoples in bad times as well as good.
Fortified by their salutary lesson, William continues his work,
'. . . ut regni Hierosolymorum status omnis, tam prosper quam
adversus, posteritati nostra significetur opera'.[40]

This purpose, not a common one at the time, he carries
out with great success. His education, with its solid classical
foundation, stood him in good stead, as did his apparently
inborn love of factual accuracy. His ability, and willingness,
to draw the line between fact and fable were developed to a
degree remarkable in an age when the distinction was but
vaguely made, if at all. His work does not differ, as literature,

---

[38] *RHC* i. 3. Babcock and Krey i. 53.   [39] *RHC* i. 4. Babcock and Krey i. 55.
[40] *RHC* i. 1132. Babcock and Krey ii. 506.

from that of his European contemporaries; rather it differs in the consistency of the writer's outlook. William was an ecclesiastic, by nature as well as by virtue of his office, and however he might strive for impartiality of mind, he was bound in the end to take a basically theocratic view of history. To him Outremer was not primarily a Frankish colony, but the Holy Land; if the City of God was to exist anywhere on earth it must surely be at Jerusalem. It was even more clear to William than to his contemporaries in general, that kings ruled under God, and this must be true particularly of those who ruled in God's country. When therefore having recorded faithfully the history of that country over some six centuries he comes to a time, in the last decades of the twelfth century, when God is clearly allowing His people, the liberators of the Holy Places, to be gradually dispossessed of the land they had won in God's name, William is understandably distressed. But his system does not fail. God will preserve Palestine for those who obey Him, and this is what the Franks are not doing. The old generation is dead, and the new one is quite different:

> Considerantibus ergo nobis et statum nostrum diligenter discutientibus prima occurit causa in Deum auctorem omnium respiciens, quod pro patribus nostris, qui fuerunt viri religiosi et timentes Deum, nati sunt filii perditissimi, filii scelerati, fidei Christianae praevaricatores, et sine delectu per omnia currentes illicita: tales aut talibus pejores, qui dixerunt domino Deo suo, Recede a nobis; scientiam viarum tuarum nolumus.[41]

So William works out his story to the end in terms of his religious belief and consequent theocratic political theory, and it is all very consistent. He would doubtless have been distressed but little surprised had he lived to see the fall of Jerusalem, the loss of the Holy Cross, and the subsequent downfall of Christian rule in Palestine. In fact he died in 1184 or 1185, in Rome, in dubious circumstances. Some said that he had gone there on family business and died a natural death, but others alleged that he was on his way to the Holy See, there to denounce the scandalous way of life of Heraclius, Patriarch of Jerusalem; and that Heraclius, realizing that if William reached his destination it would mean his own certain ruin, bribed a Syrian physician to follow William and to poison him. This is the story the abrégé gives,[42] and it fits in well with the flattering

---

[41] *Historia* xxi. 7. *RHC* i. 1015. Babcock and Krey ii. 406.   [42] M-L p. 85.

picture that chronicle paints of William, ending violently the
virtuous life of the man than whom no better clerk was known
in Christendom in his days, with murder at the hands of his
evil opponent.

However that may be, the *Historia* ends in 1184, with the
arrangements for the regency after the death of William's pupil,
Baldwin IV. As it stands, the *Historia* is a model of the medieval
Latin chronicle at its best: informative without being dry,
ordered, varied in its narrative, and polished in language and
style. William saw himself in the tradition of classical writers,
and in particular of classical historiographers like Livy, and in
that sense the *Historia* was backward-looking, anchored firmly
in an ancient tradition. When it was translated into the vernacular
it was precipitated into the present, and associated with a tradition hardly well enough established to justify the name. The
dignity, the measured phrases, the painstaking detail of the
original, all went by the board, for the translator had in mind
a public who would not bear with *longueurs* for the sake of
fine phrases. And yet the gain was almost as great as the loss.
Vast popularity followed, and who can say whether the inclusion of the *Historia* in the admittedly inferior compilations
of the *Eracles* did not somehow help to preserve interest in
the original?

The most interesting fact about the translation, from the
point of view of the development of the vernacular chronicling
tradition, is its date. If the most recent dating is correct (early
1220s *terminus ad quem* 1223)[43] then it post-dates not only
Villehardouin, but also proto-Ernoul and probably de Clari too.
This suggests that direct translation from Latin to French is
perhaps less important to the evolution of vernacular prose
writing than is generally believed, for here is one corpus in
which we find that a good deal of the vernacular material,
indeed one of the main vernacular sources, was in existence
some time before the bulk of the translated material. Vernacular histories of the crusades seem in fact to have been a
fairly well-established part of the literary scene before anyone
thought of translating into French the standard Latin history
of the crusades. This is not to say that the translation of Latin
works did not in general help to get the vernacular recognized

[43] O.G. Goulden's dating.

as the language of serious writing, and to fit it for its task, nor that the existence of a Latin prose chronicle tradition was without influence in making authors aware of the possibility of writing chronicles also in vernacular prose; but it does suggest that the influence was a more indirect one than is usually assumed.

So we have in the corpus of the *Eracles* examples of Latin prose chronicling and of translation from Latin to French. We have also, though fragmentarily, a very early vernacular chronicle, that of Ernoul, which we must class in kind with Joinville's life of Saint Louis. Ernoul's chronicle was evidently like the work of Joinville in two respects: it was an eye-witness account, and derives its historical value from that fact, and it was a eulogy, almost an apologia, for one family, as Joinville's work is a hagiography. We have already seen that Ernoul's merits as a writer are considerable; as an example of historiography the value of his work is less, for it tells us nothing that we could not have already learned from Joinville—that bias of attitude towards the subject not only affects the content of the work but makes it sympathetic to the reader, who borrows his involvement from that of the author himself. The way in which each of the compilers who used Ernoul's work adapts it is on the other hand illuminating. Each imposes on it his own style, with varying success—the compiler of *a-b* for example often casts it in a formal mould which cramps the essential informality of the source, while the abrégé author preserves the informality better, but obscures his source in a mass of extraneous information which evidently appeals to his taste, and is fortunately absent in the continuations. Most significant of all, the most personal elements in Ernoul's chronicle have apparently been suppressed to a greater or lesser degree by all the compilers. We cannot judge of course how much *d* omitted in this respect— we can only say it was less than the other compilers chose to cut out—but who knows how much information on the Ibelins that the modern historian would have prized has been lost even in this version? These omissions have an objective reason, and are not merely the result of the compilers' whim: as we saw in analysing the variants of *d*, much of their material is very nearly risible unless one assumes an intense interest in the Ibelin family.

Apart from this, the adaptations we can trace by comparing the continuations one with another give us some indications

of the range of taste of the compilers, and the tastes they
attributed to their public. Evidently there was a lot of variation,
as we might expect. The abrégé is apparently intended as a
short guide to the period 1185-1231 approximately, whereas
the *Eracles* is a more heavy-weight book in every sense. We
might deduce from this that the abrégé was a popularizing
work; if it was, it was a resounding failure in that respect, for
there are extant almost six times as many manuscripts of the
Eracles as of the abrégé, a difference which, even allowing for
the accidents of preservation, is still a very significant one. It
is also interesting that the manuscripts of the *Eracles* include
numerous very finely written and beautifully illuminated specimens, among them that made for the English court which
nowadays would be called a coffee-table edition.[44] The abrégé
manuscripts are by contrast utilitarian affairs, though Arsenal
4797 is elegantly enough written and set out on the page. Not
one has miniatures of any merit, and few have even storied
capitals.

Looking now at the progress of the chronicles over the
thirteenth century, one hesitates to use the term progress at
all, for they make virtually none in any direction. The later
phases of the *Eracles*, compared to the earlier, do not seem
more lucid, more accurate, or more gracefully expressed. If
anything the compilation degenerates as it goes on, becoming
less and less a narrative, and more like annals. In Book xxxiv,[45]
contained only in *gG* and *b*, one finds whole chapters consisting
entirely of lists of events without further comment, and where
there is something like a historical narrative it is episodic and
disjointed. Taking the *Eracles* as a whole, the first period of
the continuations, up to 1232, strikes the reader as undoubtedly
the most meritorious, from the historical point of view, and even
more so from the aesthetic.

Indeed, taking thirteenth-century French chronicles as a
whole, what is true of the *Eracles* as it develops seems true of
the whole genre too at this period. Before the last version of
the *Eracles* was finished, Joinville had already written his biography of S. Louis.[46] This, though hardly a model of well-
ordered narrative, is certainly a less haphazard work than the

---

[44] Brit. Mus. Royal 15.E.1.   [45] *RHC* ii. 436 ff.
[46] Jean, Sire de Joinville, *Histoire de Saint Louis*, ed. Natalis de Wailly (Paris, 1874).

Eracles, but then it is conceived on a far smaller scale, and produced entirely by one man. Allowing for that, it is not in any way a superior piece of work, and if it is compared with the section of *d* drawn from Ernoul, that is the part covering 1184-97, it comes off distinctly worse. We must wait for the next century and for Froissart to see style and stamina combined, and for another century again to see a change in content and presentation, when Commynes at last produces something like modern historiography in French. Even then, Commynes, admirable as his work is, cannot match the verve, the directness, the uncontrived racy narrative of Ernoul.

So the *Eracles* demonstrates in its various phases the evolution and development of the vernacular chronicle in France over the thirteenth century. Some dependence on Latin chronicles, though less and of a less direct kind than we might suppose, contributes to its range. The independent chronicles, that is those which are as far as we know the work of one man, tend to be short, but still plagiarize earlier works to a noticeable extent. In fact the freedom to plagiarize apparently contributes a great deal to the progress made in the chronicles, for it allows the author, or compiler, to exercise his abilities in the direction of arrangement of the material, construction, and expression, without the extra task of composing fresh material at the same time. What progress is made in this way is made early, say before 1250 or so, and once a fairly satisfactory standard has been evolved, it stays, the only modifications made being to suit the individual talent of the author: Joinville is largely original, Froissart extremely long and somewhat episodic. But neither of them is doing anything basically very different from what the many authors involved ultimately in the production of the *Eracles* had already done before them. The *Eracles* writers between them, from William of Tyre and Ernoul to the anonymous compiler who put together the enormous length of *gG*, had explored and exploited all the possibilities there were, or would be for some time to come, and their works between them typify everything that we find in the works of their contemporaries. The *Eracles* is not so much a collection of fossils in which we trace the history of its species; rather it is a complete demonstration of its own evolution, which we can see going on before our eyes. To the literary historian it is, as far as chronicles are concerned, what the Galápagos islands were for Charles Darwin.

X

THE TEXTS AS HISTORICAL EVIDENCE

IT REMAINS to ask: what are the implications of this study for the historians who are accustomed to use these texts as sources? In what ways, if any, do the conclusions drawn alter our view of the texts as historical evidence? As we have already seen,[1] all the texts have served very frequently as source material for historians of the crusades and the crusader states. The *Historia* itself we need hardly mention; the *Eracles* and the abrégé have also been much used—among general histories of the crusades all the major ones, those of Röhricht, Grousset, Richard, Runciman, Prawer, draw on these two texts to a greater or lesser degree, and in several cases they serve as the main source for the late twelfth and early thirteenth centuries. More specialized works too have drawn heavily on them: those of Lane Poole, Smail, and Cahen spring immediately to mind. Nor is this state of affairs surprising when we remember how valuable these chronicles are as sources of information on the Ibelins, vital characters in any account of the Latin Kingdom at this period, and also on more day-to-day matters, political, military, economic.

But the question which at present concerns us is not so much the extent as the manner of their use, and it is here that the conclusions which have emerged suggest that some fairly major modifications need to be made. In this respect the chronicles are in somewhat the same case as the *Livre de Jean d'Ibelin*,[2] another text which, though indeed a rich mine of information, is not exactly what it at first appears, and has been largely at the bottom of the belief that the Kingdom of Jerusalem presents a kind of fossilized feudalism, so static that it can be formulated in, and defined by, the books of the *Assises*. As Prawer pointed out,[3] Jean d'Ibelin was not writing about the constitution of the Kingdom since time immemorial, but about the state of customary law as obtaining in this day. Similarly, we must ask ourselves, what kind of texts are we here dealing with? what did their authors and compilers want

---

[1] Cf. Introduction.   [2] *RHC Lois* i. 7-430.

[3] J. Prawer, 'Les Premiers Temps de la féodalité dans le royaume latin de Jérusalem', *Tijdschrift voor Rechtsgeschiedenis,* xxii (1954).

to achieve in their writings? The changes in the use at present
made of the texts which these questions will suggest fall into
four broad categories: first, the texts must be dealt with in a
fragmentary way and not treated as unities in themselves;
secondly, the emphasis laid on some texts at the expense of
others must be shifted; thirdly the customary system of
nomenclature must be at least seriously modified; and last but
not least by any means, an attitude of greater caution must
be adopted towards these protean chronicles.

The most striking feature of the chronicles, from the textual
point of view, and the one most fundamentally affecting their
value as sources, is the composite nature of each of them, and
though this is universally recognized by historians[4] there is
inevitably a tendency to treat each book as a single unit. This
kind of use can best be characterized as resembling the funda-
mentalists' use of Scripture, which depends on the belief that
not only are all parts of Scripture equally true, they are, more
vitally, true in the same way. As we have seen in the preceding
chapter, our chronicles in fact vary very much in their approach
to their subject. What is more, among all the French texts of the
William of Tyre corpus there is not one that is not either a compilation from several sources, or a translation done with very
varying degrees of closeness, or an adaptation of an earlier work.
In no case are we dealing with a chronicle like that of say Joinville—
the work of one man on a single topic, planned and executed by
him in the form in which we now possess it. So it is above all
things essential to treat the abrégé, the *Estoires d'Oultremer,*
and the several versions of the *Eracles* as being each a collection
of sources rather than each a source. This approach simplifies,
indeed as far as historians are concerned it effectively solves,
the ever-troublesome question of the relatedness of the texts
to each other: that is, by considering the whole corpus as a
collection of fragments, each of which may appear in one
text only or in several, we emphasize simultaneously two vital
characteristics—the independent nature of each fragment, and
the relatedness of the various texts in which these fragments
constantly reappear. Hence it is very desirable to try to avoid
making general statements about the value of a whole text as
a source of authoritative information, and to concentrate

---

[4] See for example Runciman ii. 477-8.

rather on evaluating the various sections we have already marked off; in other words, to look at the texts horizontally, taking the same fragment across all of them, rather than vertically at one text along the whole of its length. To give an example, for the Fourth Crusade all the texts are of identical value, since all give substantially the same account, whereas for the 1184-97 period we can say that the *d* version approximates more closely to the original chronicle of Ernoul than the others, and for the conquest of Cyprus *a-b* has material not found elsewhere at all. We must take each of these elements on its own merits, making always a conscious effort to dissociate it in our estimation from the other components with which each compiler has elected to surround it.

Taking the negative points first, we can practically discount, for straightforward historical evidence, as historians nearly always have done,[5] all that part of the *Eracles* which is a translation of the *Historia*: clearly historians will not normally read a translation when the original is available. Other parts of the compilations are so thin as to be almost useless. The early part of the abrégé, for example, is so sketchy that it is hardly any use even as a check on other fuller sources. If we found a conflict between it and say William, we should be ill advised to take the abrégé's point of view very seriously, since the author clearly does not consider this period his main business, but treats it rather as a run-in to his real subject. Of these early chapters as evidence of taste, of the contemporary Western image of the Latin Kingdom, and of the abrégé compiler's view of the value of his work, we shall have more to say later. As sources of pure information they are well described by Baldwin[6] as possibly of use in supplementing the *Historia*, but never to be accepted without question.

The same is true, if not quite to the same extent, of the account of the Fourth Crusade found in all the texts.[7] It is, as far as we can possibly tell, quite independent of the written sources already known, that is principally de Clari and Villehardouin, and so might provide a different view of the

---

[5] There is one important exception to this rule, which will be discussed fully in this chapter. Cf. below, pp. 185-6.

[6] M.W. Baldwin, *Raymond III of Tripolis and the fall of Jerusalem* (Princeton, N. J., 1936), p. 163.

[7] *RHC* ii. 243 ff. M-L p. 336 para. 2 et sqq.

same events, always a useful thing to have, since it permits as
it were a stereoscopic view of the subject. But compared with
these two, the continuations give so much less attention to
this crusade that a comparison can hardly be either fair or
enlightening. The lack of detail is, however, by no means on
the same scale as that displayed in the first part of the abrégé,
so that we cannot entirely rule out the possibility that the
continuations may prove to be of some interest on this topic.
We can only say that they should be treated with some caution
in a section in which their authority is neither proved from
external evidence, nor implicit in their treatment of their
subject.

On other topics the continuations do have precisely this
value, that they offer a different perspective on events about
which we already had quite a lot of information. Into this category fall the two accounts of the siege of Damietta[8] and the
various accounts of the crusade of Frederick II and his wars
against Cyprus and against Jean de Brienne. We cannot claim
that the continuations in any way supersede what is already
known, nor that they are outstandingly valuable sources in
these respects, but they are, as far as we can tell, reasonably
well informed, and give a reasonable amount of detail, so that
in these sections we should be justified in taking them seriously
if they disagreed with another source, and also they are very
likely to be able to fill in gaps left in our information by the
other sources available. Again, they can offer us not only different information on occasion, but, more consistently, and
perhaps more important, a different interpretation of events.
Given that no chronicle offers pure information without any
interpretation added on the part of the compiler, it is vital for
the historian, if he is to weigh up his evidence as impartially
as possible, to have available sources representing more than
one allegiance. The abrégé and the continuations agreeing with
it at this point are, for example, virulently opposed to
Frederick II, and so provide a useful counterbalance to the
numerous sources which take his part.

These eliminations leave us, needless to say, with those
parts of the chronicles which are dependent on the chronicle
of Ernoul, and which derive their exceptional value in every

[8] *RHC* ii. 326 ff. main text, 315 ff. variants; M-L pp. 414 ff.

respect from that dependence, that is the sections covering the period 1184-97, and it is here that the second implication of our conclusions applies: shift of emphasis. For it is this fragment, since this is the one most certainly drawn from Ernoul's chronicle, which is the richest source of all, and it is also this fragment which varies most in its several appearances in the versions of the *Eracles* and the abrégé.

It will by now be evident what shift in emphasis I am about to advocate: a shift towards MS *d*, for this period 1184-97. The sad neglect of this manuscript has been the regrettable but perhaps inevitable result of its relegation to footnotes, often very unsatisfactory ones, in the *Recueil*. Runciman alone has made any significant use of some of its important variants;[9] many others remain entirely unexploited. This is not to say of course that the other versions in this period are worthless. The Colbert-Fontainebleau (*a-b*) version for example contains, especially on the conquest of Cyprus,[10] information not found in any other version, and which, though it has nothing to do with proto-Ernoul, is still valuable as another account of the same events, which at least one compiler thought preferable to that offered by Ernoul. For Ernoul was not an eye-witness of all the events he recounts. The value of *d* is simply that it is in this period the closest reproduction remaining to us of the chronicle of Ernoul. Within this section there are of course some parts more valuable than others, the value varying according to two factors: whether the information is eye-witness or not, and how much is known from other sources of proven reliability. Thus although we have from other sources vast quantities of information about the battle of Hattin and the fall of Jerusalem, and about the period immediately before and after those events, Ernoul's account, as transmitted by the *Eracles* and the abrégé compilers and especially by the *d* compiler, is immensely valuable for two reasons: that it is an eye-witness account, and that it gives us the singular interpretation put on events by a *Polain*, and a supporter of Raymond of Tripoli.

On the early part of the Third Crusade, on the other hand, as we have already said, Ernoul must be assumed to be less

---

[9] See for example iii. 89, 91, 93.   [10] *RHC* ii. 163-9, and cf. above, pp. 70 ff.

reliable, though his interpretation is still interesting, but from
the point where Richard and Philippe-Auguste arrive in Palestine,[11]
where Ernoul was, we have both factors in operation again. The
portrait of Richard in particular sheds some new light on a well-
known character, for the qualities which made Richard unpopular
with other European monarchs—his cunning, often bordering
on treachery, his singleness of purpose, otherwise called ruth-
lessness, and his subtlety in dealing with the Saracens for
example—were precisely those which guaranteed him popular
success with the *Polains*. Idealistic notions of a Holy War were
all very well in Europe; in Syria sound military and political
strategy was more to the point.

A topic on which the *Eracles* and the abrégé and especially
MS *d* give us quite a lot of information, and which is very little
mentioned in the general run of Western (as opposed to Arabic)
chronicles, is the internal politics of the Middle East, particularly
the state of Armenia and its relations with the crusader states.
Here the value of the chronicles is enhanced more by the dearth
of other sources than by anything else, but is not to be despised
on that account. Above all, it is here perhaps more than anywhere else that we gain our best insight into the situation of the
Kingdom of Jerusalem and the Principality of Antioch among
their neighbour states. Here we realize how far from Europe
and European politics they were, and how much involved in
a totally different continent, different in its mentality, in its
political machinery, in its culture as a whole. This in turn alters
our view of Ernoul and his chronicle, making us see that for
all it was written in French, it is worlds apart from the truly
French chronicles of the period, from those of say Villehardouin
or Joinville, for though the one settled in the East and the other
spent a number of years there, they both remain French not
merely in language but in mentality also. For the Western
reader, the chronicle of Ernoul, as traceable in MS *d* especially,
opens up a new world just as surely as do the writings of his
Arab contemporaries.

In short then, the chronicle of Ernoul is extremely valuable
as a historical source because it gives us information not obtain-
able anywhere else, and because it is almost unique in its
interpretation, standing in this respect half-way between the

[11] *RHC* ii. 170; M-L p. 273.

two main bodies of chronicles, Arabic and European. The
various versions of the *Eracles* and the abrégé are valuable
primarily in the measure in which they are faithful reproductions of Ernoul, and therefore the 1184-97 section of the
d version is by far the most valuable of all. Though Ernoul's
chronicle has long been appreciated by historians, that appreciation has been hampered, and the full extent of Ernoul's
merits largely obscured, by emphasis on the wrong texts, and
hence a very much watered-down and westernized Ernoul has
emerged, from the universal practice of referring to the abrégé
as 'Ernoul', presumably on account of the first half of the
title of Mas-Latrie's edition. In fact all historians since Mas-
Latrie have been inclined to accept his conclusions on the
authorship of the abrégé with much more certainty than he
himself ever claimed. As for the *Eracles,* it is the main version
of the *Recueil* edition, that is the version of *a-b*, which has
been the principal focus of the historians' attention, the reason
being presumably the same, that they have followed the lead
implicitly given by the format of the edition. Such is the power
of an editor to create and uncreate his text, and such the
optimism with which his readers accept his conclusions, however
tentatively he himself may present them. It was not on a whim
that Mas-Latrie gave his edition the cautious double title
'Chronique d'Ernoul et de Bernard le Trésorier', and further
examination of the text has shown that caution to be well
justified. But the title was a long one, bound to be shortened
by constant use, and the inevitable result is that Mas-Latrie's
caution has gone largely unheeded.

Ideally, to implement the third implication of this study,
one would like to see a complete revision of the misleading
system of names by which the texts have gradually come to
be known, for it is clear that the name given to a text is a
prime factor in determining the degree of authority the
reader attributes to it, and will always in the end outweigh
anything the editor may say in the preface. So it would be
best not to call any text by the name of Ernoul, since no text
now extant can carry the full authority of Ernoul's own un-
altered work. Even the *d* version is at very best an adaptation
of the 1184-97 section, the pre-1184 part is known to us only
in the very much abbreviated and adulterated version of the

abrégé, and as the stemma[12] shows, the pedigree of these texts
is very far from simple. Moreover, the stemma shows only the
derivation of one text from another; the existing MS *d* may
well be at one or several removes from the original manuscript
of its text, with all the intervening scribal hazards that this
implies. So while recognizing the text of MS *d* as being from
1184 to 1197 the nearest we have to Ernoul, we must still
emphasize that there is a certain distance, possibly a considerable
distance, between them. The real chronicle of Ernoul is lost to
us.

What then are we to call the texts? The *Estoire d'Eracles* is
a harmless enough title for the body of translation and continuations, since it says nothing about that text's authorship, provenance, or content, or indeed about anything except the opening words, and so we need have no reservations about continuing
to use a name whose familiarity alone strongly recommends it.
It can be adapted in various ways to describe the several versions:
the *a-b* text for example can be called (as it often is already) the
Colbert-Fontainebleau *Eracles*, the *gG* text might well come to
be known as the Noailles *Eracles*, taking its name, as does the
so-called *continuation de Rothelin*, from the earliest known
owner of the manuscript, and the *d* text should certainly be
called the Lyon *Eracles*. More difficult is the problem raised
by the several versions of the abrégé. In the case of the 1232
version[13] the obvious title is 'Chronicle of Bernard the Treasurer'
since we know for a certainty that he compiled it, and that
'Ernoul' served only as a source, but it has been known as
'Ernoul' for so long, to be precise just a hundred years now,
that such a total change of name would doubtless cause endless
confusion and do more harm than good on balance. At the
same time, it really is extremely undesirable to go on calling
it 'Ernoul', for not only is it not his chronicle, it is not even
a good likeness of it for the most essential part, that is 1184-
97, and before 1184 is to be relied on only *faute de mieux*.
The best compromise seems to be to call it 'Ernoul-Bernard',
a name reasonably similar to the present one, but conveying,
if not the whole truth, at least some truth about the text,
that Ernoul is one of its major sources, and Bernard its compiler.

---

[12] Above, p. 96.   [13] i.e. the whole text of *A*, as in Mas-Latrie's edition.

The shorter versions of the abrégé, ending in 1227 and 1229,[14] are not usually used separately from the 1232 version, since they offer nothing significant that is not in Ernoul-Bernard, but if some distinguishing name is needed, for example to facilitate a discussion of these three texts, it might be 'the Ernoul abrégé'—again providing both a link with past identifications and also a modification in the interests of accuracy. If a full range of names can be evolved and adopted in this way, it will mean that much more discriminating use can be made of the texts, especially in the vital places where they clash with each other, since we should then be sure what anyone meant by, say, 'Ernoul-Bernard', whereas at present one of the most confusing aspects of the textual discussions is that one can never be quite certain what any single critic means by, for example, 'the chronicle of Ernoul'. The system of names proposed here is by no means ideal, but would at least mean that the issue of the authority of the texts would not be entirely prejudged in the reader's mind by the titles used to designate them.

The fourth and last of the implications mentioned above is that a much more cautious approach to the chronicles is desirable, and one which bears in mind what kind of texts they really are. What did each of their authors intend to write? The simplest way to answer this essential question is to suppose a continuum having at one end sources which are purely contemporary records of events or states of affairs—a parish register for example—and at the other all kinds of purely literary creations, whose authors had no notion of their work as the repository of accurate information, but intended simply to catch the interest of their audience. Their writings can nevertheless serve incidentally as sources, though in an entirely different way from the first kind of document. As Gladstone puts it: '. . . the poems of Homer are in the highest sense historical, as a record of "manners and characters, feelings and tastes, races and countries, principles and institutions." '[15]

[14] At M-L pp. 458 and 467 respectively.
[15] Preface to *Homeric Synchronism: an Enquiry into the Time and Place of Homer* (London, 1879), p. 9. The quotation is from his own work *Studies on Homer and the Homeric Age* (Oxford, 1858), i. 36. Cf. also the argument in *Juventus Mundi* (London, 1869), pp. 7-9.

This is evidence, but of the most indirect kind, and must be very differently interpreted from the evidence of the more straightforwardly and intentionally factual documents. Between these two extremes we may place all the texts at present under consideration, at varying points; nor will any one text necessarily have a constant place on this continuum. The analysis of the abrégé for example has shown how its author's preoccupation with accurate facts varies enormously from one part of the text to another.[16] But it is essential to ask ourselves before using any text, 'What did this author intend to write?' The failure to ask this question, and to distinguish between texts which though superficially related to each other are fundamentally different in kind, can have undesirable results, of which we shall now examine one instance.

Only one historian has paid any attention to the French translation of the *Historia*, namely Prawer. In his essay on the colonization of the Latin Kingdom[17] he makes quite frequent use of differences between the *Historia* and its translation, but his most extensive use of this evidence relates to the foundation of Montréal in 1115. William of Tyre relates how the king brought inhabitants to the castle: '. . . in quo post operis consummationem tam equites quam pedites ampla illis conferans praedia habitatores locat'.[18]

This is Prawer's comment on *pedites*:

For who are the *pedites* of William of Tyre? The French translator and interpreter removes all doubts. He adds, commenting the event, 'Il [i.e. rei] i fist remanoir de sa gent chevaliers, sergens, villains gaengneors, et à toz douna granz teneures en la terre selonc ce que chascun estoit.' So among the *pedites* are peasants, and it is of importance to note that they are not the indigenous inhabitants of the area, they are *de sa gent*, i.e. men whom the king has brought along in his campaign in the south.[19]

Now what did the translator want to achieve in his work? Prawer here assumes that he was producing as accurate a translation as he could of the *Historia*, indeed better still, that his not infrequent additions to his text are intended as glosses;

---

[16] Cf. above, pp. 156-7.
[17] 'Colonization Activities in the Latin Kingdom of Jerusalem' in *Revue Belge de Philologie et d'Histoire*, xxix (1951), 1063-1118.
[18] *RHC* i. 500; cf. Babcock and Krey i. 506.   [19] Ibid., p. 1074.

not departures from the sense of his text, but clarifications of it, made from knowledge. It is in fact evident from what we know of him and his work that his concern was to popularize rather than to transmit accurately, and that as he was a Frenchman, and working in the second quarter of the thirteenth century, he was not in any case in a position to know very precise details of this kind. He had probably very little idea of who these *pedites* were, and no single Old French word presents itself as a straight translation of *pedites*; so he produced this free rendering, supplementing a deficiency of knowledge from his fertile imagination, and producing a more colourful version than his dignified original had been. He was presenting to a French audience a work too famous to have any need of the outward signs of respectability that high style might be thought to confer, and which he sought rather to make as agreeable as possible for a public which was of course interested in the history William had written, but more as an enthralling story of deeds of arms done beyond the sea than as an absolutely faithful record of facts. The *Estoire d'Eracles* has sometimes been known as the *Roman d'Eracles*; not an accurate title, for it is still fundamentally history, but not an entirely un-indicative one.

This example serves to show how the different approach of two writers (in this case William and his translator) to the same material can mean that a different approach is also required of whoever tries to interpret their meaning, and the examination of this corpus of chronicles has shown that they cover the whole range from the most sober historiography to the lightest of fiction. In the *Historia* William makes plain to us that he sees himself as a historian, that his purpose in writing is to make a record for posterity, as accurately and impartially as possible, regardless of his own feelings in the matter. His patently theocratic standpoint does not damage his vision of history as a process of cause and effect; he is indeed, as Runciman puts it, 'one of the greatest of mediaeval historians',[20] and we need only allow for his avowed sympathies—ecclesiastical and royalist—and for some inevitable inaccuracies, before putting our trust in his work. His translator, by contrast, is in occupation and preoccupation a literary man and no historian

[20] Runciman ii. 477.

His work can tell us indirectly a good deal about the variations in taste of the reading public, as between that assumed by the *Historia*'s author and that assumed by its translator, and also something about how thirteenth-century France envisaged twelfth-century Outremer, but as a source of factual information it does not at all recommend itself, and if it is used as such, it must be only with the greatest reservations.[21]

This comparison of the *Historia* and its French translation shows plainly how very different products can spring from the same basic material simply because it is used in a different manner and with a different intention. This becomes even more evident when we contemplate the gulf that divides the 'pure' histories, the continuations proper, and the 'mixed' compilations, the abrégé and the *Estoires d'Oultremer*. It is simplistic but not unhelpful to think of the first as comparable (though vastly inferior) to the *Historia*, and the second as having been composed in a spirit more like that of William's translator. Of course, the distinction between the two *genres* of history and romance in the minds of their authors must have been, like the distinction between fact and fiction in general, so blurred as to be practically imperceptible. But it is still necessary for us to ask ourselves, when we use these texts, towards which polarity they most strongly tend, and consequently what kind of evidence we can legitimately expect from them. Thus the abrégé, being as we have seen a work of popularization, albeit rather an unsuccessful one, can on a factual plain do no more than supplement other fuller sources. But it does also give us, by the prominence it accords to the year 1187,[22] some inkling of the vast importance attached in the West to the loss of Jerusalem and the Holy Cross, and by the dramatic way in which it deals with these events, the stage-setting it gives them (and the metaphor is deliberately chosen), shows us too how the story of Jerusalem came to be seen in a light not unlike the half-mystic, half-heroic atmosphere that surrounded the story of Arthur, an aspect which was to find its final and clearest expression with Caxton.[23]

---

[21] For an example of proper use made of the translation in this way, see Smail, pp. 76-7, and notes 8 and 9.
[22] Cf. above, p. 121.   [23] Cf. above, pp. 24-5.

Similarly, in the case of the *Estoires d'Oultremer,* the compiler's protestations of disdain for 'ces roumans rimés' cannot disguise his own penchant for them, as evidenced by the two fictitious interpolations we have described.[24] The apparently historical material this text offers us, which is not found elsewhere, is well worth examining, though in the most sceptical spirit, but what the author really wanted to produce was a romance of Salahadin, and in this he has succeeded admirably. His regard for the distinction between fact and fiction is so slight that we cannot afford to believe without especially careful examination anything he says. But what he wanted us to believe was true, particularly about Salahadin himself, is the most interesting aspect of his work, and the one that most repays close study. In other words, this text has not, apparently, a great deal to contribute to our knowledge of the political history of the Latin Kingdom, but does add new evidence to the equally interesting question of the popular image of Salahadin in the West.

With the continuations, as opposed to these short chronicles, we are on somewhat safer ground. The chief trap to be avoided here is that of thinking, or assuming, that the continuations were written as such, for although this is true of some of them, it is not true of all. One of the major sources the continuation compilers drew on, the chronicle of Ernoul, appears to have been written, as we have seen, as an apologia for the Ibelins' policies in a crucial period of their country's history, and this aspect has survived the neutralizing effects of revision in varying degrees in the several versions which use it. But far from detracting from its value as evidence, Ernoul's partiality, simply by being so evident, loses most of its danger, and adds to the informative value of his work the chance for us to see the Latin Kingdom through the eyes of a *Polain.* This in turn adds a little to our meagre knowledge of a community who have left so little cultural trace that, although European by extraction, they are really more mysterious to us than their totally alien Arab neighbours, whose cultural heritage is so strong. As well as being a record of how Jerusalem and the Holy Cross fell to the Saracens, the chronicle of Ernoul, as far

[24] Cf. above, pp. 14-15.

as we can trace it, is also a record of the 'manners and characters, feelings and tastes' of a short-lived but distinctive civilization.

We cannot repeat too often the sad fact that, until new manuscripts appear, and most probably for ever, Ernoul's chronicle is lost. But we can mitigate the loss of that work somewhat by paying to its most direct descendant, the 1184-97 section of the Lyon *Eracles* (the *d* version), the attention it deserves and has not hitherto received. We can also avoid doing Ernoul the disservice of lending his name to a short work of popularization which in no way merits it, or his authority to other pieces of text which only the hazards of fortune have juxtaposed with his. We must not put our faith in any of these chronicles, at least not the faith that asks no questions, for we must always bear in mind that of all their authors and compilers, only the first and greatest, William of Tyre, wrote consciously and conscientiously as a historian of his times. All his successors had motives very much less pure, and we must not let the conviction of their style lull us into unguarded acceptance of all they would have us believe. That is not to say that the aim (or, it is to be hoped, the result) of this study has been that of 'Proving absurd all written hitherto, And putting us to ignorance again', but rather of offering some clues to the construction of a highly complex maze, and at the same time exphasizing that we can never afford to underestimate its complexity. But judicious use of these chronicles can allow us to extract from them something which, though it is not the story that Ernoul caused to be set down in writing, can tell us a great deal both of what happened in his time, and how it seemed to his contemporaries, and so his work like William's, though in a less direct fashion, can in the end serve as a record of the prosperity and the downfall of the Latin Kingdom of Jerusalem.

APPENDIX I

MSS SAINT-OMER 722 AND LYON 828

The MS no. 722 of the Bibliotheque Municipale of Saint-Omer is a folio
volume of 163 leaves, plus two fly-leaves. Its contents are as follows:
(i) A fragment of the *Historia Hierosolymitana* of Jacques de Vitry,
   Bishop of Acre. Incipit (f.1a): Innocens li apostoles de Rome vaut
   savoir les usages et les costumes les contrees des passages de le terre
   des Sarrasins. Explicit (f.4a): Toutes ces choses manda li patriarches
   al apostole Innocent et a l'eglyse de Rome.
(ii) The *Olimpiades*, or *Les Prises de Jerusalem*, by Pierre de Beauvais.
   Incipit (f.4a): Lonc tans devant l'incarnation Nostre Segnor fu une
   chités en Gresse qui avoit non Elyde. Explicit (f.4b): A m ans et
   IIII vins et vii le reprist Salehadins. Or sont xiij fois. Encore le
   tiennent Sarrasin, Dieus par sa debonaireté le nous rende.
(iii) The chronicle of Ernoul, with the name of the author. Incipit
   (f.4b): Or entendés conment le terre de Iherusalem et le Sainte
   Crois fu conquise des Sarrasins sor Crestiiens. This version contains
   (ff. 39b ff.) the descriptions of Palestine and of Jerusalem, and
   mentions Ernoul by name f. 32b, col. 2: Dont fist descendre i sien
   vallet qui avoit non Ernous. Ce fu cil qui cest conte fist metre en
   escrit. Explicit (f.91b): Apres s'amassa grant gens et grant ost et
   ala encontre le roi Jehan. Et manda son fil en Alemaigne.
(iv) Life of Charlemagne. Incipit (f.92a): Ci commence le vie KM si
   come il conquist Espaigne.

This manuscript was not known to Mas-Latrie when he prepared his
edition of the abrégé in 1871, but it was known to Riant, who includes
it, as no. 13, in his *Inventaire sommaire des manuscrits de l'Eracles*,
published in the *Archives de l'Orient Latin* for 1880-1. It is interesting
from several points of view, which all add up to make it an important
missing piece in our total picture of the abrégé's development.
Saint-Omer 722 provides us with our third copy of the 1229 abrégé,
the others being Brussels 11142 (Mas-Latrie's base manuscript) and
B.N.f.fr. 781, and with a fourth mention of the name of Ernoul as author,
in addition to these two, and to the 1227 abrégé contained in Berne 41.
It is unlike the other two copies of the 1229 abrégé, however, in one
important respect, namely it does not have attached to it m any form
the fragment beginning 'L'an de l'Incarnation Nostre Segnor'. Brussels
11142 has this, in the form in which it is printed by Mas-Latrie, attached
at the end of the text of the abrégé, and B.N. 781 has it, also at the end,
in an even longer form, running on for some way after the end of the
Brussels version. So Saint-Omer 722 is the only copy of the 1229 abrégé
in which this fragment is not found, and which permits us to see the
fragment for what it is—a piece of text unrelated to the abrégé except
by the identity of their subjects, and gratuitously tacked on to the end
of it by some scribe, who had copied the text as found in Saint-Omer 722,

and thought it suitable to go on to something similar, which he apparently never finished in Brussels 11142, in view of the longer version extant in B.N.781. In a way, then, Saint-Omer 722 represents by itself a different family. of texts (if can use the word 'family' where there is only one known member), that is, the 1229 abrégé before the unrelated fragment had been added to it and had confused the issue of the relationship between them. Saint-Omer 722 demonstrates that the 1229 abrégé had a completely independent existence, and represents the text at an earlier stage of its development than any of the manuscripts known to Mas-Latrie. Any new editor of the abrégé would have to take the Saint-Omer manuscript very seriously, and there is a strong possibility that a new edition ought in fact to be based on it, rather than on Brussels 11142, which must give a later text, regardless of the dates of the manuscripts, since here the fragment is already added. One should add that it is not demonstrably impossible that a compiler copied a text of the family of Brussels 11142 omitting the fragment, and thus produced the Saint-Omer text; but it seems to say the least extremely unlikely.

As for the date of Saint-Omer 722, it is given in the catalogue, and by Riant, who probably relied in this on the dating of the librarian, as fourteenth century. But Dr. Jaroslav Folda of the University of North Carolina, Chapel Hill[1] has established that the miniatures, and hence the manuscript itself, cannot possibly be later than the thirteenth century.

One last point about the manuscript is that it comes from the abbey of Saint-Bertin, a Benedictine house (only the ruins now remain) situated at Saint-Omer. This fixes even more clearly the association of the abrégé with this region of France, and what is more, Saint-Omer is situated less than a hundred kilometres as the crow flies from another more famous Benedictine house, Corbie. We know that it was common practice for religious houses to lend each other books, sometimes to enable a copy to be made for the monastery library, and we now have two texts—Saint-Omer 722 and the chronicle of Bernard the Treasurer—firmly fixed in houses of the same Order, and relatively close together. Moreover, the identification (again by Dr. Folda) of the two manuscripts of the *Estoires d'Oultremer*, B.N.f.fr. 770 and 12203, as having been illustrated in this same part of France, gives us another related text associated with the same district. It seems that north-east France and Flanders not only produced many crusaders, but many crusading chronicles too, for reasons which there is here only time to mention speculatively—the general prosperity of the region perhaps, the existence there of large Benedictine houses whose scriptoria could provide all the necessary facilities, and above all the way in which crusading tended to become a family tradition, as it did in the family of Joinville, and in that of the castellans of Saint-Omer itself, the Fauquembergues. In short, considering all in all the value of the Saint-Omer text in itself, and the evidence it offers when viewed in relation to the other texts and what is already known about them, we

---

[1] In a doctorate thesis hitherto unpublished.

see that Riant was not in the least exaggerating when he described it as
'ce très précieux manuscrit'.[2]

Turning now to the Lyon manuscript, we find even more to be learnt
from it, and of even more value, as has become evident in the course of
this study. It is a large quarto volume (measuring about 12 in. by 8½ in.)
of 381 folios plus three fly-leaves. It is written in several hands, in two
columns, with thirty-nine lines to the column, and has twenty-three
miniatures. These are all fairly large, typically about three inches deep
and the width of the whole column, and are of particular interest to the
art historians, who identify them as the work of the Acre atelier.[3] It is
noticeable that the miniatures occur only in the translation of William and
not in the continuation part of the text. The manuscript is not precisely
dated, but the illustrations are thought by Buchthal to be so similar to
those of another Acre manuscript as to be conceivably the work of the
same master, and this second manuscript he dates about 1280. The manuscript belonged at one time to the Jesuit College in Lyon, and a bookplate
in the front states that it was given to them in 1698, by one Melchior
Philibert. It now belongs to the municipal library, and is numbered 828
(formerly 815 and 732) in their collection.

The script is for the most part large and clearly legible. But a number
of pages are seriously faded and difficult, occasionally impossible, to read.
The difficulties are by no means as great, however, as might reasonably
be concluded from a reading of the edition of this manuscript in variant
form in the *Recueil*, where they are many unnecessary blanks and many
grossly mistaken readings. There is no need to dwell on the importance
of this manuscript to historian and textual critic alike—we have already
seen that its text is unique, and vital to our understanding of the multiplicity of the versions of the *Eracles*. Obviously a new edition is needed,
indeed one might well say simply an edition, since the *Recueil* editing of
it is both unreadable in its format and unreliable too. But the question
is, what precisely is to be edited? For the historians, what is needed is a
partial edition of that part of the text which is directly and closely dependent on the chronicle of Ernoul, and which contains so much valuable
information for them, that is the 1184-97 section. This is also the section
in which the textual scholar would be most interested, but the fact remains
that a partial edition is in many ways very unsatisfactory for him. The
alternative, however, is to edit the entire text, all 381 folios of it, and
that would be both long and to a quite large extent unrewarding, in that
no one would be very interested in reading the translation proper, the
1197-1231 section is not substantially different from the abrégé, already
edited perfectly adequately by Mas-Latrie, and the 1231-48 section is
almost identical with the same section of the base manuscripts of the
Recueil, which is again perfectly sufficient in this respect. The problems
thus raised by the question of editing this manuscript are in themselves
not a bad indication of the wide variety of interests it serves. When we

---

[2] See preface to Michelant et Raynaud.
[3] See Buchthal, Miniature Painting, pp. 87 ff.

ask ourselves what would be the state of our knowledge about the *Eracles* without this manuscript, the answer is depressing enough; as for tracing the original form of the chronicle of Ernoul, that would be impossible. Mas-Latrie made but a passing comment about the text[4] but he was right once again.

[4] M-L p. xxiij.

APPENDIX II

POLAINS

The sense commonly attributed to this word by the compilers of dictionaries does not correspond precisely with the usage made of it by Old French authors. Tobler-Lommatsch and Godefroy, and the note to the Rothelin continuation (*RHC* ii, 633, note b) all agree in describing the *Polains* as the children of mixed marriages between Franks and Syrians. But the texts do not bear this out. Both Tobler-Lommatsch and Godefroy quote a passage from Joinville in which he says, 'On appelle les païsans dou païs poulains,' Nothing is stated about their mixed descent. It is obvious from the context that the term *païsans* here means simply the indigent population of Palestine, those of the *païs*, as opposed to Europeans like Joinville himself, and does not denote a social class. It does not exclude people of high rank born in the crusader states, nor does it exclude those of purely French descent. This agrees with the use of the term in the *d* version of the *Eracles* (see *RHC* ii, 63, *d* variant), where the *Polains* are described as 'ciaus de cest païs' and as the 'genz dou reaume', as opposed to the Poitevins who had not been born in the Kingdom, but had come over from Europe with Guy of Lusignan. Again, nothing is specified about the descent of the *Polains*, and it is certain that the anti-Poitevin faction included many men whose purely French descent was not in any doubt, for example the Ibelin brothers, and Raymond of Tripoli, to name but the most famous.

The most detailed and explicit description of the *Polains* is found, however, in Jacques de Vitry's *Historia Orientalis*, or *Historia Hierosolymitana*, where a whole chapter (73 in the 1597 edition, 72 in the version included in Bongars's *Gesta Dei per Francos*) is devoted to describing the *Pullani*. There are several points to be noted here. First, like the other texts, de Vitry does not say anything about the *Pullani* being of mixed descent. He says simply that they were descendants of the original crusaders, 'ex supradictis peregrinis . . . procedentes', albeit unworthy inheritors of their fathers' conquests:

> Generatio enim prava atque perversa, filii scelerati et degeneres, homines corrupti, et legis divinae praevaricatores, ex supradictis peregrinis, viris religiosis Deo acceptis, et hominibus gratiosis, tanquam faex ex vino, et amurca ex oleo, quasi lolium ex frumento, et rubigo ex argento procedentes, paternis possessionibus, sed non moribus successerunt; bonis temporalibus abutentes, quae parentes eorum ad honorem Dei contra impios strenue dimicantes, proprii sanguinis effusione sunt adepti. *Filii autem eorum, qui Pullani nominantur* . . . (Bongars i. 1088-9, my italics.)

This passage is strikingly similar to William of Tyre's description of his countrymen, degenerate sons of noble fathers, indeed the two authors use almost the same words in several places:

> Considerantibus ergo nobis et statum nostrum diligenter discutientibus prima occurrit causa in Deum auctorem omnium respiciens, quod pro patribus nostris, qui fuerunt viri religiosi et timentes Deum, nati sunt filii perditissimi, filii scelerati, fidei Christianae praevaricatores, et sine delectu per omnia currentes illicita: tales

aut talibus pejores, qui dixerunt domino Deo suo, 'Recede a nobis; scientiam
viarum tuarum nolumus.' (*RHC* i, 1015.)

If the *Pullani* of Jacques de Vitry's account, or the *populus noster*
of the *Historia* had been of partly Syrian descent, this would have provided one of the best excuses for these two authors to offer. Neither
does so.

Secondly, de Vitry agrees with the *Eracles* in separating off the *Polains*
as a class not on the grounds of race, but rather on the grounds that they
had been born in the Orient, as opposed to the metropolitan French, or
those born in the West generally: '. . . nisi Francos et *Occidentales populos*
secum haberent, plusquam sexum foeminum non formidarent' (Bongars,
loc. cit., my italics).

Elsewhere he distinguishes them from the various Italian communities
of Palestine, which suggests perhaps that the *Polains* were of French descent,
rather than European in general.

Thirdly, de Vitry describes the political attitude of the *Pullani* to the
Saracens thus: 'Ipsi autem cum Saracenis foedus ineuntes . . . et bella
civilia inter se concitantes, et plerumque ab inimicis fidei nostrae contra
Christianos auxilium postulantes' (Bongars, loc. cit.).

These are precisely the charges which European chroniclers levelled
at the Frankish barons born in Syria, especially Raymond of Tripoli
and Balian d'Ibelin, that they made pacts with the Saracens, wasted
time and energy quarelling amongst themselves, and sought the Saracens'
help against Christians.

If de Vitry had meant by *Pullani* people of mixed Frankish-Syrian
descent, he has several obvious opportunities to say so—their partly
Syrian ancestry could be offered as the most obvious explanation of
any of the traits quoted above, and also of another of their habits he
mentions later, that of keeping their wives closely guarded at home.
This last he attributes, not to their descent from a people with whom
it was presumably normal, but to their jealous natures.

As for the derivation of the word *Polain*, Tobler-Lommatsch gives
it as an extended meaning of the common noun *polain<pullus*, the
young of an animal. This tallies exactly with what we have seen of its
use by Jacques de Vitry: the *Pullani* were the offspring of the crusaders,
whom de Vitry, like William, contrasts with their fathers, the original
crusaders. In the *Eracles* too, they are not first-generation emigrants
from Europe, like Guy and his followers, but the *genz dou reiaume*, the
offspring of emigrants. Assuming this is indeed the origin of the word,
which there seems no reason to doubt, the implication is that the
Polains were at least second-generation colonials, not at all that they
were of mixed blood.

BIBLIOGRAPHY

Texts

Albert of Aix: *Historia Hierosolymitanae Expeditionis*. In *RHC* iv.
Ambroise: *L'Estoire de la guerre sainte*. Ed. Gaston Paris, Paris, 1897.
    See also La Monte and Hubert.
Babcock (E.) and Krey (A.C.): *A History of Deeds Done Beyond the
    Sea*. Records of Civilisation, 35. New York, 1943.
Baldus (D.) ed: *Enchiridion Locorum Sanctorum*. 2nd ed. Jerusalem,
    1955.
Beha-Eddin: *Vita et Res Gesta Sultani Almalichi Alnasiri Saladini*.
    Ed. A. Schultens. Lyons, 1732. See also Wilson (C.W.).
Beugnot (A.A.), ed.: *Assises de Jérusalem*. In *RHC Lois*, i and ii.
Bongars (J.): *Gesta Dei per Francos*. Hanover, 1611.
Brochardus: *L'Advis directif pour faire le saint voyage d'Oultremer, par
    le frère Brochard Lalemant*. *RHC Documents arméniens*, ii, contains
    the Latin text (*Directorium ad passagium faciendum*) with the
    French text below.
Butler (Cuthbert, O.S.B.), ed.: *Sancti Benedicti Regula Monachorum*.
    Friburg-im-Breisgau, 1912.
Caxton (W.): *Godeffroy of Boloyne, or the Siege and Conqueste of
    Jerusalem, by William Archbishop of Tyre, translated by William
    Caxton*. London, 1481. See also Colvin (M.) and Sparling (H.H.).
Chroust (A.), ed.: *Historia de Expeditione Friderici Imperatoris*.
    Monumenta Germaniae Historiae. Berlin, 1928.
Citry de la Guette (Samuel de Broë, Seigneur de): *Histoire de la conqueste
    du royaume de Jérusalem sur les Chrestiens par Saladin. Traduite
    d'un ancien manuscrit*. Paris, 1679.
Colmenares (Diego de): *Historia de la Insigne Ciudad de Segovia, y
    conpendio de las Historias de Castilla*. 1st ed., Segovia, 1637.
Colvin (M.), ed.: *William Caxton: Godeffroy of Boloyne*. Early English
    Text Society, London, 1893.
Conder (R.E.): *The City of Jerusalem*. London, 1888. Palestine Pilgrims'
    Text Society, 6. See also Michelant and Raynaud.
Corbie. 'The Ancient Statutes of the Abbey of St. Peter of Corbie'. A
    typewritten transcription, with no name of author or date, num-
    bered 1107 b.4. in the catalogue of the Bodleian Library.
Curzon (H. de), ed.: *La Règle du Temple*. Paris, 1886.
Du Préau (G.): *L'Histoire de la Guerre Sainte*. Paris, 1573. An edition
    of the French translation of William of Tyre, with the continuation
    of Hérold.
Guizot (F.P.G.): *Collection des mémoires relatifs à l'histoire de France*.
    Paris, 1823-35.
Isidore of Seville: *Etymologiae*. In *PL* lxxxii.
Jacques de Vitry: *Epistola de Captione Damiatae*. Published by Iacobus
    Gretserus, S.J., Ingolstadt, 1610.
—— *Liber Orientalis, siue Hierosolymitanae*. Douai, 1597. Also in Vol. i
    of Bongars and Vol. xv of Guizot (qq.v.).
—— *Lettres*. Ed. R.B.C. Huygens. Leyden, 1960.

Jocelin of Brakelonde: *Chronica Jocelini de Brakelonda de rebus et gestis Samsonis Abbatis Monasterii Sancti Edmundi.* Ed. J.G. Rokewode, London 1840.

Josephus: *The Antiquities and The Jewish War of Flavius Josephus* Translated by William Whiston. London, 1963.

La Monte (J.L.) with Hubert (M.J.): *The Crusade of Richard the Lion-Heart.* Records of Civilization, 34. New York, 1941. A translation of Ambroise (q.v.).

Lodeman (F.E.), ed.: *Le Pas Salhadin.* In *Modern Language Notes,* xii (Jan. 1897).

Martène (E.) and Durand (U.): *Veterum Scriptorum et Monumentorum Historicorum, Dogmaticorum, Moralium, Amplissima Collectio.* Paris, 1724-33.

Mas-Latrie (L. de), ed.: *La Chronique d'Ernoul et de Bernard le Trésorier.* Paris, 1871.

Matthew of Edessa: *Chronicon.* In *RHC Documents Arméniens,* i.

Mayer (H.E.): *Das Itinerarium Peregrinorum.* Stuttgart, 1962. See also Richard of London.

Michelant (H.) and Raynaud (G.), eds.: *Itinéraires à Jérusalem et descriptions de la Terre Sainte rédigés en français au XIe, XIIe et XIIIe siècles.* Publications de la Société de l'Orient Latin, série géographique, 3. Geneva, 1882.

Migne (J.-P.): *Patrologiae Cursus Completus. Series Latina.* Paris, 1844-55.

Morris (William), ed. and trans.: *L'Ordène de chevalerie.* Hammersmith, at the Kelmscott Press, 1893.

Muratori (L.A.), ed.: *Rerum Italicarum Scriptores.* Milan, 1723-51.

Oliver of Paderborn: *De Captione Damiatae.* Ed. H. Hoogeweg, Tübingen, 1894. Also in Bongars, Vol. i (q.v.).

Paris (P.), ed.: *Guillaume de Tyr et ses continuateurs.* Paris, 1879-80. The French translation of William of Tyre only; the continuations were never published.

Philippe de Novare: *Mémoires 1218-1243.* Ed. Ch. Kohler, Paris, 1888.

—— *Le Livre des plaits et des us et des costumes des assises d'outre-mer et de Jérusalem et de Chypre.* In *RHC Lois,* i under the title *Le Livre de Philippe de Navarre.*

Pierre de Beauvais: 'Les Olimpiades'. Unpublished. MSS Saint-Omer 722, Berne 41 and 113, and Bodleian Hatton 77.

Pipino (Francesco, O.P.): *Chronicon.* In *RIS* vii and ix.

Ralph of Coggeshalle: *Chronicon Anglicanum,* and the *De Expugnatione Terrae Sanctae per Saladinum Libellus,* doubtfully attributed to Ralph. Ed. J. Stevenson, Rolls Series, 66. London, 1875.

Raynaud (G.), ed.: *Les Gestes des Chiprois.* Publications de la Société de l'Orient Latin, série historique, 5. Geneva, 1887.

Richard of Devizes: *Chronicon de Rebus Gestis Ricardi Primi, Regis Angliae.* Ed. J. Stevenson, London 1838.

Richard of London: *Itinerarium Peregrinorum et Gesta Regis Ricardi; auctore ut videtur Ricardo, Canonico Sanctae Trinitatis Londiniensis.* Ed. W. Stubbs, Rolls Series, 38, London, 1864. See also Mayer (H.E.)

Robert de Clari: *La Conquête de Constantinople.* Ed. P. Lauer, Paris, 1924.
Robert the Monk: *Historia Hierosolymitana.* In *RHC* iii.
Salloch (M.): *Die lateinische Fortsetzung Willelms von Tyrus.* Leipzig, 1934.
Sparling (H.H.): *William Caxton: The History of Godefrey of Boloyne and of the Conquest of Iherusalem.* Corrected by H. Halliday Sparling, printed by William Morris at the Kelmscott Press, Hammersmith, Apr. 1893.
Tobler (T.), ed.: *Descriptiones Terrae Sanctae ex saeculo VIII, IX, XII et XV.* Leipzig, 1874.
— *Topographie von Jerusalem.* Berlin, 1854.
Tudeboeuf (Pierre) or Tudebodus: *Historia de Hierosolymitano Itinere.* In *RHC* iii.
Villehardouin (Geoffroi de): *La Conquête de Constantinople.* Ed. E. Faral, Paris, 1938.
Vincent de Beauvais: *Speculum Historiale.* Augsburg, 1474.
— *Speculum Majus.* Venice, 1494.
Wailly (Natalis de), ed.: *Récits d'un menestrel de Reims.* Paris, 1876.
William of Newburgh: *Historia Rerum Anglicarum.* Ed. H.C. Hamilton, London, 1866.
William of Tyre: *Historia Rerum in Partibus Transmarinis Gestarum.* In *RHC* i. See also Babcock and Krey, Du Préau, and Paris.
Wilson (C.W.): *Saladin; or: What befell Sultan Yūsuf-Salāh-ed-Dîn.* Palestine Pilgrims' Text Society, 13. London, 1897. A translation of Beha-Eddin (q.v.).

Bibliographies

Becker (G.): *Catalogi Bibliothecarum Antiqui.* Bonn, 1885.
Carpentier (P.), ed.: *Glossarium Novum ad Scriptores Medii Aevi.* Paris, 1766. A supplement to Du Cange (q.v.).
Du Cange (Charles du Fresne, sieur): *Glossarium ad Scriptores Mediae et Infimae Latinitatis.* Paris, 1678. A revised edition of this work, by Carpentier (q.v.) and others, Niort, 1883-7.
Fabricius (J.A.): *Bibliotheca Latina mediae et infimae aetatis.* Hamburg, 1734-46.
Gröber (G.): *Grundriss der romanischen Philologie.* Strassburg, 1886-1901. 2nd ed., Berlin, 1933.
James (M.R.): *A Descriptive Catalogue of Fifty Manuscripts in the Library of Henry Yates Thompson.* Cambridge, 1898.
Lelong (J.): *Bibliothèque historique de la France.* Paris, 1719.
Manitius (M.): *Geschichte der lateinischen Literatur des Mittelalters.* Munich, 1911.
Mayer (H.E.): *Bibliographie zur Geschichte der Kreuzzüge.* Hannover, 1960.
Meusel (J.G.): *Bibliotheca Historica.* Leipzig, 1782-1802.
Michaud (J.F.): *Bibliographie des croisades.* Paris, 1822.
Montfaucon (B. de): *Bibliotheca Bibliothecarum Manuscriptorum Nova.* Paris, 1739.

Paris (P.): *Les Manuscrits français de la Bibliothèque du Roi*. Paris, 1836.
Riant (P.): *Inventaire sommaire des manuscrits de l'Eracles*. In *Archives de l'Orient Latin*, i, 1881.
Woledge (B.) and Clive (H.P.): *Répertoire des plus anciens textes en prose française*. Geneva, 1964.

Secondary Sources

Alphandéry (P.): *La Chrétienté et l'idée de croisade*. Paris, 1954.
Archer (T.A.): *The Crusade of Richard I*. London, 1888.
Baldwin (M.W.): *Raymond III of Tripolis and the Fall of Jerusalem*. Princeton, N.J., 1936.
Beaunier (Dom) and Besse (J.M.): *Abbayes et prieurés de l'ancienne France*. Archives de la France Monastique. Paris, 1905.
Bourgeat (J.B.): *Études sur Vincent de Beauvais*. Paris 1856.
Brummer (R.): *Die erzählende Prosadichtung in den romanischen Literaturen des dreizehnten Jahrhunderts*. Berlin, 1948.
Buchthal (Hugo): *Miniature Painting in the Latin Kingdom of Jerusalem*. Oxford, 1957.
Butler (Cuthbert, O.S.B.): *Benedictine Monachism*. London, 1924.
Cartellieri (A.): *Philipp II August, König von Frankreich*. Leipzig, 1899.
Chevalier (U.): *Répertoire des sources historiques du Moyen Âge*. 2nd ed., Paris, 1905-7
Cottineau (L.H.): *Répertoire topobibliographique des abbayes et prieurés*. Mâcon, 1935.
Cousin (Patrice, O.S.B.): *Précis d'histoire monastique*. Paris-Tournai, 1959.
Curtius (E.R.): *Europäische Literatur und lateinisches Mittelalter*. Berne, 1948.
Daniel (N.): *Islam and the West*. Edinburgh, 1960.
Daoust (J.) and Gaillard (L.), eds.: *Corbie Abbaye Royale. Volume du XIIIe Centenaire*. Lille, 1963.
Delatte (Paul, O.S.B.): *The Rule of St. Benedict: a Commentary by Dom Paul Delatte*. Translated by Dom Justin McCann. London, 1921.
Donovan (J.P.): *Pelagius and the Fifth Crusade*. Philadelphia, Pa., 1950.
Du Cange (Charles du Fresne, sieur): *Les Familles d'Outremer*. Published by E.G. Rey. Paris, 1869.
Erdmann (C.): *Die Entstehung des Kreuzzugsgedankens*. Stuttgart, 1935.
Fuller (Thomas): *The Historie of the Holy Warre*. Cambridge, 1639.
Grousset (René): *L'Empire du Levant: histoire de la question d'Orient*. Paris, 1946.
—— *Histoire des Croisades et du royaume franc de Jérusalem*. Paris, 1934-6.
Guérin (V.): *Description de la Palestine*. Paris, 1869.
Hackett (J.W.): 'Saladin's Campaign of 1188'. Oxford B.Litt. thesis, 1937.
Huygens (R.B.C.): *Latijn in Outremer*. Leiden, 1964.
Jenkins (C.): *The Monastic Chronicler and the Early School of St. Albans*. London, 1922.

Kestner (E.): *Der Kreuzzug Friedrichs II.* Göttingen, 1873.

Kohler (Charles): *Mélanges pour servir à l'histoire de l'Orient latin et des croisades.* Paris, 1900.

Laking (G.F.): *A Record of European Armour and Arms through Seven Centuries.* London, 1920.

Lane Poole (S.): *Saladin and the Fall of the Kingdom of Jerusalem.* Heroes of the Nations, 24, London, 1898.

Longnon (J.): *Les Français d'Outremer au Moyen Âge.* Paris, 1929.

— *L'Empire latin de Constantinople et la principauté de Morée.* Paris, 1949.

Luchaire (A.): *La Société française au temps de Philippe-Auguste.* Paris, 1909.

Maimbourg (L.): *Histoire des croisades.* In *Les Histoires du sieur Maimbourg.* Paris, 1686.

Maître (L.): *Les Écoles épiscopales et monastiques en occident avant les universités.* Archives de la France Monastique, 26. Ligugé, 1924.

Mas-Latrie (L. de): *Histoire de l'île de Chypre.* Paris, 1852-61.

Mercuri (P.) and Bonnard (C.): *Costumes historiques du XIIIe XIVe et XVe siècles.* 2nd ed., Paris, 1860-1.

Michaud (J.F.): *Histoire des croisades.* Paris, 1841.

Montalembert (C.F.R.): *Les Moines d'Occident depuis S. Benoît jusqu'à S. Bernard.* Paris, 1860-77.

Ost (F.): *Die altfranzösische Übersetzung der Geschichte der Kreuzzüge Wilhelms von Tyrus.* Halle, 1899.

Pihan (A.P.): *Glossaire des mots français tirés de l'arabe, du persan et du turc.* Paris, 1847.

Prawer (J.): *Histoire du royaume latin de Jérusalem.* French translation by G. Nahon, Paris, 1969.

Prutz (H.): *Kulturgeschichte der Kreuzzüge.* Berlin, 1883.

— *Quellenbeiträge zur Geschichte der Kreuzzüge.* Danzig, 1876.

Richard (J.): *La Royaume latin de Jérusalem.* Paris, 1953.

Riley-Smith (J.S.C.): *The Knights of St. John in Jerusalem and Cyprus.* London, 1967.

Röhricht (R.): *Die Kreuzfahrt Kaiser Friedrich des Zweiten.* Berlin, 1872.

— *Quellenbeiträge zur Geschichte der Kreuzzüge.* Berlin, 1875.

— *Zusätze und Verbesserungen zu Du Cange: Les Familles d'Outremer.* Berlin, 1886.

— *Studien zur Geschichte des fünften Kreuzzuges.* Innsbruck, 1891.

— (ed.): *Regesta regni Hierosolymitani.* Innsbruck, 1893.

— *Geschichte des Königreichs Jerusalem 1100-1291.* Innsbruck, 1898.

Runciman (Sir Steven): *A History of the Crusades.* Cambridge, 1952-3.

— *The Families of Outremer. The Feudal Nobility of the Crusader Kingdom of Jerusalem 1099-1291.* Creighton Lecture, London 1960.

Schon (P.M.): *Studien zum Stil der frühen französischen Prosa.* Frankfurt, 1960.

Setton (K.M.), ed.: *A History of the Crusades.* Vol. i: *The First Hundred Years,* ed. M.W. Baldwin. Pennsylvania, Pa., 1955. Vol. ii: *The Later Crusades,* ed. R.L. Wolff and H.W. Hazard. Pennsylvania, Pa., 1962.

Smail (R.C.): *Crusading Warfare, 1097-1193.* Cambridge, 1956.
Smalley (B.): *The Study of the Bible in the Middle Ages.* 2nd ed., Oxford, 1952.
Southern (R.W.): *Western Views of Islam in the Middle Ages.* Cambridge, Mass., 1962.
Streit (L.): *De rerum transmarinarum qui Guilelmum Tyrium excepisse fertur Gallico auctore specimen.* Greifswald, 1861.
Vasiliev (A.A.): *History of the Byzantine Empire, 324-1453.* 2nd English ed., Oxford 1952.

Articles

Archer (T.A.): 'On the Accession Dates of the Early Kings of Jerusalem', *English Historical Review,* iv (1889).
Cahen (C.): 'Indigènes et Croisés; quelques mots à propos d'un médecin d'Amaury et de Saladin', *Syria,* xv (1934).
Delisle (L.): 'Recherches sur l'ancienne bibliothèque de Corbie', *Bibliothèque de l'École des Chartes,* 5th Ser. i (1860).
Duval (A.): 'Auteur anonyme de l'Ordène de chevalerie', *HLF* xviii (1835).
Edwards (J.C.): 'The *Itinerarium Regis Ricardi* and the *Estoire de la guerre sainte'.* In *Historical Essays in Honour of James Tait.* Manchester, 1933.
Giry (A.): 'Les Châtelains de Saint-Omer 1042-1386', *Bibliothèque de l'École des Chartes,* xxxv (1874).
Hellweg (M.): 'Die ritterliche Welt in der Geschichtschreibung des vierten Kreuzzugs', *Romanische Forschungen* lii (1938).
Huygens (R.B.C.): 'La Tradition manuscrite de Guillaume de Tyr', *Studi Medievali,* 3e série, v, 1 (June 1964).
—— 'Guillaume de Tyr étudiant. Un chapitre (XIX, 12) de son "Histoire" retrouvé', *Latomus,* xxi (1962).
Jones (L.W.): 'The Scriptorium at Corbie', *Speculum,* xxii (1947).
Köhler (E.): 'Zur Entstehung der altfranzösischen Prosaromans', *Wissenschaftliche Zeitschrift der Friedrich-Schiller-Universität Jena,* v (1955-6).
Krey (A.C.): 'William of Tyre: the Making of a Historian in the Middle Ages'. *Speculum,* xvi (1941).
La Monte (J.L.) and Downs (N.): 'The Lords of Bethsan in the Kingdoms of Jerusalem and Cyprus', *Medievalia et Humanistica,* vi (1950).
La Monte (J.L.): 'John d'Ibelin, the Old Lord of Beirut, 1177-1236', *Byzantion,* xii (1937).
—— 'The Lords of Caesarea in the Period of the Crusades', *Speculum,* xxii (1947).
Lesne (E.): 'L'Économie domestique d'un monastère au IXe siècle d'après les statuts d'Adalhard, abbé de Corbie.' In *Mélanges Offerts à F. Lot.* Paris, 1925.
Levillain (L.): 'Les Statuts d'Adalhard', *Le Moyen Âge,* 2e Sér. iv (1900).
Manzoni (L.): 'Frate Francesco Pipino da Bologna dei pp. Predicatori, geografo, storico e viaggiatore', *Atti e Memorie della R. Deputazione di Storia Patria per le Provincie di Romagna. Terza serie,* xiii (Bologna, 1896).

Mayer (H.E.): 'Zum Tode Wilhelms von Tyrus', *Archiv für Diplomatik*, v-vi (1959-60).

Mayer (P.): 'Notice et extraits du MS 8336 de la Bibliothèque de Sir Thomas Phillips à Cheltenham', *Romania*, xiii (1884). See especially p. 530 on the *Ordene de Chevalerie*.

—— 'Les MSS français de Cambridge', *Romania*, viii (1879) and xv (1886). See especially description of MS GG 6.28 of the University Library.

Munro (D.C.): 'The Western Attitude towards Islam during the Crusades', *Speculum* vi (1931).

Ohly (F.): Vom geistigen Sinn des Wortes im Mittelalter', *Zeitschrift für deutsches Altertum*, lxxxix (1958).

Ortroy (F. van): S. François d'Assise et son voyage en Orient', *Analecta Bollandiana*, xxxi (1912).

Paris (G.): 'La Légende de Saladin', *Journal des Savants* May to August inclusive, 1893. Ostensibly a review of Fioravanti: *Il Saladino nelle legende del medioevo*. Reggio-Calabria, 1891.

Paris (P.): Untitled article on *Histoire d'Outremer* in a collection under the general heading of 'Chroniques'. In *HLF* xxi (1847), 679-85.

Pastouret (E.C.J.P.): 'Guillaume de Tyr. Sa Vie', *HLF* xiv (1817).

Petit-Radel (L.C.F.): 'Bernard, dit le Trésorier, traducteur et continuateur de Guillaume de Tyr', *HLF* xviii (1835).

Prawer (J.): 'Assise de Teneure et Assise de Vente: a Study of Landed Property in the Latin Kingdom', *Economic History Review*, 2nd Ser. iv (1951-2).

—— 'The Settlements of the Latins in Jerusalem', *Speculum*, xxvii (1952).

—— 'Colonization Activities in the Latin Kingdom of Jerusalem', *Revue Belge de Philologie et Histoire*, xxix. 2 (1951).

—— 'La Noblesse et le régime féodal du royaume latin de Jérusalem', *Le Moyen Âge*, 4e série, xiv (1959).

—— 'La Bataille de Hattin', *Israel Exploration Journal*, xiv (1964).

—— 'Les Premiers Temps de la féodalité dans le royaume latin de Jérusalem—une réconsidération', *Tijdschrift voor Rechtsgeschiedenis*, xxii (1954).

Prutz (H.): 'Studien über Wilhelm von Tyrus', *Neues Archiv der Gesellschaft für ältere deutsche Geschichtskunde*, viii (1883).

Richard (J.): 'An Account of the Battle of Hattin referring to the Frankish Mercenaries in Oriental Moslem Sates', *Speculum*, xxvii (1952).

Smail (R.C.): 'Crusaders' Castles of the Twelfth Century', *Cambridge Historical Journal*, x (1951).

Woledge (B.): 'La Légende de Troie et les débuts de la prose française.' In *Mélanges Offerts à Mario Roques*. Paris, 1950.

Wolff (R.L.): 'Baldwin of Flanders and Hainault', *Speculum*, xxvii (1952).

INDEX

DATE DUE

NOV 17			